Henry Wilson

History of the Anti-Slavery Measures of the 37th and 38th United-States Congresses

Henry Wilson

History of the Anti-Slavery Measures of the 37th and 38th United-States Congresses

ISBN/EAN: 9783744732345

Printed in Europe, USA, Canada, Australia, Japan

Cover: Foto ©ninafisch / pixelio.de

More available books at **www.hansebooks.com**

ANTISLAVERY MEASURES IN CONGRESS.

a

HISTORY

OF THE

ANTISLAVERY MEASURES

OF THE

THIRTY-SEVENTH AND THIRTY-EIGHTH
UNITED-STATES CONGRESSES,

1861–64.

By HENRY WILSON.

BOSTON:
WALKER, WISE, AND COMPANY,
245, WASHINGTON STREET.
1864.

Entered, according to Act of Congress, in the year 1864, by
WALKER, WISE, AND COMPANY,
In the Clerk's Office of the District Court of the District of Massachusetts.

BOSTON:
STEREOTYPED AND PRINTED BY JOHN WILSON AND SON,
No. 5, Water Street.

PREFACE.

Since the adoption of the Federal Constitution, questions pertaining to slaves and slavery have often been pressed upon the Congress of the United States. Those questions, generally, originated by the slaveholding class, have, down to the 4th of March, 1861, almost uniformly resulted in the success of measures tending to the perpetuity and extension of slavery, and to the increase of its influence over the National Government. Since the breaking-out of the Rebellion, the exigencies of the nation have forced upon the 37th and 38th Congresses the consideration of a series of antislavery measures. These measures, so comprehensive in their scope and character, cannot fail to have a lasting influence upon the future of the country. I have sought, in this volume, to narrate, with brevity, fairness, and impartiality, the history of the antislavery legislation of Congress during the past three years of civil war. In tracing the words of the actors in these great measures of legislation, I have endeavored faithfully to give their ideas, or to quote their words, so as to present to the reader their position, feelings, and opinions. Trusting that I have not wholly failed in my endeavors to record with fidelity this antislavery legislation, I present this volume to the public, in the hope that it will be of some little interest, especially to those who, amid years of obloquy and reproach, have labored and hoped for the dawning of that day, when, in all the wide circuit of our land, "the sun will not rise upon a master, or set upon a slave."

CONTENTS.

CHAPTER I.

SLAVES USED FOR INSURRECTIONARY PURPOSES MADE FREE.

Slaves used in the Rebel Forces. Mr. Trumbull's Proposition to free Slaves used for Military Purposes. Mr. Trumbull's Speech. Mr. Breckinridge's Speech. Mr. Wilson's Speech. Mr. Breckinridge's Reply. Mr. M'Dougall's Speech. Mr. Ten Eyck's Speech. Mr. Pearce's Speech. Adoption of Mr. Trumbull's Amendment freeing Slaves used for Military Purposes. Substitute reported by the Judiciary Committee of the House. Substitute Rejected. Mr. Bingham's Speech. Mr. Burnett's Speech. Mr. Crittenden's Speech. Mr. Kellogg's Speech. Mr. Cox's Motion to lay the Bill on the Table. Mr. Pendleton's Speech. Mr. Stevens's Speech. Mr. Diven's Speech. Mr. Pendleton's Motion to recommit the Bill carried. Bill reported back with an Amendment. Mr. Holman's Motion to lay the Bill on the Table. Passage of the Bill. . . . . pp. 1-16.

CHAPTER II.

FUGITIVE SLAVES NOT TO BE RETURNED BY PERSONS IN THE ARMY.

Surrender of Slaves coming within the Lines of the Union Armies. Mr. Lovejoy's Resolution. Notice of a Bill by Mr. Wilson. Mr. Lovejoy's Bill. Mr. Sumner's Resolution. Mr. Cowan's Speech. Resolution of Mr. Wilson of Iowa. Bill of Mr. Wilson of Massachusetts. Mr. Wilson's Bill considered. Mr. Saulsbury's Motion to postpone indefinitely. Mr. Collamer's Amendment. Mr. Powell's Speech. Mr. Collamer's Speech. Mr. Wilson's Speech. Mr. Pearce's Speech. Mr. Blair's Bill to make an additional Article of War. Mr. Bingham's Speech. Mr. Vallandigham's Motion to lay the Bill on the Table. Passage of the House Bill. Reported by Mr. Wilson in the Senate. Mr. Davis's

viii   CONTENTS.

Amendment. Mr. Saulsbury's Amendment. Mr. M'Dougall's Speech. Mr. Howard's Speech. Passage of the Bill. Mr. Wilson's Resolution concerning the Surrender of Fugitives. Mr. Grimes's Amendment. Mr. Grimes's Speech. Mr. Sumner's Speech. Mr. Saulsbury's Speech.
pp. 17-37.

CHAPTER III.

THE ABOLITION OF SLAVERY IN THE DISTRICT OF COLUMBIA.

The National Capital. Slavery. Mr. Wilson's Resolution. The District Committee. Mr. Wilson's Bill. Mr. Morrill's Report, with Amendments. Mr. Wilson's Bill to repeal the Slave Code. Committee's Amendments adopted. Mr. Morrill's Amendments. Mr. Davis's Amendments. Mr. Doolittle's Amendment. Remarks by Mr. Davis. Mr. Hale. Mr. Doolittle. Mr. Pomeroy. Mr. Willey. Mr. Saulsbury. Mr. King. Mr. Davis. Mr. Wilson. Mr. Kennedy. Mr. Saulsbury. Mr. Harlan. Mr. Wilkinson. Mr. Saulsbury's Amendment. Mr. Sumner. Mr. Wright. Mr. Fessenden. Mr. Davis's Amendment. Mr. Clark's Amendment. Mr. Willey's Amendment. Mr. Clark's Amendment. Mr. Davis. Mr. Morrill. Mr. M'Dougall. Mr. Sumner's Amendment. Mr. Wright's Amendment. Mr. Browning's Amendment. Mr. Wilmot. Mr. Collamer's Amendment. Mr. Doolittle's Amendment. Mr. Powell. Mr. Bayard. Passage of the Bill. House. Mr. Stevens's Motion. Mr. Thomas. Mr. Noxon. Mr. Blair. Mr. Crittenden. Mr. Riddle. Mr. Fessenden. Mr. Rollins. Mr. Blake. Mr. Van Horn. Mr. Ashley. Mr. Hutchins. Mr. Wright's Amendment. Mr. Hickman. Mr. Wadsworth. Mr. Harding's Amendment. Mr. Train's Amendment. Mr. Lovejoy. Mr. Wickliffe's Amendment. Mr. Holman's Amendment. Mr. Cox. Mr. Menzies' Amendment. Passage of the Bill. . . . . pp. 38-78.

CHAPTER IV.

THE PRESIDENT'S PROPOSITION TO AID STATES IN THE ABOLISHMENT OF SLAVERY.

The President's Special Message. Mr. Roscoe Conkling's Resolution. Mr. Richardson's Speech. Mr. Bingham's Speech. Mr. Voorhees' Speech. Mr. Mallory's Speech. Mr. Wickliffe's Speech. Mr. Diven's Speech. Mr. Thomas's Speech. Mr. Biddle's Speech. Mr. Crisfield's Speech. Mr. Olin's Speech. Mr. Crittenden's Speech. Mr. Fisher's Speech. Mr. Hickman's Speech. Passage of the Bill in the House. In the Senate,

CONTENTS. ix

the Resolution reported without Amendment by Mr. Trumbull. Mr. Saulsbury's Speech. Mr. Davis's Amendment. Mr. Sherman's Speech. Mr. Doolittle's Speech. Mr. Willey's Speech. Mr. Browning's Speech. Mr. M'Dougall's Speech. Mr. Powell's Speech. Mr. Latham's Speech. Mr. Morrill's Speech. Mr. Henderson's Amendment. Mr. Sherman's Speech. Passage of the Resolution. . . . . pp. 79-91.

CHAPTER V.

THE PROHIBITION OF SLAVERY IN THE TERRITORIES.

Mr. Arnold's Bill. Mr. Lovejoy's Report. Motion to lay the Bill on the Table. Mr. Lovejoy's Substitute. Remarks of Mr. Cox. Mr. Diven. Mr. Olin. Mr. Crisfield. Mr. Kelley. Mr. Sheffield. Mr. Stevens. Mr. Thomas. Mr. Bingham. Mr. Fisher. Passage of the Bill in the House. In the Senate. Mr. Browning's Report. Mr. Browning's Amendment. Mr. Carlile's Speech. Mr. Wade's Speech. Passage of the Bill as amended. Amendment of the Senate concurred in.
pp. 92-109.

CHAPTER VI.

CERTAIN SLAVES TO BE MADE FREE.

Mr. Pomeroy's Bill. Mr. Trumbull's Bill. Mr. Morrill's Joint Resolution. Report of the Judiciary Committee. Mr. Sumner's Amendment. Mr. Sherman's Amendment. Remarks of Mr. Willey. Mr. Hale's Reply. Mr. Harris's Amendment. Remarks of Mr. Howard. Mr. Collamer's Amendment. Motion to refer to a Select Committee. Remarks of Mr. Wilmot. Mr. Wilson's Amendment. Mr. Collamer. Motion to refer to a Select Committee by Mr. Clark. Remarks of Mr. Hale. Mr. Wilson's Reply. Select Committee. Mr. Clark's Report. Mr. Sumner's Amendment. Mr. Davis's Amendment. Mr. Saulsbury's Amendment. Mr. Wilson's Amendment. Mr. Clark's Amendment. Mr. Sumner's Amendment. Passage of the Bill. House. Mr. Eliot's Resolution. Mr. Roscoe Conkling's Amendment. Mr. Campbell's Resolution. Mr. Stevens's Resolution. Mr. Conway's Resolution. Bills referred to Judiciary Committee. Mr. Hickman's Report. Mr. Bingham's Substitute. Mr. Porter's Amendment. Mr. Eliot's Report. Bill defeated. Reconsideration. Recommitted on Motion of Mr. Porter. Reported back by Mr. Eliot. Mr. Clark's Amendment. Senate Amendment lost in the House. Senate Conference Committee. House Conference Committee. Report of Conference Committee. Mr. Clark's Senate Amendment adopted. . . . . pp. 110-174.

CHAPTER VII.

HAYTI AND LIBERIA.

Mr. Sumner's Bill to authorize the Appointment of Diplomatic Representatives to Hayti and Liberia. Mr. Sumner's Speech. Mr. Davis's Amendment. Mr. Davis's Speech. Passage of the Bill. The Bill reported in the House. Mr. Gooch's Speech. Mr. Cox's Amendment. Mr. Cox's Speech. Mr. Biddle's Speech. Mr. Kelley's Speech. Mr. M'Knight's Speech. Mr. Eliot's Speech. Mr. Thomas's Speech. Mr. Fessenden's Speech. Mr. Maynard's Speech. Mr. Crittenden's Speech. Passage of the Bill. . . . . pp. 175–183.

CHAPTER VIII.

EDUCATION OF COLORED YOUTH IN THE DISTRICT OF COLUMBIA.

Mr. Grimes's Bill. Mr. Grimes's Report. Mr. Wilson's Amendment. Remarks of Mr. Wilson. Passage of the Bill. Bill reported in the House by Mr. Rollins. Passage of the Bill. Mr. Lovejoy's Bill. Reported by Mr. Fessenden. Passage of the Bill. Bill reported in the Senate by Mr. Grimes. Passage of the Bill. Mr. Wilson's Bill. Reported from the District Committee. Remarks by Mr. Carlile. Mr. Grimes. Mr. Davis. Mr. Morrill. Passage of the Bill in the Senate. Passage in the House. Mr. Wilson's Bill. Mr. Grimes's Bill. Passage in the Senate. Mr. Patterson's Substitute. Passage of the Bill. . . . pp. 184–194.

CHAPTER IX.

THE AFRICAN SLAVE-TRADE.

The Treaty between the United States and Great Britain for the Suppression of the Slave-trade. Mr. Sumner's Bill. Remarks of Mr. Saulsbury. Passage of the Bill. Mr. Foster's Bill. Passage of the Bill.
pp. 195–197.

CHAPTER X.

ADDITIONAL ACT TO ABOLISH SLAVERY IN THE DISTRICT OF COLUMBIA.

Mr. Wilson's Bill. Reported back with Amendments by Mr. Grimes. Mr. Grimes's Speech. Mr. Wilson's Speech. Committee's Amendments. Mr. Sumner's Amendment. Passage of the Bill. Bill in the House. Remarks of Mr. Wickliffe. Motion to lay on the Table by Mr. Cox. Remarks by Mr. Crisfield. Passage of the Bill. . pp. 198–202.

CHAPTER XI.

COLORED SOLDIERS.

Mr. Wilson's Bill. Mr. Grimes's Amendment. Remarks of Mr. Saulsbury. Mr. Carlile. Mr. King's Amendment. Mr. Sherman's Speech. Mr. Fessenden's Speech. Mr. Rice's Speech. Mr. Wilson's Speech. Mr. Davis's Amendment. Mr. Collamer's Speech. Mr. Ten Eyck's Speech. Mr. King's Speech. Mr. Henderson's Amendment. Mr. Sherman's Amendment. Mr. Browning's Amendment. Mr. Lane's Speech. Mr. Harlan's Speech. Mr. Wilson's Bill. Remarks by Mr. Sherman. Mr. Lane. Speech of Mr. Howard. Mr. Sherman's Amendment. Mr. Browning's amendment. Remarks of Mr. Henderson. Mr. Wright. Mr. Doolittle. Mr. Powell. Passage of the Bill. Mr. Stevens's Amendment. Remarks of Mr. Clay. Mr. Boutwell. Mr. Davis's Amendment. Mr. Mallory's Speech. Mr. Webster's Amendment. Mr. Scofield's Speech. Mr. Wood's Speech. Mr. Whalley's Amendment. Mr. Stevens's Amendment adopted. Conference Committee. Report adopted.
pp. 203–223.

CHAPTER XII.

AID TO THE STATES TO EMANCIPATE THEIR SLAVES.

Mr. Wilson's Joint Resolution. House Committee on Emancipation. Mr. White's Bill. Mr. Wilson's Resolution. Mr. Henderson's Bill. Mr. Noell's Bill. Mr. White's Report. Remarks of Mr. Clements. Mr. Wickliffe. Mr. Noell. Passage of the Bill. House Bill reported by Mr. Trumbull. Remarks of Mr. Henderson. Mr. Wilson's Amendment. Remarks of Mr. Fessenden. Mr. Trumbull. Mr. Foster. Mr. Wilson. Mr. Sherman. Mr. Cowan. Mr. Bayard. Mr. Clark. Mr. Lane of Kansas. Mr. Morrill. Mr. Wilson's Amendment. Mr. Grimes's Speech. Mr. Kennedy's Speech. Mr. Harris's Report. Mr. Wilson of Missouri. Mr. Wall's Speech. Mr. Richardson's Amendment. Mr. Collamer's Amendment. Mr. Sumner's Amendment. Remarks of Mr. Powell. Mr. Sumner's Amendment. Mr. Sumner's Speech. Passage of the Bill as amended. Mr. White's Report in the House. Bill referred to Committee of the Whole. . . . . pp. 224–248.

CHAPTER XIII.

AMENDMENT OF THE CONSTITUTION.

Mr. Ashley's Bill. Mr. Wilson's Joint Resolution. House Committee on the Judiciary. Mr. Henderson's Joint Resolution. Mr. Sumner's Resolution. Mr. Henderson's Amendment reported with an Amendment.

Remarks of Mr. Trumbull. Mr. Wilson. Mr. Davis's Amendment. Remarks of Mr. Saulsbury. Mr. Clark. Mr. Howe. Mr. Johnson. Mr. Davis's Amendments. Mr. Powell's Amendment. Remarks of Mr. Harlan. Mr. Hale. Mr. M'Dougall. Mr. Hendricks. Mr. Henderson. Mr. Sumner. Mr. Sumner's Amendment. Remarks of Mr. Trumbull. Mr. Howard. Passage of the Joint Resolution in the Senate. Mr. Morris's Speech. Remarks of Mr. Herrick. Mr. Kellogg. Mr. Pruyn. Mr. Wood. Mr. Higby. Mr. Wheeler's Amendment. Mr. Kellogg of Michigan. Mr. Ross. Mr. Holman. Mr. Thayer. Mr. Mallory. Mr. Ingersoll. Mr. Pendleton's Amendment. Joint Resolution defeated. Mr. Ashley's Motion to reconsider. . . pp. 249–272.

CHAPTER XIV.

REPEAL OF FUGITIVE-SLAVE LAWS.

Mr. Howe's Bill. Mr. Wilmot's Bill. Mr. Wilson's Bill. Mr. Stevens's Bill. Mr. Ashley's Bill. Mr. Julian's Bill. Special Committee on Slavery. Mr. Sumner's Bill and Report. Mr. Foster's Speech. Mr. Sherman's Amendment. Mr. Johnson's Speech. Mr. Sumner's Speech. Mr. Saulsbury's Amendment. Mr. Brown's Speech. Mr. Howard's Amendment. Remarks of Mr. Conness. Mr. Morris's Bill. Remarks of Mr. Mallory. Mr. Morris. M. Wilson. Mr. Pendleton. Mr. King. Mr. Cox. Mr. Hubbard. Mr. Farnsworth. Passage of Mr. Morris's Bill in the House. Mr. Morris's Bill reported by Mr. Sumner. Mr. Saulsbury's Amendment. Mr. Johnson's Amendment. Passage of the Bill.
pp. 273–292.

CHAPTER XV.

PAY OF COLORED SOLDIERS.

Mr. Wilson's Bill. Mr. Grimes's Amendment. Mr. Wilson's Joint Resolution. M. Conness's Amendment. Remarks of Mr. Fessenden. Mr. Wilson. Mr. Foster. Mr. Sumner. Mr. Johnson. Mr. Grimes. Mr. Howe. Mr. Wilson. Mr. Grimes. Mr. Cowan's Amendment. Mr. Sumner's Amendment. Mr. Wilson's Amendment. Mr. Doolittle's Amendment. Mr. Sumner's Amendment to Mr. Cowan's Amendment. Mr. Wilson's Amendment. Remarks of Mr. Clark. Mr. Davis's Amendment. Mr. Collamer's Amendment. Remarks of Mr. Foot. Mr. Sumner's Amendment. Remarks of Mr. Wilkinson. Mr. Wilson. Mr. Howard. Mr. Johnson. Mr. Fessenden. Mr. Wilson's Bill. Mr. Davis's Amendment. Passage of the Bill. Mr. Wilson's Amendment to the Army Appropriation Bill. Mr. Stevens's Amendment. Remarks of Mr. Holman. Mr. Price. Mr. Holman's Amendment. Conference Committees. Report accepted. . . . . pp. 293–312.

CONTENTS. xiii

CHAPTER XVI.

TO MAKE FREE THE WIVES AND CHILDREN OF COLORED SOLDIERS.

Mr. Wilson's Bill to promote Enlistments. Mr. Powell's Motion to strike out the Section to make free the Mothers, Wives, and Children of Colored Soldiers. Mr. Henderson's Amendment. Remarks of Mr Grimes. Mr. Wilkinson. Remarks of Mr. Johnson. Mr. Sherman's Speech. Mr. Carlile's Speech. Remarks of Mr. Doolittle. Mr. Brown's Amendment. Mr. Wilson's Amendment. Mr. Wilkinson's Amendment. Remarks of Mr. Sherman. Mr. Grimes. Mr. Conness's Motion to refer the Bill. Remarks of Mr. Clark. Mr. Howard. Mr. Fessenden. Mr. Davis's Amendment. Mr. Wilkinson's Speech. Mr. Wilson's Joint Resolution.
pp. 313-327.

CHAPTER XVII.

A BUREAU OF FREEDMEN.

Memorial of the Massachusetts Emancipation League. Mr. Eliot's Bill. Select Committee on Emancipation. Freedmen's Bill reported by Mr. Eliot. Remarks of Mr. Eliot. Mr. Cox. Mr. Cole. Mr. Brooks. Mr. Kelley. Mr. Dawson. Mr. Price. Mr. Knapp. Mr. Pendleton. Passage of Mr. Eliot's Bill. Mr. Sumner's Bill. Mr. Eliot's Bill reported by Mr. Sumner, with an Amendment. Mr. Sumner's Speech. Mr. Sumner's Amendment amended and adopted in the Senate. The House postpone the Bill to the next Session. . . . . pp. 328-336.

CHAPTER XVIII.

RECONSTRUCTION OF REBEL STATES.

Mr. Harlan's Bill. Mr. Sumner's Resolutions. Mr. Ashley's Bill. Mr. Harris's Bill. Mr. Winter Davis's Resolution. Select Committee on Reconstruction. Mr. Davis's Bill. Remarks of Mr. Davis, Mr. Beaman, Mr. Allen, Mr. Smithers, Mr. Norton, Mr. Broomall, Mr. Scofield, Mr. Dawson, Mr. Williams, Mr. Baldwin of Massachusetts, Mr. Donnelly, Mr. Perham, Mr. Gooch, Mr. Fernando Wood, Mr. Kelley, Mr. Boutwell, Mr. Pendleton. Mr. Davis's Substitute. Passage of Mr. Davis's Bill. House Bill reported by Mr. Wade. Mr. Brown's Amendment. Mr. Sumner's Amendment. Passage of Mr. Brown's Substitute. House non-concur. Senate recede. Passage of the Bill. The President refuses to approve it. . . . . pp. 337-347.

xiv   CONTENTS.

CHAPTER XIX.

CONFINEMENT OF COLORED PERSONS IN THE WASHINGTON JAIL.

Mr. Wilson's Joint Resolution. Remarks of Mr. Wilson, Mr. Clark, Mr. Hale, Mr. Wilson, Mr. Fessenden, Mr. Sumner. Mr. Clark's Resolution. Mr. Grimes's Bill. Remarks of Mr. Grimes. Mr. Powell's Amendment. Remarks of Mr. Pearce, Mr. Powell, Mr. Carlile, Mr. Wilson, Mr. Fessenden, Mr. Latham, Mr. Cowan. Passage of the Bill. Mr. Wilson's Bill. Remarks of Mr. Wilson. Mr. Grimes's Amendment. Remarks of Mr. M'Dougall, Mr. Hale, Mr. Wilson, Mr. Pearce, Mr. Sumner. Mr. Bingham's Bill. . . . . pp. 348–357.

CHAPTER XX.

NEGRO TESTIMONY.

The Bill to abolish Slavery in the District of Columbia. Mr. Sumner's Amendment. Supplementary Bill to abolish Slavery in the District of Columbia. Mr. Sumner's Amendment. Mr. Sumner's Bill. Mr. Sumner's Amendment to the Civil Appropriation Bill. Remarks of Mr. Sumner. Mr. Sherman. Mr. Buckalew's Amendment. Remarks of Mr. Saulsbury. Mr. Howard. Mr. Sumner's Amendment adopted.
pp. 358–361.

CHAPTER XXI.

THE COASTWISE SLAVE-TRADE.

Mr. Sumner's Bill. Mr. Sumner's Amendment to the Civil Appropriation Bill. Remarks of Mr. Sherman, Mr. Sumner, Mr. Johnson, Mr. Hendricks, Mr. Collamer, Mr. Johnson, Mr. Saulsbury, Mr. Doolittle. Adoption of Mr. Sumner's Amendment. . . . . pp. 362–366.

CHAPTER XXII.

COLOR NO DISQUALIFICATION FOR CARRYING THE MAILS.

Mr. Sumner's Bill. Passage in the Senate. Reported by Mr. Colfax in the House. Remarks of Mr. Colfax. Mr. Dawes. Mr. Wickliffe. Bill laid on the Table. Mr. Sumner's Bill. Mr. Collamer's Amendment. Remarks of Mr. Collamer. Mr. Lane of Indiana. Mr. Lane of Kansas. Mr. Saulsbury. Mr. Sumner. Mr. Powell. Mr. Hendricks. Mr. Powell's Amendment. Remarks of Mr. Conness. Mr. Johnson.
pp. 367–370.

CHAPTER XXIII.

NO EXCLUSION FROM THE CARS ON ACCOUNT OF COLOR.

Mr. Sumner's Amendment. Remarks of Mr. Saulsbury, Mr. Johnson, Mr. Sumner, Mr. Morrill. Mr. Sumner's Amendment. Remarks of Mr. Sherman, Mr. Hendricks, Mr. Willey, Mr. Sumner, Mr. Wilson, Mr. Trumbull, Mr. Sumner, Mr. Wilson, Mr. Grimes, Mr. Powell. Amendment agreed to. . . . . pp. 371–376.

CHAPTER XXIV.

CONCLUSION. . . . . pp. 377–384.

ANTISLAVERY MEASURES IN CONGRESS.

CHAPTER I.

SLAVES USED FOR INSURRECTIONARY PURPOSES MADE FREE.

SLAVES USED IN THE REBEL FORCES. — MR. TRUMBULL'S PROPOSITION TO FREE SLAVES USED FOR MILITARY PURPOSES. — MR. TRUMBULL'S SPEECH. — MR. BRECKINRIDGE'S SPEECH. — MR. WILSON'S SPEECH. — MR. BRECKINRIDGE'S REPLY. — MR. M'DOUGALL'S SPEECH. — MR. TEN EYCK'S SPEECH. — MR. PEARCE'S SPEECH. — ADOPTION OF MR. TRUMBULL'S AMENDMENT FREEING SLAVES USED FOR MILITARY PURPOSES. — SUBSTITUTE REPORTED BY THE JUDICIARY COMMITTEE OF THE HOUSE. — SUBSTITUTE REJECTED. — MR. BINGHAM'S SPEECH. — MR. BURNETT'S SPEECH. — MR. CRITTENDEN'S SPEECH. — MR. KELLOGG'S SPEECH. — MR. COX'S MOTION TO LAY THE BILL ON THE TABLE. — MR. PENDLETON'S SPEECH. — MR. STEVENS'S SPEECH. — MR. DIVEN'S SPEECH. — MR. PENDLETON'S MOTION TO RECOMMIT THE BILL CARRIED. — BILL REPORTED BACK WITH AN AMENDMENT. — MR. HOLMAN'S MOTION TO LAY THE BILL ON THE TABLE. — PASSAGE OF THE BILL.

AT the opening of the Rebellion, slaves were used by their masters for insurrectionary purposes. Wherever armed rebels gathered, officers, and in many instances privates, brought their slaves with them as servants. Slaves were put at work on fortifications, and employed by thousands as laborers in various capacities in the rising forces of the insurgents. They were used in the erection of the works in the harbor of

Charleston, on which were planted the batteries whose fires demolished Sumter, and kindled the devastating flames of civil war. In Virginia, where the rebel forces were massing for the contest, the labor of slaves lightened the toils of rebel soldiers, and augmented the powers of rebel armies.

In the Senate, on the 20th of July, 1861, Mr. Trumbull (Rep.) of Illinois, Chairman of the Committee on the Judiciary, reported, by order of that committee, a bill to confiscate the property used for insurrectionary purposes. The bill provided, that if during the present or any future insurrection against the Government of the United States, after the President shall have declared by proclamation that the laws of the United States are opposed, and the execution obstructed, by combinations too powerful to be suppressed by the ordinary course of judicial proceedings, any person or persons, his, her, or their agent, attorney, or *employé*, shall purchase or acquire, sell or give, any property, of whatsoever kind or description, with intent to use or employ the same, or suffer the same to be used or employed, in aiding, abetting, or promoting such insurrection, or any person or persons engaged therein; or if any person or persons, being the owner or owners of any such property, shall knowingly use or employ, or consent to the use or employment of, the same, — all such property is to be declared to be lawful subject of prize and capture wherever found.

Mr. Fessenden (Rep.) of Maine thought it a very important bill, that had better be postponed for consideration. Mr. Trumbull did not care to have the bill considered at that time; but he would like to offer an amendment, not reported from the committee, with the view of having it before the Senate. He then proposed as an additional section, —

"That whenever any person claiming to be entitled to the service or labor of any other person, under the laws of any State, shall employ such person in aiding or promoting any insurrection, or in resisting the laws of the United States, or shall permit or suffer him to be so employed, he shall forfeit all right to such service or labor; and the person whose labor or service is thus claimed shall be henceforth discharged therefrom, any law to the contrary notwithstanding."

Mr. Ten Eyck (Rep.) of New Jersey did not understand the Chairman of the Committee on the Judiciary to offer the amendment from that committee. Mr. Trumbull replied, that he had already stated that he offered the amendment himself, not from the committee.

On the 22d of July, the day following the battle of Bull Run, the bill to confiscate property used for insurrectionary purposes was taken up for consideration; the pending question being Mr. Trumbull's amendment freeing slaves used for military purposes. Mr. Breckinridge (Dem.) of Kentucky said, "This amendment strikes me as very objectionable. I do not propose to argue it, for I am aware it will probably command a decided majority in the Senate; but I ask for the yeas and nays on the amendment." Mr. Trumbull, Chairman of the Judiciary Committee, in reply to Mr. Breckinridge, said, "As the yeas and nays are called for, I will state simply what it is, and all there is of it. The amendment provides, that if any person held to service or labor in any State, under the laws thereof (by which, of course, is meant a slave in any of these

States), if employed, in aid of this Rebellion, in digging ditches or intrenchments, or in any other way, or if used for carrying guns, or if used to destroy this Government, by the consent of his master, his master shall forfeit all right to him, and he shall be for ever discharged; and I am glad the yeas and nays are called to let us see who is willing to vote that the traitorous owner of a negro shall employ him to shoot down the Union men of the country, and yet insist upon restoring him to the traitor that owns him. I understand that negroes were in the fight which has recently occurred. I take it that negroes who are used to destroy the Union, and to shoot down the Union men by the consent of traitorous masters, ought not to be restored to them. If the senator from Kentucky is in favor of restoring them, let him vote against the amendment. To these remarks of Mr. Trumbull, Mr. Breckinridge replied, with some warmth of manner, " The line of remarks made by the senator appears to me to be altogether uncalled for. I expect to do my duty here as a senator, upon my own conscience and upon my own judgment, according to the Constitution. I shall enter into no argument in reply. I showed my willingness to vote by asking for the yeas and nays. In my opinion, the amendment will be one of a series which will amount, before we are done with it, — if, unhappily, we have no settlement or adjustment soon, — to a general confiscation of all property, and a loosing of all bonds. The inferences the senator draws are not deducible from my motives and purpose in calling for the yeas and nays on this amendment, and the vote I shall give."

"I shall vote," said Mr. Wilson (Rep.) of Massachusetts, "with more heart than I vote for ordinary measures, for this proposition. I hope the Senate and the House of Representatives will sustain it, and that this Government will carry it out with an inflexibility that knows no change. The idea that men who are in arms destroying their country shall be permitted to use others for that purpose, and that we shall stand by and issue orders to our commanders, that we should disgrace our cause and our country by returning such men to their traitorous masters, ought not longer to be entertained. The time has come for that to cease; and by the blessing of God, as far as I am concerned, I mean it shall cease. If there is anybody in this Chamber that chooses to take the other path, let him do it: let him know what our purpose is. Our purpose is to save this Government and save this country, and to put down treason; and, if traitors use bondmen to destroy this country, my doctrine is that the Government shall at once convert those bondmen into men that cannot be used to destroy our country. I have no apologies to make for this position. I take it proudly. I think the time has come, when this Government, and the men who are in arms under the Government, should cease to return to traitors their fugitive slaves, whom they are using to erect batteries, to murder brave men who are fighting under the flag of their country. The time has come when we should deal with the men who are organizing negro companies, and teaching them to shoot down loyal men for the only offence of upholding the flag of their country. I hope further, sir, that there is a public sentiment in this country that will blast men who will rise in the Senate, or out of it, to make apologies for treason, or to defend or to maintain the doctrine that this Government is bound to protect traitors in converting their slaves into tools for the destruction of the Republic."

"One single word, sir," said Mr. Breckinridge in reply. "The senator from Massachusetts is a senator from that Commonwealth, and, I presume, discharges what he believes to be his duty. I am a senator from Kentucky, and I do the same thing; and when the senator attempts to deter me from doing my duty in my place, by intimating to me that the public sentiment, here or elsewhere, will blast any man who votes as he believes in his conscience to be right, I tell him that he speaks to the wind. I will utter no unparliamentary language; but I give that senator notice now, that it is perfectly idle to attempt to influence the conduct of senators, in the discharge of their public duties, by any such course of remark."

"I understand this amendment," said Mr. M·Dougall (Dem.) of California, "to be in the nature of a confiscation for treason. I am in favor of it; but I ask the senator from Illinois to make one modification in it. As it now reads, it makes the confiscation where the masters 'permit or suffer' the employment of these parties. 'Suffer' may be something he is compelled to do, and therefore I object to that term." Mr. Trumbull would agree to that amendment.

Mr. Ten Eyck of New Jersey said, "No longer ago than Saturday last, I voted in the Judiciary Committee against this amendment, for two reasons: first, I did not believe that persons in rebellion against this Government would make use of such means as the employment of persons held to labor or service in their armies; secondly, because I did not know what was to become of these poor wretches if they were discharged. God knows, we do not want them in our section of the Union. But, sir, having learned, and believing, that these persons have been employed with arms in their hands to shed the blood of the Union-loving men of this country, I shall now vote in favor of that amendment, with less regard to what may become of these people than I had on Saturday. I will merely instance that there is a precedent for this. If I recollect history aright, Gen. Jackson, in the Seminole War, declared that every slave who was taken in arms against the United States should be set free."

"It will not be surprising to the Senate," said Mr. Pearce (Dem.) of Maryland, "if those who come from the section of the country in which I reside should be a little sensitive at any thing which proposes, as this amendment does, an act of emancipation, however limited and qualified. That is my objection to it. Besides, I think it will be *brutum fulmen*. Nothing will come of it but more of that irritation of which it is my earnest prayer there shall be as little as possible. I think it is the part of statesmen, in managing the concerns of the country at this dreadful crisis, to observe all possible toleration, all conciliation, all liberality; not looking merely at the events of the day, but at the great events that may crowd upon us for years, and upon which the fate of the country, for weal or for woe, may depend for a century. I am not insensible to the magnitude of this occasion. I look at all its aspects, and at all the consequences which may result from that which is now in progress.. No man deplores it more deeply than I do. No man sought more earnestly to shun it. I only ask now, that this measure, which cannot be of any very active force, may not be adopted; because it will only add one more to the irritations which are already exasperating the country to far too great an extent. It will inflame suspicions which have had much to do with producing our present evils; will disturb those who are now calm and quiet; inflame those who are restless; irritate numbers who would not be exasperated by any thing else; and will, in all probability, produce no other real effect than these. Being, then, useless, unnecessary, and irritating, it is, in my opinion, unwise."

The question, being taken by yeas and nays, resulted — yeas 33, nays 6 — as follows: —

YEAS. — Messrs. Anthony, Bingham, Browning, Chandler, Clark, Collamer, Cowan, Dixon, Doolittle, Fessenden, Foot, Foster, Grimes, Hale, Harlan, Harris, Howe, Johnson of Tennessee, King, Lane of Kansas, M'Dougall, Morrill, Nesmith, Pomeroy, Sherman, Simmons, Sumner, Ten Eyck, Trumbull, Wade, Wilkinson, Wilmot, and Wilson, — 33.

NAYS. — Messrs. Breckinridge, Johnson of Missouri, Kennedy, Pearce, Polk, and Powell, — 6.

So the amendment was agreed to, the bill was reported to the Senate as amended, the amendments were concurred in, and the bill passed the Senate.

In the House of Representatives, on the 2d of August, Mr. Bingham (Rep.) of Ohio, from the Committee on the Judiciary, reported back, with an amendment in the nature of a substitute, the Senate bill to confiscate property used for insurrectionary purposes.

It provided that whenever hereafter, during the existence of the present insurrection against the Government of the United States, any person held to labor or service under the laws of any State shall be required or permitted, by the person to whom such labor or service is due, or his legal agent, to take up arms against the United States, or to work or be employed in or about any fort, navy-yard, armory, dock-yard, ship, or in any military or naval service, against the Government of the United States, or as the servant of any person engaged in active hostilities against the United States, then the person to whom such labor is due shall forfeit all claim to such service or labor, any law of any State or of the United States to the contrary notwithstanding; and, in case of a claim for such labor, such facts shall be a full and sufficient answer.

Mr. Bingham said, "The substitute is the instruction of a majority of the committee, from which I dissent." Mr. Sheffield (Dem.) of Rhode Island desired "to know to whom this right of property is to be forfeited." To this question Mr. Bingham replied, "The forfeiture is simply a forfeiture of all claim, under any State laws or under any laws of the United States, of the person so offending, to any person hitherto held to service by him."

Mr. Kellogg (Rep.) of Illinois proposed an amendment to the original bill, — to strike out, in the fourth section, all after the sixth line, as follows: "And the person whose labor or service is thus claimed shall be thenceforth discharged therefrom, any law to the contrary notwithstanding;" and insert, in lieu thereof, as follows: "And such claim to service or labor shall be confiscated."

Mr. Bingham demanded the previous question on the substitute reported by the Judiciary Committee, and the substitute was rejected.

Mr. Bingham then remarked, that "the Senate bill is a sweeping declaration, that whenever any person claiming to be entitled to the service or labor of any other person, under the laws of any State, shall employ such person in aiding or promoting any insurrection, or in resisting the laws of the United States, or shall permit him to be so employed, he shall forfeit all right to such service or labor; and the person whose labor or service is thus claimed shall be thenceforth discharged therefrom, any law to the contrary notwithstanding."

Mr. Burnett (Dem.) of Kentucky understood that "the use of a slave, by authority of the owner, in any mode which will tend to aid or promote this insurrection, will entitle that slave to his freedom."—"Certainly it will," replied Mr. Bingham. "Or with his consent," inquired Mr. Burnett, "or the consent of his agent, in any mode whatever, then the negro is entitled to his freedom?"—"Yes, sir," replied Mr. Bingham. "Then," exclaimed Mr. Burnett, "that amounts to a wholesale emancipation of the slaves in the seceding or rebellious States."—"No just court in America," replied Mr. Bingham, "will ever construe this fourth section, if it becomes a law, to the effect, that because it happens that citizens of the United States, residing in a seceding State, hold slaves, this law amounts to an emancipation of their slaves. By the express words of the bill, it is limited in its effect to those persons, who themselves, by their own direct acts, for the purpose of overturning the powers of the Government, employ, or consent that others shall employ, the services of their slaves to that end. I aver that a traitor should not only forfeit his slaves, but he should forfeit his life as well." — "It has been conceded," said Mr. Crittenden of Kentucky, "in all time, that the Congress of the United States had no power to legislate upon the subject of slavery within the States. Absence of all power of legislation in time of peace must be the absence of the same power at all times. You have no power, by your Constitution, to touch slavery at all."

Mr. M'Clernand (Dem.) of Illinois inquired "if it would not be competent, according to the laws of war, for the Government to forfeit the ownership of a horse found in the use of the enemy in war, and if a law which would forfeit the ownership of a horse would not forfeit the title to a negro found engaged in military service." — "I am not inquiring," replied Mr. Crittenden, "nor am I prepared to make an argument, as to powers in a state of war, — as to national law, world-wide law. I am interposing a positive statute; and I say, if there is no power to do this thing in time of peace, there is no such power at any time."

Mr. Kellogg (Rep.) of Illinois suggested to Mr. Crittenden, "whether it is not competent to forfeit the claim that a man has to his slaves, for treason in the master, in the same way that he would forfeit his claim to his horse, and yet not at all conflict with or abrogate the law that authorizes the holding of slaves." — "If you have no power," replied Mr. Crittenden, "there the question ends. Well, have you a power to legislate concerning a slave in Kentucky, as to his rights present or future? Have you a right to impose any terms or conditions on the master, in time of peace, on which the slave shall be entitled to his liberty?"

Mr. Kellogg, in answer, said, "My idea on that point is simply this: that the citizen of Kentucky, like the citizen of any State, by an infraction of law,—of the highest law of the country,—is liable to penalties and forfeitures. It operates on the person to forfeit his right by his own crime, and does not at all attack or invalidate the right to hold slaves or abolish slavery in Kentucky.

Mr. Cox (Dem.) of Ohio moved that the bill be laid upon the table, and demanded the yeas and nays on his motion. The question was taken; and it was decided in the negative,—yeas 57, nays 71. Mr. Pendleton (Dem.) of Ohio moved to recommit the bill to the Judiciary Committee. "I may be asked," said Mr. Diven (Rep.) of New York, "'What would you do with negroes taken in actual arms against the country? What would you do with negroes found employed in building ships-of-war, fighting battles against the country, rearing fortifications from which shots are to be fired on the soldiers of the Union?' Why, sir, I would treat them as men in arms against the country. I would treat them as prisoners of war. Then I admit that a question, entirely novel in the usages of war, at once occurs. You have then got a species of men as prisoners whom the usages of war, in no place that I have ever seen, treat as such. I proposed in committee, as a substitute for this bill, to relieve the Government and the war-power of the country from the attitude in which the seizure of these men thus employed against the Government would place them, by providing the simple penalty, that any man taken in arms against the Government is taken as a prisoner of war, whether he be black or white or tawny, or whatever may be his complexion. Afterwards, when you come to determine on an exchange of prisoners, you can determine on what terms they should be released. I would have a law by which our generals, when they come to settle on the release as to prisoners, shall make the release of those black men thus employed dependent on the master's losing all right to them. For such a law, and such a bill, I will go most cordially."

Mr. Stevens (Rep.) of Pennsylvania said, "When a country is in open war with an enemy, every publicist agrees that you have the right to use every means which will weaken him. Vattel says, that in time of war, if it be a just war, and there be a people who have been oppressed by the enemy, and that enemy be conquered, the victorious party cannot return that oppressed people to the bondage from which they have rescued them. I wish gentlemen would read what Vattel says upon this subject. I wish the gentleman from New York, especially, would read the remark of Vattel, that one of the most glorious consequences of victory is giving freedom to those who are oppressed." — "I agree to it," replied Mr. Diven. "Then how is it," asked Mr. Stevens, "that if we are justified in taking property from the enemy in war, when you have rescued an oppressed people from the oppression of that enemy, by what principle of the law of nations, by what principle of philanthropy, can you return them to the bondage from which you have delivered them, and rivet again the chains you have once broken? It is a disgrace to the party which advocates it. It is against the principle of the law of nations. It is against every principle of philanthropy. I, for one, shall never shrink from saying, when these slaves are once conquered by us, 'Go, and be free.' God forbid that I should ever agree that they should be restored again to their masters! I warn Southern gentlemen, that, if this war is to continue, there will be a time when my friend from New York (Mr. Diven) will see it declared by this free nation, that every bondman in the South — belonging to a rebel, recollect; I confine it to them — shall be called upon to aid us in war against their masters, and to restore this Union."

On Mr. Pendleton's motion to recommit the bill to the Committee on the Judiciary, the House voted, — ayes 69, noes 48. Mr. Stevens moved to reconsider the vote by which the bill was recommitted. Mr. Kellogg moved that the motion be laid on the table. Mr. Burnett demanded the yeas and nays; and they were ordered, — yeas 71, nays 61.

On the 3d of August, Mr. Bingham, from the Committee on the Judiciary, reported back the Senate bill to confiscate property used for insurrectionary purposes, with an amendment, and demanded the previous question on the third reading of the bill. The amendment proposed to strike out all of section four of the Senate bill after the enacting clause, and insert, —

"That whenever hereafter, during the insurrection against the Government of the United States, any person claimed to be held to labor or service under the laws of any State shall be required or permitted by the person to whom such labor or service is claimed to be due, or by the lawful agent of such person, to take up arms against the United States, or shall be required or permitted by the person to whom such service or labor is claimed to be due, or his lawful agent, to work or to be employed in or upon any fort, navy-yard, dock, armory, ship, or intrenchment, or in any military or naval service whatever, against the Government and lawful authority of the United States, then, and in every such case, the person to whom such service is claimed to be due shall forfeit his claim to such labor, any law of the State or of the United States to the contrary notwithstanding; and, whenever thereafter the person claiming such labor or service shall seek to enforce his claim, it shall be a full and sufficient answer to such claim, that the person whose service or labor is claimed had been employed in hostile service against the Government of the United States, contrary to the provisions of this act."

Mr. Vallandigham (Dem.) of Ohio called for tellers on ordering the previous question: they were ordered, the House divided, and the tellers reported, — ayes 53, nays 42. Mr. Holman (Dem.) of Indiana moved to lay the bill on the table. Mr. Sheffield of Rhode Island demanded the yeas and nays. Mr. M'Pherson (Rep.) of Pennsylvania asked Mr. Holman to withdraw the motion to lay on the table, to enable him to move to postpone the bill until December next. The question was taken on Mr. Holman's motion, and lost, — yeas 47, nays 66. The question recurring on the amendment of the Committee on the Judiciary, Mr. Mallory (Dem.) of Kentucky moved the House do now adjourn, and demanded the yeas and nays; and they were ordered, — yeas 30, nays 75. Mr. Bingham demanded the previous question on the passage of the bill; and it was ordered. Mr. Burnett demanded the yeas and nays on the passage of the bill; and they were ordered. The question was taken, and it was decided in the affirmative, — yeas 60, nays 48, — as follows: —

YEAS. — Messrs. Aldrich, Alley, Arnold, Ashley, Babbitt, Baxter, Beaman, Bingham, Francis P. Blair, Samuel S. Blair, Blake, Buffinton, Chamberlain, Clark, Colfax, Frederick A. Conkling, Covode, Duell, Edwards, Eliot, Fenton, Fessenden, Franchot, Frank, Granger, Gurley, Hanchett, Harrison, Hutchins, Julian, Kelley, Francis W. Kellogg, William Kellogg, Lansing, Loomis, Lovejoy, M'Kean, Mitchell, Justin S. Morrill, Olin, Potter, Alexander H. Rice, Edward H. Rollins, Sedgwick, Sheffield, Shellabarger, Sherman, Sloan, Spaulding, Stevens, Benjamin F. Thomas, Train, Van Horn, Verree, Wallace, Charles W. Walton, E. P. Walton, Wheeler, Albert S. White, and Windom, — 60.

NAYS. — Messrs. Allen, Ancona, Joseph Baily, George H. Browne, Burnett, Calvert, Cox, Cravens, Crisfield, Crittenden, Diven, Dunlap, Dunn, English, Fouke, Grider, Haight, Hale, Harding, Holman, Horton, Jackson, Johnson, Law, May, M'Clernand, M'Pherson, Mallory, Menzies, Morris, Noble, Norton, Odell, Pendleton, Porter, Reid, Robinson, James S. Rollins, Sheil, Smith, John B. Steele, Stratton, Francis Thomas, Vallandigham, Voorhees, Wadsworth, Webster, and Wickliffe, — 48.

So the Senate bill to confiscate the property used for insurrectionary purposes, with the provision moved by Mr. Trumbull, making free the slaves used by the rebel forces, amended by the amendment reported by Mr. Bingham from the Judiciary Committee, was passed. It received the approval of the President on the 6th of August, and became, in the words of Mr. Breckinridge, the first " of a series of acts loosing all bonds."

CHAPTER II.

FUGITIVE SLAVES NOT TO BE RETURNED BY PERSONS IN THE ARMY.

SURRENDER OF SLAVES COMING WITHIN THE LINES OF THE UNION ARMIES. — MR. LOVEJOY'S RESOLUTION. — NOTICE OF A BILL BY MR. WILSON. — MR. LOVEJOY'S BILL. — MR. SUMNER'S RESOLUTION. — MR. COWAN'S SPEECH. — RESOLUTION OF MR. WILSON OF IOWA. — BILL OF MR. WILSON OF MASSACHUSETTS. — MR. WILSON'S BILL CONSIDERED. — MR. SAULSBURY'S MOTION TO POSTPONE INDEFINITELY. — MR. COLLAMER'S AMENDMENT. — MR. POWELL'S SPEECH. — MR. COLLAMER'S SPEECH. — MR. WILSON'S SPEECH. — MR. PEARCE'S SPEECH. — MR. BLAIR'S BILL TO MAKE AN ADDITIONAL ARTICLE OF WAR. — MR. BINGHAM'S SPEECH. — MR. VALLANDIGHAM'S MOTION TO LAY THE BILL ON THE TABLE. — PASSAGE OF THE HOUSE BILL. — REPORTED BY MR. WILSON IN THE SENATE. — MR. DAVIS'S AMENDMENT. — MR. SAULSBURY'S AMENDMENT. — MR. M'DOUGALL'S SPEECH. — MR. HOWARD'S SPEECH. — PASSAGE OF THE BILL. — MR. WILSON'S RESOLUTION CONCERNING THE SURRENDER OF FUGITIVES. — MR. GRIMES'S AMENDMENT. — MR. GRIMES'S SPEECH. — MR. SUMNER'S SPEECH. — MR. SAULSBURY'S SPEECH.

IN the outset of the Rebellion, slaves inspired by the hope of freedom came within the lines of the Union armies. Their masters often sought for them within the encampments, where they had hoped for protection and freedom, and demanded their surrender as escaped bondmen. While many officers refused to surrender these persons claimed as slaves, or to permit slave masters to seek for them within their camps, other officers readily permitted them or their agents, weaponed for violence, to search their camps, seize, bind, and bear away their trembling, despairing victims. In many instances, slaves, who had brought to the officers of the Union armies intelligence of great value, were given up on the demand of rebel claimants. These slaves surrendered by officers of the army were often most mercilessly punished by their enraged masters, whose arms were doubtless nerved by the malignity of their hearts toward the country and its defenders. This revolting practice of arresting and surrendering fugitives coming within the lines of the armies demoralized the soldiers, and outraged the moral sense of the nation.

In the House of Representatives, on the 9th of July, 1861, Mr. Lovejoy (Rep.) of Illinois introduced the following resolution, and demanded the previous question upon its passage: "That, in the judgment of this House, it is no part of the duty of the soldiers of the United States to capture and return fugitive slaves." Mr. Mallory (Dem.) of Kentucky moved to lay it upon the table, — yeas 66, nays 81. The question recurring on agreeing to the resolution, Mr. Logan (Dem.) of Illinois demanded the yeas and nays, and they were ordered, — yeas 93, nays 55.

In the Senate, on the 4th of December, 1861, Mr. Wilson (Rep.) of Massachusetts gave notice of his intention to introduce a bill to punish officers and privates of the army for arresting, detaining, or delivering persons claimed as fugitive slaves. Mr. Lovejoy (Rep.) of Illinois, on the 4th of December, introduced a bill making it a penal offence for any officer or private of the army or navy to capture or return, or aid in the capture or return of, fugitive slaves. It was read twice, and its consideration postponed to the 10th of December.

In the Senate, on the 17th of December, Mr. Sumner (Rep.) of Massachusetts introduced, and asked for its immediate consideration, a resolution, — "That the Committee on Military Affairs and the Militia be directed to consider the expediency of providing, by additional legislation, that our national armies shall not be employed in the surrender of fugitive slaves." Mr. M'Dougall (Dem.) of California objecting, the resolution went over under the rule; but it came up for consideration the next day, and Mr. Sumner stated that he had received communications in regard to the outrages perpetrated in the armies. He said, "With these communications which I have received, some of an official character and others of a private character, I have felt that I should not do my duty if I did not call the attention of the Senate to this outrage. It must be arrested. I am glad to know that my friend and colleague, the chairman of the Committee on Military Affairs, promises us at once a bill to meet this grievance. It ought to be introduced promptly, and to be passed at once. Our troops ought to be saved from this shame." Mr. Cowan (Rep.) of Pennsylvania apprehended that "there need be no possible difficulty whatever upon this question in any of its aspects." He thought "we had nothing in the world to do with all these questions. We send a general," he said, "to suppress this insurrection. What is his duty? If he meets a negro upon his errand, and that negro is an enemy, he treats him as an enemy; if the negro is a friend, he treats him as a friend, and uses him as such. Nothing, to my mind, can be simpler. How is he to determine the title to that negro? Suppose, Mr. President, you were to go into his camp, and say, 'Sir, here is my negro: I want him.' The obvious answer of the general is, 'My dear sir, that may be all true; I have no desire to raise any issues of fact with you: it may be that this is your negro; but I cannot determine that question; I cannot try the title to him; I am not a court; I am not a jury,'—a great many of them, indeed, are not even lawyers. How are they to determine whether this negro is a slave or not? They cannot determine it; they have no right to determine it. If the master, being a loyal man, in that camp insists, and says, 'This is my negro;' I do not know what other men might do, but, if I were the general, I would say to him, 'If this is your negro, your "boy," as you call him,—this man that you are educating to civilization and Christianity,—if he will go with you, if he is willing to submit to your guardianship in this behalf, take him, in God's name, and be away with him.' Suppose the claimant says, 'He will not go, and I want to force him:' what then? I would say to him, 'No, you cannot do that; because that presumes that I decide the very question which I am incompetent to decide. I cannot allow you to use force here, because I am the constable of the nation, and I am the repositary of its force in this behalf, and you cannot use it.'" The resolution was agreed to.

Mr. Wilson (Rep.) of Iowa, on the 23d of December, offered the following resolution, and demanded the previous question upon it: "That the Committee on Military Affairs be requested to report a bill to this House for the enactment of an additional article of war, whereby all officers in the military service of the United

States shall be prohibited from using any portion of the forces under their respective commands for the purpose of returning fugitives from service or labor, and provide for the punishment of such officers as may violate said article by dismissal from the service." Pending the question, the House, on the motion of Mr. Cox (Dem.) of Ohio, adjourned, — yeas 58, nays 53.

Mr. Wilson (Rep.) of Massachusetts, on the 23d of December, introduced a bill in relation to the arrest of persons claimed to be held to service or labor by the officers of the military and naval service of the United States; which was read twice, and referred to the Committee on Military Affairs. It declared that officers in the military service of the United States have, without the authority of law, and against the plainest dictates of justice and humanity, caused persons claimed as fugitives from service or labor to be seized, held, and delivered up; and that such conduct has brought discredit upon our arms, and reproach upon our Government; and it therefore proceeded to enact, that any officer in the military or naval service of the United States, who shall cause any person, claimed to be held to service or labor by reason of African descent, to be seized, held, detained, or delivered up to or for any person claiming such service or labor, shall be deemed guilty of a misdemeanor, and shall be dishonorably discharged, and for ever ineligible to any appointment in the military or naval service of the United States.

. On the 6th of January, 1862, Mr. Wilson reported back his bill from the Committee on Military Affairs, with an amendment. On the 7th of January, Mr. Wilson called it up; and the Senate, as in Committee of the Whole, proceeded to its consideration. The Committee on Military Affairs reported an amendment to strike out all of the original bill, and insert as a substitute, "That it shall be unlawful for any officer in the military or naval service of the United States to cause any person claimed to be held to service or labor by reason of African decent to be seized, held, detained, or delivered up to or for any person claiming such service or labor; and any officer so offending shall be discharged from service, and be for ever ineligible to any appointment in the military or naval service of the United States." Mr. Saulsbury (Dem.) of Delaware moved its indefinite postponement, — yeas 13, nays 23. On motion of Mr. Carlile (Dem.) of Virginia, it was temporarily laid on the table.

The Senate, on the 16th of January, on motion of Mr. Wilson, took from the table and resumed the consideration of the bill to punish persons in the military and naval service for arresting and delivering fugitive slaves. The pending question being on the amendment reported from the Committee on Military Affairs to strike out the original bill, and insert the amendment as a substitute, Mr. Collamer (Rep.) of Vermont said, "Without criticising at all the form of expression of the proposed amendment, I offer a substitute for it, which I send to the Chair, — 'No officer of the army or navy of the United States, or of the volunteers or militia in the service of the United States, shall assume or exercise any military command or authority to arrest, detain, hold, or control any person, on account of such person being holden to service as of African descent; and any such officer so offending shall be dismissed from service.'" Mr. Wilson accepted the amendment proposed by the senator from Vermont. Mr. Powell said, "This is a very important measure; and, as the amendment of the senator from Vermont has only been this moment presented, I ask that the bill be postponed, and the amendment be printed, in order that we may have some time to look into it." — "The amendment," replied Mr. Wilson, "is very plain and simple: a child can comprehend its import. I hope that this important bill, which ought to have been passed on the second day of this session, for the honor of the country, will not be postponed any longer." — "I have drawn up," said Mr. Saulsbury, "very hurriedly, an amendment, which I propose to insert as an additional section, — 'Nor shall any soldier or officer, under like penalty, entice away or detain any person held to service or labor in the United States from his or her master or owner.'" Mr. Collamer thought the amendment hardly german to the subject. "I believe," he said, " we are generally agreed that there is great impropriety in military men exercising military authority within the States, in relation to their internal and municipal affairs: it is very likely to produce collisions, that ought to be avoided. . . . The amendment reported by the committee made it unlawful for an officer to do any thing in regard to the seizure or delivery of a person held to service by reason of African descent: it seemed to direct the individual action of the man as a man; which is, I think, hardly legitimate and proper on this occasion. I do not know but that we have officers in our army who are themselves the owners of slaves. According to the provision reported by the committee, such an officer could not even arrest his own slave under the laws of the State in which he was holden. It seems to me, that, in dealing with officers of the army, our business is to deal with them in their official capacity. Therefore, to strip the subject of all sort of question about that, I have drawn and presented the amendment which the Senate have adopted, and which, I think, should pass into a law, — that no officer shall use any military power over this subject. As to his own individual action, that is a matter which must be left to him." — "If you adopt," said Mr. Saulsbury, "the amendment of the senator from Vermont, you make it penal for a soldier or officer to return, even to a loyal master or owner, his slave; but you provide no penalty against any soldier or any officer for depriving even a loyal master of the services of his slave. My amendment proposes to prohibit, under the same penalty, an officer or a soldier of the army from decoying or enticing away from the service of his master a slave, or from harboring a slave."

Mr. Rice (Dem.) of Minnesota proposed to amend Mr. Saulsbury's amendment by adding, "who may be a loyal citizen of the United States;" and the amendment to the amendment was agreed to. Mr. Collamer thought, that, under Mr. Saulsbury's amendment, "if any soldier wanted to get dismissed from the service, he would have nothing to do but to entice a slave, and he would get himself and the slave both dismissed." — "I am opposed," said Mr. Wilson, "to this amendment in every shape and form, and to any legislation protecting, covering, or justifying slavery for loyal or disloyal masters. The laws on that subject are all that ought to be given at this time. What I want to do is to put upon the statute-book of this country a prohibition to the officers of the army of the United States from arresting, detaining, and delivering up persons claimed as fugitives by the use of military power. There is no law for it. They have acted in violation of law. Some of these officers have dishonored the profession, and disgraced the country: and I mean, if God is willing and I have the power, to reject their confirmation here for that reason; and I give them the notice now." Mr. Pearce (Dem.) of Maryland said, "The senator from Massachusetts objects to a proposition which forbids officers and soldiers of the army from enticing, harboring, or preventing the recovery — that is the amount of it — of a fugitive slave, known to be such, upon the application of his master, known to be his lawful owner, according to the laws of the State in which he lives. What is the effect of that? It is an invitation to all the slaves of the State of Maryland, who can do so, to resort to the camp, sure of protection there, first, because no officer of the army can order their delivery up to their master, however loyal or however indisputable his title may be to that slave. It is an invitation, therefore, to all such people to resort to the lines of the army as a harbor of refuge, a place of asylum, a spot where they can be safe from the operation of the undoubted legal rights of the owner. That is the effect of it; and that is an invitation to the whole body of such people, within the loyal State of Maryland, to accomplish their freedom by indirection. It is not an act of emancipation in its terms; but so far as it can operate, and does operate, it leads directly to that result." The bill was then reported to the Senate; and, pending the question of concurring in Mr. Collamer's amendment, the Chair announced the special order of the day.

In the House, Mr. Blair (Rep.) of Missouri, on the 25th of February, reported from the Committee on Military Affairs a bill to make an additional article of war. The bill provided, that hereafter the following shall be promulgated as an additional article of war for the government of the army of the United States, and shall be obeyed and observed as such: "All officers are prohibited from employing any of the forces under their respective commands for the purpose of returning fugitives from service or labor who may have escaped from any persons to whom such service or labor is claimed to be due. Any officer who shall be found guilty by court-martial of violating this article shall be dismissed from the service." Mr. Bingham (Rep.) of Ohio moved to add, after the word "officers," the words "or persons in the military and naval service of the United States;" and the amendment was agreed to. "You," said Mr. Mallory (Dem.) of Kentucky, "are deciding, by this article of war, that the President of the United States shall not be permitted to send a military force into a State to aid the authorities of that State in enforcing a national law which stands on your statute-book. I ask the gentleman from Missouri whether it is the fixed determination to repeal the Fugitive-slave Law."—"I do not propose," replied Mr. Blair, "to decide the question the gentleman has raised, as to whether this bill, if it becomes a law, will repeal the Fugitive-slave Law or not. I believe, in common with a great many others, that the army of the United States has a great deal better business than returning fugitive slaves." Mr. Mallory wished to postpone the bill to the third Wednesday in March. Mr. Lovejoy objected to Mr. Blair yielding the floor. Mr. Blair would yield the floor to Mr. Mallory for the purpose indicated. Mr. Bingham hoped Mr. Blair would not yield the floor to allow this bill to be postponed to the end of March. He denounced the practice of arresting and returning fugitive slaves by officers of the army, as " a military despotism that the American people should not tolerate for a moment, nor lose a moment in ending it by the enactment of this bill into a law. I say, that a military officer who assumes, wrongfully assumes, to exercise the functions of civil magistracy, and undertakes to sit upon the right of any human being, born within the limits of this Republic, to the possession of his own person and his own soul, and against whom no offence is charged, is worse than a kidnapper. He has no right to do it; and, by so doing, commits a crime, a great crime. Some of your military officers of high and low degree have been detailing their men for the purpose of seizing, and have seized, persons not accused of crime, but *suspected* of the virtue of preferring liberty to bondage. Are we to revive here, in this land, the hated rule of the Athenian ostracism, by which men were condemned, not because they were charged with crime or proved guilty of crime, but because they were *suspected* to possess and practise the virtues of justice and patriotism in such degree as rendered their presence in the State dangerous to republican equality? Aristides was condemned because he was just; and Themistocles, because he was the savior of the city. I have read in the papers, and I believe it is true, that one of these persons *suspected* of escaping from bondage to liberty swam across the Ohio River, making for an encampment upon the Indiana shore, where he saw the banner of Liberty flying, which he fondly looked upon as consecrating that place, at least, as sacred to the rights of person, and where even the rights of a hunted bondman would be respected. After having been beaten about, bruised and mangled against the rocks in the channel of the river, to whose rushing waters he committed his life that he might regain his liberty, he reached the opposite shore. Somebody went into the camp, and reported that this man was suspected of the crime of having run away from chains and slavery. A company of soldiers, it is said, were detailed to seize him, and did seize and return him as a slave to the man who claimed him. If that practice is to be pursued by the army and navy under the American flag, it ought to cover with midnight blackness every star that burns upon its field of azure, and with everlasting infamy the men who dare to desecrate it to such base uses."

Mr. Wickliffe (Dem.) of Kentucky said, "I see, by the evidence which has been furnished, that Gen. Grant captured — at Fort Donelson I think it was — twelve negro slaves among the prisoners there taken. They were returned by him to their loyal owners in Kentucky, from whom they had been forced by the rebel power. Would this bill prevent a military commander from the exercise of such a power?"—"I am informed by a letter from my neighborhood," said Mr. Grider

(Dem.) of Kentucky, " that, within three counties in my district, the rebel army have impressed and run off slaves to the value of about three hundred thousand dollars. Now, sir, does this article of war propose that these servants shall not be returned, and shall not be intercepted?" Mr. Vallandigham (Dem.) of Ohio moved to lay the bill on the table; upon which Mr. Bingham demanded the yeas and nays, — yeas 44, nays 87. Mr. Blair demanded the previous question upon the bill and amendment; and it was ordered. He did not wish to press the bill to a vote to-night, and moved an adjournment; but the motion was lost, — ayes 59, nays 61. The question was taken on the passage of the bill, — yeas 83, nays 42. So the bill passed the House.

In the Senate, on the 4th of March, Mr. Wilson reported back from the Military Committee, without amendment, the House bill providing for the promulgation of an additional article of war, forbidding officers or persons in the military and naval service, on pain of dismissal from the service, to arrest or return fugitive slaves. Mr. Davis (Opp.) of Kentucky would like to offer an amendment, and desired that the bill should go over until to-morrow. Mr. Wilson would, with the understanding that we take up the bill and act on it to-morrow, withdraw his motion to proceed to its consideration; and the proposition was assented to.

On the 10th of March, Mr. Wilson moved to take up the bill from the House of Representatives to make an additional article of war. The motion was agreed to, and the consideration of the bill was resumed as in Committee of the Whole. "I move to amend the bill," said Mr. Davis, "by inserting after the word 'due,' in the eleventh line of the first section, the words, 'and also from detaining, harboring, or concealing any such fugitives;' so that the proposed article will read: 'All officers or persons in the military or naval service of the United States are prohibited from employing any of the forces under their respective commands for the purpose of returning fugitives from service or labor who may have escaped from any persons to whom such service or labor is claimed to be due, and also from detaining, harboring, or concealing any such fugitive.'" The yeas and nays were ordered; and, being taken, resulted — yeas 10, nays 29 — as follows: —

YEAS. — Messrs. Bayard, Carlile, Davis, Henderson, Latham, M'Dougall, Powell, Rice, Saulsbury, and Wilson of Missouri, — 10.

NAYS. — Messrs. Anthony, Browning, Chandler, Clark, Collamer, Cowan, Dixon, Doolittle, Fessenden, Foot, Foster, Grimes, Hale, Harlan, Harris, Howard, Howe, King, Lane of Indiana, Lane of Kansas, Morrill, Pomeroy, Sherman, Sumner, Ten Eyck, Trumbull, Wade, Wilson of Massachusetts, and Wright, — 29.

Mr. Saulsbury moved to amend by adding at the end of the first section, "That this article shall not apply in the States of Delaware, Maryland, Missouri, and Kentucky, nor elsewhere where the Federal authority is recognized or can be enforced." Yeas 7, nays 30. "I wish," remarked Mr. Carlile, "to make an inquiry of the patron of this bill. The President, under his proclamation in April, among other things, called for the services of the militia to aid him in the execution of the laws. One of the laws upon our statute-book is for the return of fugitive slaves. If the President shall find it necessary to call upon the military power of the country to enable him to discharge his sworn duty in this respect, — for he swears, as I understand, when he enters upon the duties of his office, to see that the laws are faithfully executed, — I desire to know if this bill will not interfere with that in this particular, and what effect this bill would have upon any military authorities of the country who should obey the call."—" I suppose," said Mr. Wilson in reply, "the senator from Virginia clearly understands this matter. The case he supposes, if I understand it, would be a case where the authorities would call out the military for the purpose of enforcing the decision of the judicial tribunals, — a mere civil process. The return of fugitive slaves is a civil question, a judicial one, not a military one." — " Then," said Mr. Carlile, " I am to understand that this will not interfere with that?" Mr. M'Dougall said, "It is, I understand, a mere measure to prevent the interference of the army in these matters. As such, I am prepared to vote for it; but, in voting for it, I wish to say here, that I understand it to be simply a provision to prevent the interference of army officers in this matter; not impairing the obligation on the part of an army officer, as well as a private citizen, to surrender a fugitive from service or labor, under the Constitution and laws of the United States." The amendment was then rejected. Mr. Saulsbury said, " I move to amend the bill by inserting after the word ' due,' in the eleventh line of the first section, the words, ' or for the purpose of enticing or decoying such persons, held to service or labor, from the service of their loyal masters.' I ask for the yeas and nays on the amendment." Mr. Anthony inquired " if officers of the army, and all other persons, are not already prohibited from enticing or decoying slaves." Mr. Howard replied, " They are, by heavy penalties." Mr. Saulsbury remarked, " If you say you intend to keep your army aloof from this question, but do not intend that they shall return fugitive slaves, then all I ask of you is, that, when they come into a loyal community, it shall not be lawful for them, nor for any person acting under Federal authority, to entice or decoy my slave or the slave of my constituents away." — " If he did, I suppose," replied Mr. Howard, " he would simply make himself liable to the severe and almost inhuman penalties of the fugitive-slave law of 1850." Mr. Sherman observed, that " the laws of the State would operate also." Mr. Howard said he " would be subject also to the penalty prescribed by the law of the State where he is. I understand this bill as simply prohibiting military men from disgracing the uniform they wear, by engaging in the business of slave-catching, and delivering slaves to their owners, — a disreputable business, in which no gentleman, North or South, military or civil, I undertake to say, will willingly engage." — " In voting," said Mr. Anthony, " against this amendment, which I shall do, I certainly do not wish it to be understood that I would vote to give any officer the right to entice a slave from a loyal master ; but I understand that the law already prohibits it : it is already an offence, and we are only re-enacting another law." Mr. M'Dougall could see no mischief in the amendment of the senator from Delaware. The question, being taken by yeas and nays, resulted — yeas 10, nays 29. The bill was then passed, — yeas 29, nays 9, — as follows : —

YEAS. — Messrs. Anthony, Browning, Chandler, Clark, Collamer, Dixon, Doolittle, Fessenden, Foot, Foster, Grimes, Hale, Harlan, Harris, Howard, Howe, King, Lane of Indiana, Lane of Kansas, M'Dougall, Morrill, Pomeroy, Sherman, Sumner, Ten Eyck, Trumbull, Wade, Wilson of Massachusetts, and Wright, — 29.

NAYS. — Messrs. Bayard, Carlile, Davis, Henderson, Latham, Powell, Rice, Saulsbury, and Wilson of Missouri, — 9.

So the bill passed, and was approved by the President on the 13th of March, 1862.

The 14th of April, on motion of Mr. Wilson of Massachusetts, the Senate proceeded to consider the following resolution, submitted by him on the 3d of April : "*Resolved*, That the Committee on Military Affairs and the Militia be directed to consider and report whether any further legislation is necessary to prevent persons employed in the military service of the United States from aiding in the return or control over persons claimed as fugitive slaves, and to punish them therefor." — " I propose," said Mr. Grimes (Rep.) of Iowa, " to amend the resolution by adding to it, 'and to report what re-organization of the army, in its *personnel* or otherwise, may be necessary to promote the public welfare, and bring the Rebellion to a speedy and triumphant end.'" — " One would think," said Mr. Grimes, " that all men would agree in pronouncing that a cruel and despotic order which repeals the divine precept, 'Inasmuch as ye did it not to one of the least of these, ye did it not to me,' and arbitrarily forbids the soldier to bestow a crust of bread or a cup of water upon a wretched, famishing fugitive escaping from our own as well as from his enemy. Yet, Mr. President, I grieve to say that there are those, high in rank in the service of the United States, who have sought to break down the spirit of manhood, which is the crowning glory of true soldiers, by requiring them to do acts, outside of their profession, which they abhor, and to smother all impulses to those deeds of charity which they have been taught to believe are the characteristics of Christian gentlemen. . . . It was known to the country, at an early day after the commencement of the war, that some military commanders were abusing the great power intrusted to them, and were employing the army to assist in the capture and rendition of fugitive slaves, not in aid of any judicial process, but in obedience to their own unbridled will. The effect of this assumption of unauthorized power was to incite the soldiery to disobedience, and to arouse the people to the necessity of proper legislative restraints. It was in compliance with the popular sentiment on this subject that Congress enacted the additional article of war, which was approved on the 13th of March last. . . . In the month of February last, an officer of the third regiment of Iowa infantry, stationed at a small town in Missouri, succeeded in capturing several rebel bridge-burners, and some recruiting officers belonging to Price's army. The information that led to their capture was furnished by two or three remarkably shrewd and intelligent slaves, claimed by a lieutenant-colonel in the rebel army. Shortly afterwards, the master despatched an agent, with instructions to seize the slaves, and convey them within the rebel lines: whereupon the Iowa officer himself seized them, and reported the circumstances to headquarters. The slaves soon understanding the full import of Gen. Halleck's celebrated order No. 3, two of them attempted an escape. This was regarded as an unpardonable sin. The Iowa officer was immediately placed under arrest, and a detachment of the Missouri State militia — men in the pay of this Government and under the command of Gen. Halleck — were sent in pursuit of the fugitives. The hunt was successful. The slaves were caught, and returned to their traitor master, but not until one of them had been shot by order of the soldier in command of the pursuing party. . . . How long, think you, will this method of dealing with the rebels be endured by the freemen of this country? Are our brothers and sons to be confined within the walls of the tobacco-warehouses and jails of Richmond and Charleston, obliged to perform the most menial offices, subsisted upon the most stinted diet, their lives endangered if they attempt to obtain a breath of fresh air or a beam of God's sunlight at a window, while the rebels captured by those very men are permitted to go at large upon parole, to be pampered with luxuries, to be attended by slaves, and the slaves guarded from escape by our own soldiers?"

On the 1st of May, the Senate, on motion of Mr. Wilson, resumed the consideration of the resolution; the pending question being the amendment moved by Mr. Grimes. Mr. Sumner was "grateful to the senator from Iowa for the frankness with which he exposed and condemned the recent orders of our generals." Mr. Sumner then examined and condemned the orders of Generals Hooker, M'Cook, Buel, Halleck, and the Provost Marshal of Louisville. He contrasted and commended the action of Gen. Doubleday and Gen. M'Dowell. He closed his speech by saying, "Sir, we are making history now. Every victory adds something to that history; but such an order is worse for us than a defeat. More than any defeat, it will discredit us with posterity, and with the friends of liberal institutions in foreign nations. I have said that Gen. Halleck is reputed to be an able officer; but most perversely he undoes with one hand what he does with the other. He undoes by his orders the good he does as a general. While professing to make war upon the Rebellion, he sustains its chief and most active power, and degrades his gallant army to be the constables of slavery. Slavery is the constant rebel and universal enemy. It is traitor and belligerent together, and is always to be treated accordingly. Tenderness to slavery now is practical disloyalty, and practical alliance with the enemy. Against these officers to whom I have referred to-day I have no personal unkindness. I should much prefer to speak in their praise; but, sir, I am in earnest. While I have the honor of a seat in the Senate, no success, no victory, shall be any apology or any shield to a general who undertakes to insult human nature. From the midst of his triumphs, I will drag him forward to receive the condemnation which such conduct deserves."

Mr. Saulsbury moved to amend the resolution by adding to it, "and what further legislation is necessary to prevent the illegal capture and imprisonment of the free white citizens of the United States." In support of the amendment, he said, "But, while we are entertained every morning with a narrative of the grievances of the black men of this country, the free negroes and the slaves of this country, thinking equally as much, and — although it may be an infirmity and a weakness at the present time to say it — thinking a little more, of the free white citizens of my country, I will, in my place, demand that justice shall be done them, and that free *white* men, who have done nought to injure their country, to destroy its institutions or its Union, shall be protected, and that inquiry shall be made to see if further legislation is necessary to secure them in *their* rights." Pending the question, the President called up the Confiscation Bill, which was the order of the day: the bill went over, and was not again taken up.

CHAPTER III.

THE ABOLITION OF SLAVERY IN THE DISTRICT OF COLUMBIA.

THE NATIONAL CAPITAL. — SLAVERY. — MR. WILSON'S RESOLUTION. — THE DISTRICT COMMITTEE. — MR. WILSON'S BILL. — MR. MORRILL'S REPORT, WITH AMENDMENTS. — MR. WILSON'S BILL TO REPEAL THE SLAVE CODE. — COMMITTEE'S AMENDMENTS ADOPTED. — MR. MORRILL'S AMENDMENTS. — MR. DAVIS'S AMENDMENTS. — MR. DOOLITTLE'S AMENDMENT. — REMARKS BY MR. DAVIS. — MR. HALE. — MR. DOOLITTLE. — MR. POMEROY. — MR. WILLEY. — MR. SAULSBURY. — MR. KING. — MR. DAVIS. — MR. WILSON. — MR. KENNEDY. — MR. SAULSBURY. — MR. HARLAN. — MR. WILKINSON. — MR. SAULSBURY'S AMENDMENT. — MR. SUMNER. — MR. WRIGHT. — MR. FESSENDEN. — MR. DAVIS'S AMENDMENT. — MR. CLARK'S AMENDMENT. — MR. WILLEY'S AMENDMENT. — MR. CLARK'S AMENDMENT. — MR. DAVIS. — MR. MORRILL. — MR. M'DOUGALL. — MR. SUMNER'S AMENDMENT. — MR. WRIGHT'S AMENDMENT. — MR. BROWNING'S AMENDMENT. — MR. WILMOT. — MR. COLLAMER'S AMENDMENT. — MR. DOOLITTLE'S AMENDMENT. — MR. POWELL. — MR. BAYARD. — PASSAGE OF THE BILL. — HOUSE. — MR. STEVENS'S MOTION. — MR. THOMAS. — MR. NOXON. — MR. BLAIR. — MR. CRITTENDEN. — MR. RIDDLE. — MR. FESSENDEN. — MR. ROLLINS. — MR. BLAKE. — MR. VAN HORNE. — MR. ASHLEY. — MR. HUTCHINS. — MR. WRIGHT'S AMENDMENT. — MR. HICKMAN. — MR. WADSWORTH. — MR. HARDING'S AMENDMENT. — MR. TRAIN'S AMENDMENT. — MR. LOVEJOY. — MR. WICKLIFFE'S AMENDMENT. — MR. HOLMAN'S AMENDMENT. — MR. COX. — MR. MENZIES' AMENDMENT. — PASSAGE OF THE BILL.

THE first Congress under the Constitution was deeply absorbed by the question of the permanent location of the seat of the Federal Government. The Eastern States would have been content to let it remain in New York. Pennsylvania sought to win it back to Philadelphia. Maryland, Virginia, the Carolinas, and Georgia would fix it on the Potomac. . The conflicting claims of sections defeated, in 1789, all propositions for the permanent location of the seat of Government; but it was determined at the next session, by three majority in the House of Representatives, to locate it on the banks of the Potomac. Clothed by the Constitution with the "power to exercise exclusive legislation in all cases whatsoever" over the District, Congress, instead of providing a code of humane and equal laws for the government of the national capital, enacted, in 1801, that the laws of Maryland and Virginia should continue in force. By this act, the colonial slave-codes of Maryland and Virginia were accepted, reaffirmed, and re-enacted. Washington and Georgetown adopted oppressive and inhuman ordinances for the government of slaves and free persons of color. For half a century the slave-trade was carried on, to the lasting dishonor of the nation; and for two generations the public men of the country were surrounded by an atmosphere tainted by the breath of the slave, and by the blinding and perverting influences of the social life of slaveholding society.

On the 4th of December, 1861, after the announcement of the Standing Committees of the Senate, Mr. Wilson (Rep.) of Massachusetts introduced a resolution, that all laws in force relating to the arrest of fugitives from service, and all laws concerning persons of color, within the District, be referred to the Committee on the District of Columbia; and that the committee be instructed to consider the expediency of abolishing slavery in the District, with compensation to loyal holders of slaves. The committee to whom the resolution was referred consisted of Mr. Grimes (Rep.) of

Iowa, Mr. Dixon (Rep.) of Connecticut, Mr. Morrill (Rep.) of Maine, Mr. Wade (Rep.) of Ohio, Mr. Anthony (Rep.) of Rhode Island, Mr. Kennedy (Dem.) of Maryland, and Mr. Powell (Dem.) of Kentucky. Mr. Grimes, chairman of the committee, Mr. Morrill, and Mr. Wade, were recognized by their associates and by the country as thorough and uncompromising opponents of slavery in every form. Mr. Dixon and Mr. Anthony were fair representatives of the feelings and views of conservative Republicanism. Mr. Kennedy came into the Senate a type of the moderate, conservative, respectable Whigism of the Border slave States; but was soon borne, like many others of that halting, timid school, by the current of events, into the ranks of Democracy. Mr. Powell was an original Democrat, of the faith and creed of the slaveholding school, and an earnest, bold, and adroit advocate of its policy. In moving the reference of his resolution to this committee, Mr. Wilson expressed the hope that the chairman "would deal promptly with the question."

Mr. Wilson of Massachusetts, on the 16th of December, obtained leave to introduce a bill for the release of certain persons held to service or labor in the District of Columbia; which was read twice, and ordered to be printed. The bill provided for the immediate emancipation of the slaves, for the payment to their loyal owners of an average sum of three hundred dollars, for the appointment of a commission to assess the sum to be paid, and the appropriation of one million of dollars. On the 22d of December, on the motion of Mr. Wilson, the bill was referred to the District Committee.

Mr. Morrill, on the 13th of February, 1862, reported back from the Committee on the District of Columbia the bill, introduced by Mr. Wilson on the 16th of December, for the release of certain persons held to service or labor in the District of Columbia, with amendments. Mr. Wilson, on the 24th of February, introduced a bill to repeal certain laws and ordinances in the District of Columbia relating to persons of color, and moved its reference to the District Committee. This bill proposed to repeal the act of Congress extending over the District the laws of Maryland concerning persons of color, to annul and abrogate those laws, to repeal the acts giving the cities of Washington and Georgetown authority to pass ordinances relating to persons of color, to abrogate those ordinances, and to make persons of color amenable to the same laws to which free white persons are amenable, and to subject them to the same penalties and punishments. Mr. Wilson briefly recited the laws and ordinances it was intended to repeal and abrogate. Mr. Wilmot (Rep.) of Pennsylvania thought the Senate should act promptly upon the bill for the abolition of slavery in the District. "We should be the most derelict in our duty of any body that ever sat in the seats of power, if we adjourn this Congress without the abolition of slavery in the District of Columbia." Mr. Wilson would say to the senator from Pennsylvania, that the bill was very carefully prepared; that it had been reported, with very slight amendments, by the committee; and that it should be taken up for action at an early day. "The bill," he said, "which I have introduced this morning, is only following up that bill, and repealing the black code of the District, — the laws applicable to persons of color in the District. It is a necessary bill to be passed also; and I hope, when we have done that, we shall go a step further, and offer to the State of Maryland the same terms that we offer to the people of the District, and clear this thing out of our neighborhood."

On the 27th of February, the Senate, on motion of Mr. Morrill, made the bill for the abolition of slavery in the District the special order for the 5th of March. The bill on the 12th, on motion of Mr. Morrill, was taken up; and the Senate, as in Committee of the Whole, proceeded to its consideration. The amendments reported by the committee were agreed to: and Mr. Morrill then moved to add an amendment, that no claim shall be paid for any slave brought into the District after the passage of the act, or which originates in or by virtue of any transfer heretofore made, or which shall hereafter be made, by any person who has in any manner aided or sustained the Rebellion against the Government of the United States; and it was agreed to. Mr. Morrill moved still further to amend the bill by adding, that any person who shall kidnap or in any manner transport out of said District any person discharged or freed by the provisions of this act, or any free person, with intent to re-enslave or sell such person into slavery, or shall re-enslave any of said persons, the person so offending shall be deemed guilty of a misdemeanor; and, on conviction, shall be imprisoned in the penitentiary not less than five nor more than twenty years. Mr. Howard (Rep.) of Michigan would strike out "misdemeanor," and insert "felony."

Mr. Morrill accepted the suggestion; and the amendment as modified was agreed to. Mr. Morrill then moved that all acts of Congress and all laws of the State of Maryland in force in said District, and all ordinances of the cities of Washington or Georgetown, inconsistent with the provisions of this act, are hereby repealed; and the amendment was agreed to.

Mr. Davis (Opp.) of Kentucky moved to add as a new section, that all persons liberated under this act shall be colonized out of the limits of the United States; and the sum of a hundred thousand dollars, out of any money, shall be expended, under the direction of the President of the United States, for that purpose. Mr. Doolittle (Rep.) of Wisconsin "understood the effect of this amendment to be to colonize them, whether they are willing to be colonized or not. If the amendment of the senator was to offer to appropriate the sum of a hundred thousand dollars to be used for transporting and colonizing such of the free colored persons of this District as might desire to be colonized, I should vote for the amendment; but, as it is, I cannot vote for it." Mr. Davis thought he was "better acquainted with negro nature than the honorable senator from Wisconsin. He will never find one slave in a hundred that will consent to be colonized when liberated. The liberation of the slaves in this District and in any State of the Union will be just equivalent to settling them in the country where they live; and whenever that policy is inaugurated, especially in the States where there are many slaves, it will inevitably and immediately introduce a war of extermination between the two races. . . . The negroes that are now liberated, and that remain in this city, will become a sore and a burden and a charge upon the white population. They will be criminals. They will become paupers. They will be engaged in crimes and in petty misdemeanors. They will become a charge and a pest upon this society; and the power which undertakes to liberate them ought to relieve the white community in which they reside, and in which they will become a pest from their presence." Mr. Davis emphatically asserted, that "whenever any power, constitutional or unconstitutional, assumes the responsibility of liberating slaves where slaves are numerous, they establish, as inexorably as fate, a conflict between the races, that will result in the exile or the extermination of the one race or the other. I know it. We have now about two hundred and twenty-five thousand slaves in Kentucky. Think you, sir, that we should ever submit to have those slaves manumitted and left among us? No, sir; no, never: nor will any white people in the United States of America, where the slaves are numerous. If, by unconstitutional legislation, you should, by laws which you shrink from submitting to the tests of constitutionality in your courts of justice, liberate them, without the intervention of the courts, the moment you re-organize the white inhabitants of those States as States of the Union, they would reduce those slaves again to a state of slavery, or they would expel them and drive them upon you or south of you, or they would hunt them like beasts, and exterminate them. . . . I know what I talk about. Mr. President, the loyal people of the slave States are as true to this Union as any man in the Senate Chamber or in any of the free States: but never, never, will they submit, by unconstitutional laws, to have their slaves liberated and to remain domiciled among them ; and the policy that attempts it will establish a bloody La Vendée in the whole of the slave States, my own included."

On the 18th, the bill was taken up, the pending question being Mr. Davis's amendment; and Mr. Doolittle proposed to amend the amendment, so as to make it read, "with their own consent." Mr. Hale (Rep.) of New Hampshire delivered an earnest and effective speech for the passage of the bill. "I may remark," he said, "that, of all the forms scepticism ever assumed, the most insidious, the most dangerous, and the most fatal, is that which suggests that it is unsafe to perform plain and simple duty, for fear that disastrous consequences may result therefrom. This question of emancipation, wherever it has been raised in this country, so far as I know, has rarely ever been argued upon the great and fundamental principles of right. The inquiry is never put, certainly in legislative circles, What is right? what is just? what is due to the individuals that are to be affected by the measure? but, What are to be the consequences? Men entirely forget to look at the objects that are to be effected by the bill, in view of the inherent rights of their manhood, in view of the great questions of humanity, of Christianity, and of duty; but what are to be the consequences; what is to be its effect upon the price of sugar, tobacco, cotton, and other necessaries and luxuries of life. The honorable senator from Kentucky looks upon it in that point of view entirely. . . . But now, sir, let me close by reading to the senator from Kentucky predictions of the consequences that will follow emancipation, exceedingly different from those which he has predicted. He predicts pauperism, degradation, crime, burdens upon society. That is the dark picture which fills his imagination as the consequences that are to follow the putting-away of oppression from the midst of us. Let me read to him a different prediction : —

"'6. Is not this the fast that I have chosen? — to loose the bands of wickedness, to undo the heavy burdens, and to let the oppressed go free, and that ye break every yoke?

"'7. Is it not to deal thy bread to the hungry, and that thou bring the poor that are cast out to thy house? When thou seest the naked, that thou cover him; and that thou hide not thyself from thine own flesh?'

"What are to be the consequences? Not pauperism, degradation, and crime, but, —

"'8. Then shall thy light break forth as the morning, and thine health shall spring forth speedily; and thy righteousness shall go before thee. The glory of the Lord shall be thy rearward.

"'9. Then shalt thou call, and the Lord shall answer; thou shalt cry, and he shall say, Here I am. If thou take away from the midst of thee the yoke, the putting-forth of the finger, and speaking vanity;

"'10. And if thou draw out thy soul to the hungry, and satisfy the afflicted soul; then shall thy light rise in obscurity, and thy darkness be as the noonday.

"'11. And the Lord shall guide thee continually, and satisfy thy soul in drought, and make fat thy bones; and thou shalt be like a watered garden, and like a spring of water, whose waters fail not.

"'12. And they that shall be of thee shall build the old waste places. Thou shalt raise up the foundations of many generations; and thou shalt be called, The repairer of the breach, The restorer of paths to dwell in.'— *Isa.*, ch. 58.

"Now, sir, this nation has an opportunity, if I may say so, — and I say it reverently, — of putting the Almighty to the test, and of seeing whether the consequences that his prophet has foretold or his senator has predicted will follow as the result of this measure."

Mr. Doolittle then addressed the Senate in advocacy of the policy of colonizing persons made free by the enactment of the pending bill. Mr. Pomeroy (Rep.) of Kansas followed in decided opposition to the policy of making compensation to the masters for the slaves to be emancipated by the passage of the measure. "I am really," he declared, "a friend to the bill; and I desire at the proper time — I believe it is not in order now — to propose an amendment, striking out all of the bill, except the first and eighth sections. The first section of the bill extends over this District the ordinance of 1787; and I think there is no doubt as to the effect of that. The eighth section simply prohibits men from taking colored persons out of the District to sell them after they have been made free. The first section frees them: the eighth section prevents their being kidnapped. I do not know what necessity there is for any further provision in the bill." Mr. Willey (Union) of Virginia addressed the Senate on the 20th, in opposition to the measure. "This bill," he asserted, "is a part of a series of measures already initiated, all looking to the same ultimate result, — the universal abolition of slavery by Congress."

The Senate resumed, on the 24th, the consideration of the bill; the pending question being Mr. Doolittle's amendment to Mr. Davis's amendment. Mr. Saulsbury (Dem.) of Delaware was in favor, if the slaves were liberated, of colonizing them; yet, not believing that Congress has any constitutional power either to pass a bill to liberate the slaves in the District or to appropriate money to colonize them, he should vote against the amendment and the bill. Mr. King (Rep.) of New York "did intend to vote for this bill; and I prefer to vote for it in the simplest shape in which it can be presented. Although I am disposed to look with favor upon the proposition submitted by the senator from Wisconsin, when this subject comes to be considered upon a more extended scale; yet, as it relates merely to the District, I am inclined to vote against any amendments which go to extend the character of the bill beyond a simple proposition to emancipate the negroes in the District." The question being taken on Mr. Doolittle's amendment to Mr. Davis's amendment, it was agreed to, — yeas 23, nays 16. The question on Mr. Davis's amendment as amended was then taken, — yeas 19, nays 19: so it was lost.

Mr. Davis then addressed the Senate at great length in opposition to the bill. "You have originated," he said, "in the North-east, Mormonism and free love, and that sort of ethereal Christianity that is preached by Parker and by Emerson and by others, and all sorts of mischievous isms; but what right have you to force your isms upon us? What right have you to force your opinions upon slavery or upon any other subject on an unwilling people? What right have you to force them on the people of this District? Is it from your love for the slaves, your devotion to benevolence and humanity, your belief in the equality of the slaves with yourselves? Why do you not go out into this city, and hunt up the blackest, greasiest, fattest old negro wench you can find, and lead her to the altar of Hymen? You do not believe in any such equality; nor do I. Yet your emissaries proclaim here that the slaves, when you liberate them, shall be citizens, shall be eligible to office in this city. A few days ago, I saw several negroes thronging the open door, listening to the debate on this subject; and I suppose, in a few months, they will be crowding white ladies out of these galleries."

Mr. Wilson of Massachusetts, on the 25th, addressed the Senate in favor of the bill he had introduced early in the session. "This bill, to give liberty to the bondman," he said, "deals justly, ay, generously, by the master. The American people, whose moral sense has been outraged by slavery and the black codes enacted in the interests of slavery in the District of Columbia, whose fame has been soiled and dimmed by the deeds of cruelty perpetrated in their national capital, would stand justified in the forum of nations if they should smite the fetter from the bondman, regardless of the desires or interests of the master. With generous magnanimity, this bill tenders compensation to the master out of the earnings of the toiling freemen of America. . . . In what age of the world, in what land under the whole heavens, can you find any enactment of equal atrocity to this iniquitous and profligate statute, this 'legal presumption' that color is evidence that man, made in the image of God, is an 'absconding slave'? This monstrous doctrine, abhorrent to every manly impulse of the heart, to every Christian sentiment of the soul, to every deduction of human reason, which the refined, humane, and Christian people of America have upheld for two generations, which the corporation of Washington enacted into an imperative ordinance, has borne its legitimate fruits of injustice and inhumanity, of dishonor and shame. Crimes against man, in the name of this abhorred doctrine, have been annually perpetrated in this national capital, which should make the people of America hang their heads in shame before the nations, and in abasement before that Being who keeps watch and ward over the humblest of the children of men. . . . Here the oath of the black man affords no protection whatever to his property, to the fruits of his toil, to the personal rights of himself, his wife, his children, or his race. Greedy avarice may withhold from him the fruits of his toil, or clutch from him his little acquisitions; the brutal may visit upon him, his wife, his children, insults, indignities, blows; the kidnapper may enter his dwelling, and steal from his hearthstone his loved ones; the assassin may hover on his track, imperilling his household; every outrage that the depravity of man can visit upon his brother man may be perpetrated upon him, upon his family, his race: but his oath upon the Evangelists of Almighty God, though his name may be written in the Book of Life, neither protects him from wrong, nor punishes the wrong-doer. This Christian nation, in solemn mockery, enacts that the free black men of America shall not bear testimony in the judicial tribunals of the District of Columbia. Although the black man is thus mute and dumb before the judicial tribunals of the capital of Christian America, his wrongs we have not righted here will go up to

a higher tribunal, where the oath of the proscribed
negro is heard, and his story registered by the pen of
the recording angel. . . . These colonial statutes of
Maryland, re-affirmed by Congress in 1801; these ordinances of Washington and Georgetown, sanctioned in
advance by the authority of the Federal Government, —
stand this day unrepealed. Such laws and ordinances
should not be permitted longer to insult the reason, per-
vert the moral sense, or offend the taste, of the people
of America. Any people mindful of the decencies of
life would not longer permit such enactments to linger
before the eye of civilized man. Slavery is the prolific
mother of those monstrous enactments. Bid slavery
disappear from the District of Columbia, and it will
take along with it this whole brood of brutal, vulgar,
and indecent statutes. . . . This bill for the release
of persons held to services or labor in the District of
Columbia, and the compensation of loyal masters from
the treasury of the United States, was prepared after
much reflection and some consultation with others. The
Committees on the District of Columbia, in both Houses,
to whom it was referred, have agreed to it, with a few
amendments calculated to carry out more completely its
original purposes and provisions. I trust that the bill
as it now stands, after the adoption of the amendments
proposed by the senator from Maine (Mr. Morrill),
will speedily pass without any material modifications.
If it shall become the law of the land, it will blot out
slavery for ever from the national capital, transform
three thousand personal chattels into freemen, obliterate
oppressive, odious, and hateful laws and ordinances,
which press with merciless force upon persons, bond or

free, of African descent, and relieve the nation from the responsibilities now pressing upon it. An act of beneficence like this will be hailed and applauded by the nations, sanctified by justice, humanity, and religion, by the approving voice of conscience, and by the blessing of Him who bids us 'break every yoke, undo the heavy burden, and let the oppressed go free.'"

"Why," asked Mr. Kennedy of Maryland, "seek to impose upon us principles and measures of policy which we do not want, and which tend only to still further derange and embarrass us, — tend further to surround us with complicated questions from which we have no escape? Why not allow us to work out our own destiny, and to accommodate ourselves as best we can to the disadvantages which this unhappy revolution has thrown around us? . . . What possible benefit can occur to the North by the abolition of slavery in this District, when it is to be so deleterious and so injurious in its results to a sister State of this Union? What earthly consideration of good is to result to the people of the North, that does not bring a tenfold corresponding evil, not only upon the people here, but upon the people of my State?"

Mr. Saulsbury moved to amend by inserting as a new section, that "the persons liberated under this act shall, within thirty days after the passage of the same, be removed, at the expense of the Federal Government, into the States of Maine, New Hampshire, Massachusetts, Rhode Island, Connecticut, Vermont, New York, Pennsylvania, New Jersey, Ohio, Indiana, Illinois, Michigan, Iowa, Wisconsin, Minnesota, Kansas, Oregon, and California; and that said persons shall be distributed to and among the said States, *pro rata*, according to the population of the same." "If it is the spirit of philanthropy and a love of freedom," he said, "that prompts you gentlemen to set these three thousand slaves in the District of Columbia free, render that philanthropy and that love of freedom sublime in the sight of all human kind by taking into your own embrace, in your own midst, the slaves thus liberated. Prove that you are sincere."

"I regret," said Mr. Harlan (Rep.) of Iowa, "very much that senators depart so far from the proprieties, as I consider it, of this Chamber, as to make the allusions they do. It is done merely to stimulate a prejudice which exists against a race already trampled under foot. I refer to the allusions to white people embracing colored people as their brethen, and the invitations by senators to white men and white women to marry colored people. Now, sir, if we were to descend into an investigation of the facts on that subject, it would bring the blush to the cheeks of some of these gentlemen. I once had occasion to direct the attention of the Senate to an illustrious example from the State of the senator who inquired if any of us would marry a greasy old wench. It is history, that an illustrious citizen of his State, who once occupied officially the chair that you, sir, now sit in, lived notoriously and publicly with a negro wench, and raised children by her. . . . I refer to a gentleman who held the second office in the gift of the American people; and I never yet have heard a senator on this floor denounce the conduct and the association of that illustrious citizen of our country. I know of a family of colored or mulatto children,—the children, too, of a gentleman who very recently occupied a seat on the other side of the Chamber, — who are now at school in Ohio; yes, sir, the children of a senator, who very recently, not to exceed a year since, occupied a seat on this floor, a senator from a slave State. I do not desire to consume the time of the Senate and of the country in calling attention to these facts; it is humiliating enough to know that they exist: but, if senators who represent slaveholding States will perpetually drag this subject to the attention of the Senate and of the country, let them take the logical consequences of their own folly, and bear the shame which an investigation of facts must inflict on themselves and their constituents."

Mr. Saulsbury followed in reply to Mr. Harlan, and closed by saying, "Senators, abandon now, at once and for ever, your schemes of wild philanthropy and universal emancipation; proclaim to the people of this whole country everywhere, that you mean to preserve the Union established by Washington and Jefferson and Madison and the fathers of the Republic, and the rights of the people as secured by that glorious instrument which they helped to frame, and your Union never can be destroyed: but go on with your wild schemes of emancipation, throw doubt and suspicion upon every man simply because he fails to look at your questions of wild philanthropy as you do, and the God of heaven only knows, after wading through scenes before which even the horrors of the French revolution 'pale their ineffectual fires,' what ultimately may be the result."

Mr. Wilkinson (Rep.) of Minnesota addressed the

Senate, on the 26th of March, in an earnest and eloquent speech in favor of the bill. "If there be a place upon the face of the earth," he said, "where human slavery should be prohibited, and where every man should be protected in the rights which God and Nature have given him, that place is the capital of this great Republic. It is an insult to the enlightened public sentiment of the age, that those who meet here from the free States of the Union, and the representatives of the free governments of the earth, — lovers of liberty, — should be compelled, in the capital of this free Republic, daily to witness the disgusting and shocking barbarities which a state of human slavery continually presents to their view. It is a shame, that here, upon common ground, the representatives of the loyal and free North, those who have never failed to discharge every duty to their country, should be treated with contumely and contempt, and even hissed, as they have been in the Capitol of the nation and in the galleries of the Senate, by the slaveholding influence of this District." At the close of Mr. Wilkinson's speech, the vote was taken on Mr. Saulsbury's proposition to colonize the liberated slaves among the loyal States, and it was unanimously rejected; Mr. Saulsbury finally voting against his own amendment.

On Monday, the 31st of March, the Senate resumed the consideration of the bill; and Mr. Sumner addressed the Senate in an elaborate and eloquent speech in favor of its speedy passage. He said, "Mr. President, with unspeakable delight I hail this measure, and the prospect of its speedy adoption. . . . It is the first instalment of that great debt which we all owe to an enslaved race, and will be recognized in history as one of the victories of humanity. At home, throughout our own country, it will be welcomed with gratitude; while abroad it will quicken the hopes of all who love freedom. Liberal institutions will gain everywhere by the abolition of slavery at the national capital. Nobody can read that slaves were once sold in the markets of Rome, beneath the eyes of the sovereign pontiff, without confessing the scandal to religion, even in a barbarous age; and nobody can hear that slaves are now sold in the markets of Washington, beneath the eyes of the President, without confessing the scandal to liberal institutions. For the sake of our good name, if not for the sake of justice, let the scandal disappear. . . . Amidst all present solicitudes, the future cannot be doubtful. At the national capital, slavery will give way to freedom: but the good work will not stop here; it must proceed. What God and Nature decree, rebellion cannot arrest. And as the whole wide-spread tyranny begins to tumble, — then, above the din of battle, sounding from the sea and echoing along the land, above even the exultations of victory on well-fought fields, will ascend voices of gladness and benediction, swelling from generous hearts wherever civilization bears sway, to commemorate a sacred triumph, whose trophies, instead of tattered banners, will be ransomed slaves."

On the 1st of April, Mr. Wright (Union) of Indiana spoke in opposition to the enactment of the measure. He had presented a bill for the abolition of slavery in the District of Columbia, being in substance the measure proposed by Mr. Lincoln in 1848. It provided for the gradual extinction of slavery. . He thought, "if slavery was let alone, there would be no slavery here in ten years." The pending question being the amendment offered by Mr. Pomeroy "to settle the account between master and slave," he said he had offered the amendment in good faith, as a friend of the measure, so that "the commission could weigh out justice, give compensation where it was due."—"The fundamental law of the land," declared Mr. Fessenden (Rep.) of Maine, "is broad and clear. We need no excuse on the subject at all. Congress, under the Constitution, is gifted with all power of legislation over this District, and may do any thing in it that any legislature can do in any State of the Union, unless expressly restrained by the Constitution which gives it its powers; and there being a specific grant of all powers of legislation in this District, and there being no restraint upon it which would touch the question, it follows as a matter of necessity that the constitutional power exists; and it includes as well the power to vote money. . . . This question of the abolition of slavery in the District of Columbia, I have stated, has been one that has always been near to my heart. Gentlemen say it is a bad time to take it up: it will be attended with injury. With regard to one point of injury, I have spoken; but do gentlemen believe any other injury is to follow? Whom do we injure? The slaves? The slave will bear the injury. Do we injure the owner? What claim have the owners of slaves in the District of Columbia upon us? They have, in my judgment, been holding slaves here without law since the foundation of the Government; and they have been able to do it, because it has been in their power to secure a majority always in Congress which was invincible, that could not be overcome." Mr. Davis moved to strike out the proviso to the third section, limiting the average sum to be paid to three hundred dollars, — yeas 11, nays 30.

Mr. Browning (Rep.) of Illinois " never doubted the existence of the power in Congress, under the Constitution, to pass this or any other legislative measure affecting the District of Columbia. The grant of power is as broad and ample as it is possible for our language to make it." Mr. Clark (Rep.) of New Hampshire moved an amendment of eleven sections, as a substitute for the original bill. "I do not propose this amendment," he said, "for the purpose of impeding the passage of the bill, or of impeding the abolition of slavery in this District. I desire to accomplish it. It is a measure to which I gave my heart long ago, and it is a measure to which I am ready and desirous to give my hand now. I do it with the intention of offering to the Senate a better bill, as I conceive it to be." Mr. Morrill, in reply to Mr. Clark, asserted " that this bill originally, as submitted to the committee, was prepared with very great care, and it has received the best consideration that the committee was able to bestow upon it; and I will say to my honorable friend who criticises the original bill, and who thinks that his is much better, that there was not a single question to which he alludes that did not receive the attention of the committee; and, if I understand the bill of the committee, there is not a single provision of his bill but is provided for in the bill of the committee, except the feature of referring it to the Court of Claims." Mr. Willey proposed to amend Mr. Clark's amendment so as to submit the bill to the legal voters of the District. Mr. Willey averred that he intended to vote for the President's resolution tendering the aid of the Government to the loyal States. "It meets," he said, " my approbation ; and the more I think about it, the more I believe it is correct, and that it will be a balm to heal the bleeding wounds of our country at last." — " If we are going," said Mr. Pomeroy, " to leave this question to the people to vote upon it, I insist that the senator from Virginia should amend his amendment by striking out at least two words, 'free white.' If he will strike out those two words, and let every person who has arrived at the age of twenty-one years vote, there will at least be fairness in submitting this question to a vote of the people. As the question affects both parties alike, and as it is as much for the interest of the colored man as the white man, I should like to know why he may not vote on it." Mr. Willey's amendment was rejected, — yeas 13, nays 24.

Mr. Clark moved to strike out the third section of the original bill, and insert a new section in lieu of it. This amendment was advocated by Mr. Clark, opposed by Mr. Morrill, and rejected. Mr. Wright, on the 2d of April, presented the memorial of the Board of Aldermen of Washington, expressing " the opinion that the sentiment of a large majority of the people of this community is adverse to the unqualified abolition of slavery in this District at the present critical juncture in our national affairs."

Mr. Davis of Kentucky made a very long, desultory harangue against the bill and all kindred measures. "Massachusetts," he said, " was the hot-bed, the very place of origin, of every political heresy that has been set up in any part of the country. . . . I hardly know of any political, religious, or social mischievous and noxious ism but what had its origin in Massachusetts. . . . It has been frequently inquired, 'What brought about this war?' I shall not enter into that subject at any length; but I will tell you what I religiously believe, — that the States of Massachusetts and South Carolina and their mischievous isms have done more to bring about our present troubles than all other causes."

Mr. Morrill said in reply, that "the sentiments which the honorable senator puts forth here are sentiments directly adverse to the principles of the common law. I know they are opinions and principles reaching far back into the early period of the world; but allow me to say to the honorable senator, they are barbarian in their origin. They were never inculcated and never adopted in civilized nations. Where civilization has advanced, where the doctrines of Christian civilization are recognized, these notions are held to be antiquated, barbarian; and they do not enter into the jurisprudence of any civilized or Christian nation on the globe."

Mr. M'Dougall, on the 3d, addressed the Senate in an elaborate speech in opposition to the measure; and Mr. Ten. Eyck preferred a system of gradual emancipation, but would vote for the original bill as amended. He was not sure but the postponement of the measure until the Border slave States have acted on the President's proposition would cure the evil. "If Maryland and Delaware should vote to abolish slavery according to the plan proposed by the President and the resolution we passed yesterday, slavery in this District would speedily die out of itself. Like an exhausted candle, it would flicker in its socket, and soon be gone for ever, and not a single wave of popular feeling be created to disturb or agitate the surrounding sections of country interested in the institution." Mr. Sumner moved to amend, by introducing in the fifth section, after the words "courts of justice," the words "without the exclusion of any witness on account of color." Mr. Morrill said the bill provided that the claimant may be summoned before the commissioners, and that the party for whose service compensation is claimed may testify; but the amendment extends that to other persons, and he did not object to it. On motion of Mr. Saulsbury, the yeas and nays were taken on Mr. Sumner's amendment, — yeas 26, nays 10. Mr. Clark's substitute was rejected, without a division.

Mr. Wright moved to strike out all after the enacting clause of the bill, and insert as a substitute the amendment he had proposed, providing for a system of gradual emancipation. Mr. Wright declared he had offered it "because it embodies principles which I like. The object of presenting it as an amendment is, that, if adopted, it may be referred back to the committee for perfection." The amendment was rejected, — yeas 10, nays 27.

Mr. Clark moved to insert at the end of section two, " that he has not borne arms against the United States during the present Rebellion." Mr. Trumbull moved to add that " the oath of the party to the petition shall not be evidence of the facts therein stated;" and the amendment to the amendment was agreed to, and the amendment as amended adopted. Mr. Browning

moved to make the sum appraised and apportioned five
in lieu of three hundred dollars, one-half to be paid to
the master, and the other half paid to the slave, on
satisfactory evidence that he has removed and settled
outside the United States. Mr. Browning would combine emancipation and colonization. "I believe," he
declared, "that we cannot do any substantial good to
the colored people of this country without combining
with whatever action we take upon this subject a system
of colonization, or adopting measures that will lead to
voluntary colonization on their part. It is not legal
and political equality and emancipation alone that can
do much for the elevation of the character of these
people. We may confer upon them all the legal and
political rights we ourselves enjoy: they will still be in
our midst, a debased and degraded race, incapable of
making progress, because they want that best element
and best incentive to progress, social equality, which
they never can have here." — "Why does not the gentleman," asked Mr. Wilmot, "make his amendment
consistent with his argument, and propose compulsory
colonization? If the races cannot live together, then
surely we should adopt compulsory emigration. The
amendment of the senator goes but a short way towards
the argument that he advances."

"This inducement," replied Mr. Browning, "for
voluntary emigration, is perfectly consistent with all
that I have said on that point. I do not propose now
to discuss a system of compulsory emigration. We
are acting upon too small a scale to justify us in broaching so momentous a question as that is at this time.
The time may come, the time possibly will come, when

compulsory colonization may be found necessary for the good of both races; and, if it does come, I apprehend I, for one, shall be found ready to meet it, and to take my share of the responsibility of enforcing it." Mr. Browning's amendment was rejected.

Mr. Collamer (Rep.) of Vermont, for the better security of emancipated persons, moved to add two additional sections, providing that the claimants shall file, with the clerk of the Circuit Court in the District, descriptive lists of the persons for whom they claim compensation; and that the clerk shall give on demand, to each person made free or manumitted by this act, a certificate under the seal of said court, setting out the name and description of such person, and stating that such person was duly manumitted and made free by virtue of this act; and these provisions were incorporated in the bill. Mr. M'Dougall offered as a substitute the amendment previously offered by Mr. Wright and rejected, — yeas 10, nays 25. The bill was then reported to the Senate, and the amendments adopted in Committee of the Whole concurred in.

Mr. Doolittle thought his amendment appropriating a hundred thousand dollars to aid in the colonization and settlement of such free persons of African descent as may desire to emigrate to the republics of Hayti or Liberia, or such other country beyond the limits of the United States as the President may determine, had been voted down because some senators thought it connected in some way with a system of compulsory colonization. He renewed his amendment, and demanded the yeas and nays; and they were ordered, — yeas 27, nays 10. "I regard the bill," said Mr. Powell, "as unconstitutional, impolitic, unjust to the people of the District of Columbia, and bad faith to the people of Virginia and Maryland. . . . This bill is unjust to the people of the District of Columbia, because it deprives them of one of their domestic institutions. It is unjust to them in another respect; because, while you pretend to pay them, you do not give them a fourth of the value of their property. The highest amount you give a citizen for his negro is three hundred dollars, while every one in this Senate knows that many of those negroes are worth three or four times that amount." Mr. Wilson of Massachusetts remarked, that the senator from Kentucky was mistaken. "The average sum to be paid is three hundred dollars; but for some may be paid eight or nine hundred or a thousand dollars, and for others but a very small sum indeed." Mr. Bayard (Dem.) of Delaware had hoped "to obtain the floor, on the passage of the bill, at an earlier hour; and though it is certainly, personally, very inconvenient to me to speak at this time, I have to perform a duty which I owe, not to my own constituents, for they have no particular nor immediate interest in the bill, but a duty that I think I owe, as a member of this body, to my country. . . . I concede, without the slightest reservation, that the authority of the General Government over the District of Columbia is precisely the same as the authority of a State over its territory; that no constitutional objection can arise to the action of Congress in abolishing slavery in this District, other than those that could be made within the boundaries of a State under similar provisions of a State constitution. The effect of this bill, in my judgment, will be deleterious, and most deleterious first to the city of Washington, next to the State of Maryland, then to the State of Virginia, and then by the effect of its indirect influence to the State of Kentucky and the State of Missouri; and, if you succeed in compelling by force of arms the other slaveholding States to return into the Union, the effect will permeate through the entire mass of those States."

At the close of Mr. Bayard's speech, the presiding officer stated that the question was on the passage of the bill, upon which the yeas and nays had been ordered. The question was taken, and resulted — yeas 29, nays 14. Thus the bill " for the release of certain persons held to service or labor in the District of Columbia," introduced by Mr. Wilson into the Senate, Dec. 16, 1861, passed the Senate, April 3, 1862.

In the House of Representatives, on the 10th of April, Mr. Stevens (Rep.) of Pennsylvania moved that the House resolve itself into the Committee of the Whole on the State of the Union. The motion was agreed to; and Mr. Stevens moved that all the preceding bills on the calendar be laid aside, and that the committee take up the bill for the abolition of slavery in the District of Columbia. Mr. Webster (Union) of Maryland objecting, the chairman, Mr. Dawes (Rep.) of Massachusetts, stated that he would call the calendar in order. Mr. Stevens said he would move to lay the bills aside until he reached the bill he had indicated. When the Senate bill for the abolition of slavery in the District of Columbia was reached, Mr. Webster moved to lay it aside; but the motion failed, and the bill was before the Committee of the Whole for consideration. " I avail myself," said Mr. Thomas (Opp.) of Massachusetts, "of the indulgence of the committee to make some suggestions upon subjects now attracting the attention of Congress and of the country, — the relation of the 'seceded States' (so called) to the Union, the confiscation of property, and the emancipation of slaves in such States."

On the 11th, Mr. Stevens moved that the debate upon the bill be closed in one hour after the Committee of the Whole resumes its consideration; but the motion was lost, — yeas 57, nays 64. Mr. Nixon (Rep.) of New Jersey said, "The gradual emancipation of the slave would have been more in harmony with the past modes of dealing with this question, and more in accordance with my views of public policy. But if immediate emancipation, with just compensation, shall prove to be the sentiment of the House, I am prepared to exercise an express constitutional power, and vote to remove for ever the blot of slavery from the national capital." Mr. Blair (Rep.) of Missouri said, "The charge has frequently been heard here and elsewhere, that the President is without a policy in his administration. I shall endeavor to show that this imputation is unfounded, to explain my conceptions of his policy, and to demonstrate that it is wise in every aspect, and commends itself to the lovers of the Union and of freedom." Mr. Crittenden (Union) of Kentucky followed in opposition to the bill and to the policy of emancipation. "You may produce," he said, "much mischief by this measure. What is the good? Slavery has been, under one influence or another, disappearing from this district for years. It has been decaying and going out. Your bill would not, probably, have a thousand slaves to act upon. What, then, is the deep anxiety to pass this measure? Why should Congress, at a time like this, devote its attention with so much earnestness, and apparently with so much purpose, to this measure? Let slavery alone. It will go out like a candle. No disturbance will follow it. No violation of public feeling will follow. No apprehension will result from it. This measure will create discontent among the people elsewhere, and will lead them to consider it but as an augury of what is to come afterwards. The good you can do by it is little, is minute, in comparison to the great question involved." — "We are deliberating here today," said Mr. Bingham of Ohio, " upon a bill which illustrates the great principle that this day shakes the throne of every despot upon the globe; and that is, whether man was made for government, or government made for man. Those who oppose this bill, whether they intend it or not, by recording their votes against this enactment, reiterate the old dogma of tyrants, that the people are made to be governed, and not to govern. I deny that proposition. I deny it, because all my convictions are opposed to it. I deny it, because I am sure that the Constitution of my country is against it. I cannot forget, if I would, the grand utterance of one of the illustrious men of modern times, — of whom Guizot very fitly said, that his thoughts impress themselves indelibly wherever they fall, — standing amid the despotisms of Europe, conscious of the great truth that all men are of right equal before the law, that thrones may perish, that crowns may turn to dust, that sceptres may be broken and empires overthrown, but that the rights of men are perpetual, he proclaimed to listening France the strong, true words, 'States are born, live, and die upon the earth; here they fulfil their destiny: but, after the citizen has discharged every duty that he owes to the State, there abides with him the nobler part of his being, his immortal faculties, by which he ascends to God and the unknown realities of another life.' I would illustrate that utterance of the French thinker by incorporating in our legislation this day a provision, that every human being, no matter what his complexion, here within the limits of the capital of the Republic, shall be secure in the enjoyment of his inherent rights; that the citizen is more than the State; that the protection of his rights is of more concern than any or all mere State policies. I would pass this bill, not only for the sake of giving present relief to the unfortunate human beings for whose special relief it is designed, and who, if I am rightly informed, are being carried hourly away from your capital in order to perpetuate their too-long-endured captivity, not only to burst their fetters, not only to kindle a new joy in their humble homes by inspiring in them a sense of personal security and safety, but I would pass this bill for the purpose as well of giving a new assurance that the Republic still lives, and gives promise not to disappoint the hopes of the struggling nations of the earth."

"A great truth," said Mr. Riddle (Rep.) of Ohio, "is weakened by what men call elucidation. Illustration obscures it; logic and argument compromise it; and demonstration brings it to doubt. He who permits himself to be put on its defensive is a weak man or a coward. A great truth is never so strong as when left to stand on its simple assertion. The thing right for ever remains right, under all possible circumstances and conditions, in all times, places, and seasons. Nor can it be changed at all. Not all power, nor the combination of all power, no matter how employed or applied, can change it in the least. It matters not at all how men call it: though the unanimous world conspire to call it ill, and tag it out with all vile epithets; though all obscene mouths make it common, and lewd tongues toss it into sewers, and delicate and refined ears may not hear it, — it is nowise changed. No matter what ill happens to it; though cast out, exiled, banished, and outlawed, marked and for ever banned, made leprous with contumely and reproach; though prisoned, tried, condemned, and executed, and its body, like carrion, cast to vultures, — it still lives, is still right; holds its old place and old sceptre. Nor can any man, by any power, under any circumstances, for any thing, be absolved from the allegiance he owes it." — " I did not rise," said Mr. Fessenden (Rep.) of Maine, "to discuss the merits of this bill. The hour for its discussion has passed. The hour in which to put upon it the seal of the nation has come. I trust it is, indeed, the harbinger of that brighter, brightest day at hand, when slavery shall be abolished wherever it exists in the land. This will be the one finality which will give us a righteous and a lasting peace."

Mr. Rollins (Rep.) of New Hampshire said, "It is one of the most beautiful traits of human nature, that while the sons of men are struggling to bear the burdens of human life, and perform the works assigned to our common nature, they sometimes step aside, or stop in their way, to minister to the wants of the needy, who, sitting by the wayside, lift their eyes and hands to beg for charity. This nation, which, like a giant, walks along the pathway of nations, girded as with iron, sternly to meet and overwhelm its fratricidal foes, while marching steadily on to its work, feels it no hinderance to listen to the humble cry of a few hundred of its feeblest children who grind in the prison-house of its deadly foe. The abolition of slavery in the District of Columbia is, to the few slaves therein, a deed of justice and mercy that this people cannot omit to perform at this golden opportunity. Slavery has forfeited all claims to any implied obligation for immunity in the capital of the nation by its mad attempt to tear down the pillars of that Government under which it claimed protection. Justice demands that the arch enemy of our Government and instigator of all our present calamity, who still lurks in this chosen centre of the Republic, as Satan did in the garden of Eden, should be expelled, and that the glittering sword of power should guard the gate against its entrance for evermore. Mercy — if the act of emancipation may have that quality — demands for the victims of this too-long-endured oppression their restoration to the primal rights of humanity. This is the quality that will give to this act, about, as I trust, to be consummated, its crowning grace and virtue, and commend it to the admiration of good men all over the world, and win for it the approval of Heaven, where mercy has its seat." — "Of the moral effects of the measure upon the country and upon the world," said Mr. Blake (Rep.) of Ohio, "I need not speak. That it will elevate us in the eyes of all civilized nations,

is not doubted; that it will awaken a thrill of patriotic pride and enthusiasm in the great heart of the nation, no man doubts. Even the opponents of emancipation on this floor have not ventured to shock the moral sense of the House by an absolute defence of slavery as a thing desirable in itself. No man has ventured to assert that the measure will be injurious to the general interests of the District. The respected and venerable gentleman from Kentucky (Mr. Crittenden) did declare that he was no friend of slavery; that, if the adoption of slavery were now an original proposition before the House, he would vote against it. I rejoice, sir, at such declarations as these, coming, as I have no doubt they do, from a truly loyal, patriotic heart: they are the harbinger of better days for the Republic. But, sir, I expect no applause in South Carolina and Mississippi for the passage of this bill, and none from traitors anywhere. It is our duty to abolish slavery here, because Congress, by the Constitution, has the power to do it; and, slavery being a great wrong and outrage upon humanity, we should at once do right, and pass this bill."
—"I would rather close this debate," said Mr. Van Horn (Rep.) of New York, "and come directly to the vote upon it, and content myself with recording my name in its favor. Indeed, it needs no defence. Upon its face it bears the marks of humanity and of justice. Every line and every syllable is pregnant with a just and true sentiment, and already hallowed with the sublime spirit of a noble purpose. Throughout it there breathes a spirit akin to that which runs through all the wonderful teachings of Him who spake as never man spake, and inspired the hearts of those whose immortal

sayings will outlast all the monuments that time can erect." Mr. Ashley (Rep.) of Ohio said, "The struggles and hopes of many long years are centred in this eventful hour. The cry of the oppressed, 'How long, O Lord! how long?' is to be answered to-day by the American Congress. A sublime act of justice is now to be recorded where it will never be obliterated; and, so far as the action of the representatives of the people can decree it, the fitting words of the President, spoken in his recent special message, 'INITIATE AND EMANCIPATE,' shall have a life co-equal with the Republic. God has set his seal upon these priceless words; and they, with the memory of him who uttered them, shall live in the hearts of the people for ever. The golden morn, so anxiously looked for by the friends of freedom in the United States, has dawned. A second national jubilee will henceforth be added to the calendar. The brave words heretofore uttered in behalf of humanity in this hall, like 'bread cast upon the waters,' are now 'to return after many days,' and find vindication of their purposes in a decree of freedom." — " Discussion will go on," said Mr. Hutchins (Rep.) of Ohio, " should go on, till slavery is extinct. It has only a 'contraband' existence anywhere. It has rebelled against the lawful and rightful authority of the Government, and its presence is in the way of permanent peace. Our fathers honestly supposed that it would disappear before the march of Christian civilization. They were mistaken. While we strive to imitate their wisdom, and seek to emulate their patriotism, let us be warned by their mistake. I am more anxious to vote than to detain the committee longer by remarks. This bill will make the national capital *free;* and then the statue of Liberty, fashioned by our own Crawford, will be a fitting ornament on the finished dome of the Capitol."

Mr. Stevens moved that the committee rise, for the purpose of closing the debate; and the motion was agreed to. Mr. Stevens then moved that all debate close in Committee of the Whole in one minute after the committee shall resume the consideration of the question. Mr. Richardson (Dem.) of Illinois moved to amend, so as to allow one hour, — yeas 56, nays 73. Mr. Wright (Dem.) of Pennsylvania moved to amend the first section so as to provide "that this act shall not go into operation unless the qualified citizens of the District of Columbia shall, by a majority of votes polled, approve and ratify the same." — "I would recommend to my colleague," said Mr. Stevens, "with great respect, an amendment in another document. It is somewhere provided that the wicked shall be damned. I would suggest to my colleague that he propose a proviso to that, 'providing that they consent thereto.' It would be just as decent an amendment as the one which he has proposed." Mr. Wright's amendment was lost. Mr. Wadsworth (Opp.) of Kentucky moved to strike out of the second section the words, "loyal to the United States." The provision he "held to be unconstitutional." — "I oppose," said Mr. Hickman (Rep.) of Pennsylvania, "this amendment. My objection is, that a man who is disloyal forfeits the protection which he would otherwise be entitled to from the Government; that he cannot claim the protection of the Constitution which he repudiates and attempts to cast off; and it is not for us to confer rights upon him which he distinctly disclaims." Mr. Wadsworth's amendment was rejected. Mr. Train (Rep.) of Massachusetts said, "I offer the following amendment to the third section : 'That any person feeling himself aggrieved by the determination of the commissioners in the amount of compensation awarded, may, within three months from the time when the final report of said commissioners shall be filed, appeal to the Circuit Court of the United States for the District of Columbia, and either party may be entitled to a trial by jury in that court, and the judgment in the case shall be final upon all parties.' This amendment," said Mr. Train, "does not affect the bill, so far forth as it goes to the question of emancipation, but simply the proceedings in fixing the compensation." Mr. Train's amendment was lost, — ayes 53, noes 63. Mr. Harding (Opp.) of Kentucky moved to strike out the proviso limiting the sum appraised to $300. "You do not," said Mr. Harding, "consult the people of the District as to whether they are willing to sell or not. Not at all. You have the power to buy, and you will buy; you have the power to fix your own price, and you will fix it. I say I have more respect for a man who will walk up and take my property, without thus mocking me with a consideration." Mr. Lovejoy (Rep.) of Illinois opposed the amendment. He said, "The gentleman thinks it is worse to take a thing for one-half of its value than it is to rob a man of his property outright, if I understood his remarks. I wonder which is worse, — to rob a man of his horse, or to rob him of his wife and child? That is the question I would like to ask him. Look at this which I hold in my hand : —

'GEORGETOWN, D.C., June 12, 1861.

'I hereby give my consent to let James Harod have the privilege of buying his wife and child for the sum of $1,100. James Harod is himself free.

'LOUIS MACKALL, Jun.'

"Now talk about robbery. Every slave here has been robbed and stolen, and every man who holds a slave is a man-thief; and here, in this nineteenth century, in the Federal city of this Christian Republic, lofty and eminent among the nations of the earth, challenging respect and imitation, is *this* man, Mackall, who proposes to let a free man have the privilege of buying his wife and child, which he had stolen from him, for eleven hundred dollars, — this Mackall, a woman-thief, a child-thief! How much did he give for this woman? He took her for a debt. And here let me say, for fear that my time may expire, this woman-thief, Mackall, after giving a pledge that this man might buy his own wife and child, flesh of his flesh, and bone of his bone, seized the woman and child, and a babe, six months old, *born since*, and sent them into a slave-pen in Baltimore; and yet here brazen men stand up and talk about robbing, because we give only three hundred dollars apiece, on an average, to deliver these poor oppressed beings from a condition of brutism. It is the sublimity of impudence."

Mr. Wickliffe said, "I have no hope of success; but I feel it to be my duty to move to strike out the words, 'without the exclusion of any witness on account of color,' where they occur. I presume it is intended to let a man's servant come in, and swear that he is a disloyal man. I do hope the friends of this bill will not so far outrage the laws of this District as to authorize slaves or free negroes to be witnesses in cases of this kind." Mr. Stevens said, "I trust that this committee will not so far continue an outrage as not to allow any man of credit, whether he be black or white, to be a witness;" and the amendment was rejected.

Mr. Wickliffe moved to strike out all after the enacting clause, and insert the bill moved in the Senate by Mr. Wright of Indiana. Mr. Holman (Rep.) of Indiana would amend the amendment by striking out the fifth section, requiring the authorities of Washington and Georgetown to provide active and efficient means to arrest fugitive slaves. Mr. Cox (Dem.) of Ohio opposed the motion, "because, if the bill is to pass in any shape at all, I should like to see this substitute passed in its entirety." Mr. Vallandigham (Dem.) said that "there were not ten men in the Thirty-sixth Congress of the United States who would have recorded their votes in favor of the abolition of slavery in the District of Columbia. There are many on that side of the House who believe and know that assertion to be true; and yet behold, to-day, what is before the Congress of the United States! In the language of the distinguished gentleman from Kentucky, 'availing themselves of the troubles of the times,' we have this bill brought forward as the beginning of a grand scheme of emancipation; and there is no calculation where that scheme is to end." Mr. Holman's motion to amend the amendment was rejected; and Mr. Wickliffe's amendment was lost, — ayes 34, noes 84.

Mr. Menzies (Union) of Kentucky moved to amend by striking out all after the enacting clause, and inserting as follows: "That the children of persons held to service for life in the District of Columbia, who may be born after the first day of May, 1862, shall be free; and, at the age of eighteen years, may assert their freedom against all persons. Any person who may be brought into said District after the first day of May, 1862, for the benefit of his or her owner or hirer, shall thereby become free. Any person who may deprive a person entitled to freedom, according to the first section of this act, of the power and means of asserting such freedom, shall be guilty of felony, and shall be punished, on conviction thereof in any court of competent jurisdiction, by confinement in the penitentiary not less than five nor more than twenty years." The amendment was disagreed to.

The committee, on motion of Mr. Stevens, rose; and Mr. Dawes reported that the Committee of the Whole on the State of the Union had instructed him to report the bill back to the House, without amendment. Mr. Stevens demanded the previous question; and it was ordered, — yeas 92, nays 39. Mr. Holman demanded the yeas and nays on the passage of the bill. They were ordered; and the question was taken, — yeas 92, nays 38.

The bill thus passed the House, and was approved by the President on the sixteenth day of April, 1862. By the enactment of this bill, three thousand slaves were instantly made for ever free, slavery made impossible in the capital of the United States, and the black laws and ordinances concerning persons of color repealed and abrogated. The enfranchised bondmen, grateful for this beneficent act of national legislation, assembled in their churches, and offered up the homage and gratitude of their hearts to God for the boon of personal freedom.

CHAPTER IV.

THE PRESIDENT'S PROPOSITION TO AID STATES IN THE ABOLISHMENT OF SLAVERY.

THE PRESIDENT'S SPECIAL MESSAGE. — MR. ROSCOE CONKLING'S RESOLUTION. — MR. RICHARDSON'S SPEECH. — MR. BINGHAM'S SPEECH. — MR. VOORHEES' SPEECH. — MR. MALLORY'S SPEECH. — MR. WICKLIFFE'S SPEECH. — MR. DIVEN'S SPEECH. — MR. THOMAS'S SPEECH. — MR. BIDDLE'S SPEECH. — MR. CRISFIELD'S SPEECH. — MR. OLIN'S SPEECH. — MR. CRITTENDEN'S SPEECH. — MR. FISHER'S SPEECH. — MR. HICKMAN'S SPEECH. — PASSAGE OF THE BILL IN THE HOUSE. — IN THE SENATE, THE RESOLUTION REPORTED WITHOUT AMENDMENT BY MR. TRUMBULL. — MR. SAULSBURY'S SPEECH. — MR. DAVIS'S AMENDMENT. — MR. SHERMAN'S SPEECH. — MR. DOOLITTLE'S SPEECH. — MR. WILLEY'S SPEECH. — MR. BROWNING'S SPEECH. — MR. M'DOUGALL'S SPEECH. — MR. POWELL'S SPEECH. — MR. LATHAM'S SPEECH. — MR. MORRILL'S SPEECH. — MR. HENDERSON'S AMENDMENT. — MR. SHERMAN'S SPEECH. — PASSAGE OF THE RESOLUTION.

ON the 6th of March, 1862, the President sent to Congress a special message, in which he said, " I recommend the adoption of a joint resolution by your honorable bodies, which shall be substantially as follows : —

"*Resolved*, That the United States ought to co-operate with any State which may adopt gradual abolishment of slavery ; giving to such State pecuniary aid, to be used by such State in its discretion, to compensate for the inconveniences, public and private, produced by such change of system.

"If the proposition contained in the resolution does not meet the approval of Congress and the country, there is the end ; but, if it does command such approval,

I deem it of importance that the States and people immediately interested should be at once distinctly notified of the fact, so that they may begin to consider whether to accept or reject it. The Federal Government would find its highest interest in such a measure, as one of the most efficient means of self-preservation. The leaders of the existing insurrection entertain the hope, that this Government will ultimately be forced to acknowledge the independence of some part of the disaffected region, and that all the slave States north of such part will then say, 'The Union for which we have struggled being already gone, we now choose to go with the Southern section.' To deprive them of this hope, substantially ends the Rebellion; and the initiation of emancipation completely deprives them of it as to all the States initiating it. The point is, not that *all* the States tolerating slavery would very soon, if at all, initiate emancipation, but that, while the offer is equally made to all, the more Northern shall, by such initiation, make it certain to the more Southern that in no event will the former ever join the latter in their proposed confederacy. . . . While it is true that the adoption of the proposed resolution would be merely initiatory, and not within itself a practical measure, it is recommended in the hope that it would soon lead to important practical results. In full view of my great responsibility to my God and to my country, I earnestly beg the attention of Congress and the people to the subject."

Mr. Stevens (Rep.) of Pennsylvania moved its reference to the Committee of the Whole on the State of the Union. On the 10th of March, Mr. Roscoe Conkling (Rep.) of New York asked leave to introduce a joint resolution, "That the United States ought to co-operate with any State which may adopt gradual abolishment of slavery; giving to such State pecuniary aid, to be used by such State in its discretion, to compensate for the inconveniences, public and private, produced by such change of system."

Mr. Ben. Wood (Dem.) of New York objected. Mr. Conkling moved the suspension of the rules, to allow him to introduce the resolution, which was the exact resolution recommended by the President; and the rules were suspended, — yeas 86, nays 35. Mr. Grider (Opp.) of Kentucky remarked, that he had not decided whether he should vote for the resolution or not. Mr. Wadsworth (Opp.) differed from his colleague: he was now ready to vote against the resolution. Mr. Conkling moved the previous question: lost, — ayes 61, noes 68. Mr. Richardson (Dem.) of Illinois opposed the resolution. His "people were not prepared to enter upon the proposed work of purchasing the slaves of other people, and turning them loose in their midst." Mr. Bingham (Rep.) of Ohio said, "This proposition interferes with no right of any State by intendment or otherwise." Mr. Wickliffe (Opp.) of Kentucky asked Mr. Bingham to tell him under "what clause of the Constitution he finds the power in Congress to appropriate the treasure of the United States to buy negroes, or to set them free." — "I took occasion in January last," replied Mr. Bingham, "to remind the House of the words of the Father of the Constitution, uttered in the hearing of the listening nation when the Constitution was under consideration for adoption or rejection, that the power conferred upon the National Legislature by the grant of the Constitution, for the common defence, had no limitation upon it, express or implied, save the public necessity, and that their laws should not conflict with the general spirit and purpose of the Constitution; viz., the protection of the lives, liberty, and property of its loyal citizens. If the gentleman will pardon me, I beg leave to remind him again of the words of Madison, that 'it is in vain to oppose constitutional barriers to the impulse of self-preservation: it is worse than in vain.'" — "I have," declared Mr. Voorhees (Dem.) of Indiana, "taken my stand, in the name of the people I represent, against it. If there is any Border slave State man here who is in doubt whether he wants his State to sell its slaves to this Government or not, I represent a people that is in no doubt as to whether they want to become the purchasers. It takes two to make a bargain; and I repudiate, once and for ever, for the people whom I represent on this floor, any part or parcel in such a contract." Mr. Mallory (Dem.) of Kentucky wanted the resolution postponed, to give the representatives from the Border States an opportunity for consultation. "We have," he said, "agreed on the time and the manner of consultation." Mr. Diven (Rep.) of New York "hailed the introduction of this resolution, coming as it did from the Executive of the country, as a bow of hope and promise." Mr. Thomas (Opp.) of Massachusetts "intended to vote for the resolution; but I do not understand, as gentlemen seem to intimate frequently on the floor of this House, that the House is to follow the beck of the President, or any member of the Administration. It has its duties to discharge as well as the President. This House is to initiate a policy, and not the President of the United States; it is to take the responsibility as well as the President; and therefore it is to discuss and deliberate before it decides or votes." Mr. Stevens said, "I have read it over; and I confess I have not been able to see what makes one side so anxious to pass it, or the other side so anxious to defeat it. I think it is about the most diluted, milk-and-water-gruel proposition that was ever given to the American nation."

On the 11th of March, Mr. Wickliffe opposed the resolution and the policy of emancipation. Mr. Diven appealed to the representatives of the Border States. "I ask," he said, "those men of the Border States to come up and stand by us who are loyal to them, and who have testified to them our desire to maintain to them the possession of all their rights. Stand by the President, who has never had a thought of violating one of your constitutional rights. I appeal to these men; I appeal to all who would rally round the President in his desire — in his honest, earnest desire — to bring this country out from this fiery ordeal unscathed, with every star upon her flag undimmed." Mr. Biddle (Dem.) of Pennsylvania said, "If you review this subject from the adoption of the present Constitution down to the present day, — and it is a review I do not intend to inflict upon the House at the present moment, — if you review the subject, you will find, that, while State action has always been beneficent, Federal action has always been pernicious, exasperative, and, as I think, unconstitutional." — "I concede, and it gives me pleasure to concede," said Mr. Crisfield (Opp.) of Maryland, "that the President of the United States, in making this offer to the country, is actuated by a spirit of patriotism. I can understand that he offers it to the people of the slave States to produce some harmony on the agitating question of slavery, which has disturbed the whole country. I give him entire credit for honesty and good faith." Mr. Olin (Rep.) of New York inquired, " What is this resolution, in its whole scope and extent? Why, simply, that, if you gentlemen of the slave States are willing to get rid of slavery, the General Government will aid you to do it by giving you a compensation for any loss that you may sustain; and, although I am not worth much, God knows I would divide my last crust of bread to aid our Southern friends to get rid of slavery, and let us live in peace and harmony together. I have not a great deal; but, thank God! what there is of it has been earned by honest industry; and I would cheerfully divide it to aid you, gentlemen, in accomplishing that object. If these gentlemen say, ' We cannot afford to make the sacrifice of manumitting our slaves,' the President says, ' Very well: the General Government will aid you to accomplish it.' That is the magnanimous, the great, the God-like policy of the Administration." Mr. Crittenden (Opp.) of Kentucky opposed the resolution. " I avow my confidence," he declared, " in the integrity of the President. I avow my confidence in his purity of intention. I believe he means right; and it affords me pleasure to concur with him in most of the measures recommended by him : but I regret that in this my conscience and judgment will not permit it. I believe the President would not, as he says he would not, interfere.

He would leave it to the choice of the States to say whether they will enter upon the policy of emancipation or not; but do not I know, that although the President will abstain from interfering, so far as he is concerned, there are many others, who, knowing it is a favorite policy of his, desiring themselves to be in his favor, would stir up an emancipation party in Missouri, in Maryland, and in Delaware, — I will not now speak of my own State, — simply from that motive?" Mr. Fisher (Ind.) of Delaware declared his intention to vote for the resolution. Mr. Hickman (Rep.) of Pennsylvania said, "The resolution is rather a palliative and caution than an open and avowed policy; it is rather an excuse for non-action than an avowed determination to act. Neither the message nor the resolution is manly and open. They are both covert and insidious. They do not become the dignity of the President of the United States. The message is not such a document as a full-grown, independent man should publish to the nation at such a time as the present, when positions should be freely and fully defined. . . . I know no great diversity of opinion among men whose interests are identified with slavery. I have never been able to discover a difference in views or feelings between a man from Maryland and a man from South Carolina or Alabama. I have found, wherever the negro is, there is an undivided loyalty to slavery; and every day's proceedings here show it, — conclusively show it. Every fair-minded man cannot but admit it. The President knows it; the Cabinet knows it; and therefore the difficulty which the President has had for a long time in dealing with this Rebellion. Mr. Lincoln has found himself between two swords, — the sword of the party looking to a particular policy to be pursued towards a rebellion springing from slavery; and the sword in the hands of the Border States, who insist all the time that the war shall be prosecuted in such a way as to save their peculiar, divine, and humanizing institution." The question was taken on laying the resolution on the table, — yeas 34, nays 81. Mr. Wickliffe of Kentucky demanded the yeas and nays on the passage of the resolution, — yeas 89, nays 31, as follows: —

YEAS. — Messrs. Aldrich, Arnold, Ashley, Babbitt, Baker, Baxter, Beaman, Bingham, Francis P. Blair, Jacob B. Blair, Samuel S. Blair, Blake, William G. Brown, Buffinton, Campbell, Chamberlin, Clements, Colfax, Frederick A. Conkling, Roscoe Conkling, Conway, Covode, Cutler, Davis, Delano, Diven, Duell, Dunn, Edgerton, Edwards, Eliot, Ely, Fessenden, Fisher, Franchot, Frank, Gooch, Goodwin, Granger, Haight, Hale, Harrison, Hickman, Hooper, Horton, Hutchins, Julian, Kelley, Francis W. Kellogg, William Kellogg, Killinger, Lansing, Loomis, Lovejoy, M'Knight, M'Pherson, Mitchell, Moorhead, Anson P. Morrill, Justin S. Morrill, Nixon, Olin, Patton, Timothy G. Phelps, Pike, Pomeroy, Porter, Alexander H. Rice, John H. Rice, Riddle, Edward H. Rollins, Sargent, Shanks, Sheffield, Shellabarger, Sloan, Stratton, Train, Trowbridge, Van Valkenburgh, Verree, Wallace, Charles W. Walton, E. P. Walton, Whaley, Albert S. White, Wilson, Windom, and Worcester, — 89.

NAYS. — Messrs. Ancona, Joseph Baily, Biddle, Corning, Cox, Cravens, Crisfield, Crittenden, Dunlap, English, Harding, Johnson, Knapp, Law, Leary, Noble, Norton, Pendleton, Perry, Richardson, Robinson, Shiel, John B. Steele, Francis Thomas, Voorhees, Wadsworth, Ward, Chilton A. White, Wickliffe, Wood, and Woodruff, — 31.

So the joint resolution passed the House of Representatives.

In the Senate, on the 20th of March, Mr. Trumbull (Rep.) of Illinois, from the Committee on the Judiciary, to whom was referred the joint resolution of the House of Representatives, declaring that Congress ought to co-operate with, affording pecuniary aid to, any State which may adopt the gradual abolishment of slavery, reported back the joint resolution, with a recommendation that it pass. Mr. Trumbull asked the Senate to put the resolution on its passage; but Mr. Powell (Dem.) of Kentucky objected, and it went over under the rule. On the 24th, on motion of Mr. Trumbull, the Senate proceeded, as in Committee of the Whole, to consider the joint resolution of the House, declaring that Congress ought to co-operate with and afford pecuniary aid to any State which may adopt the gradual abolishment of slavery.

Mr. Saulsbury (Dem.) of Delaware pronounced it to be "the most extraordinary resolution that was ever introduced into an American Congress; extraordinary in its origin; extraordinary in reference to the source from whence it proceeds; extraordinary in the object which it contemplates; mischievous in its tendency: and I am not at all sure that it is anywise patriotic, even in its design."

Mr. Davis (Opp.) of Kentucky moved an amendment, as a substitute for the resolution, to strike out all after the word "that," and insert, "although the whole subject of slavery in the States is exclusively within the jurisdiction and cognizance of the government and people of the States respectively having slaves, and cannot be interfered with directly or indirectly by the Government of the United States, yet, when any of those States or their people may determine to emancipate their slaves, the United States will pay a reasonable price for the slaves they may emancipate, and the cost of their colonization in some other country." Mr. Sherman (Rep.) of Ohio did "not see any substantial difference between the resolution framed by the President and the resolution as proposed by the senator from Kentucky; but he should vote for it as framed by the President." — "I admit," replied Mr. Davis, that "the general principle both of the original resolution and of the substitute is the same." Mr. Doolittle (Rep.) of Wisconsin said, "As I understand it, the resolution suggested by the President covers two ideas, — first, emancipation by the States at their own pleasure, in their own way, either immediate or gradual; and, second, the idea of colonization, a thing believed to be necessary to go along side by side with emancipation by nine-tenths of the people of the States interested, and without which they declare emancipation impossible." Mr. Willey (Union) of Virginia "could not withhold the expression of his regret that the President has deemed it to be his duty to make such a proposition to Congress; but he should vote for it, not without hesitation, not without deepest regret." Mr. Browning (Rep.) of Illinois supported the original resolution. Mr. M'Dougall (Dem.) of California denied "the right of the Senate to impose upon the people on the shores of the Pacific a tax for the purpose of emancipating the slaves of Kentucky, Missouri, or Maryland." — "I regard," said Mr. Powell, "the whole thing, so far as the slave States are concerned, as a pill of arsenic, sugar-coated." He thought the language of the President's message was very artfully and cautiously couched; but the intimation was in it, that, if we did not accept this proposition, the Government would take our slaves anyhow. "I happened," he said, "a few nights ago, through curiosity, to go to the Smithsonian Institution, to hear a man of some distinction as an orator and lecturer in this country. I took my seat in the gallery; and there I heard this man, Wendell Phillips, for half an hour; and he distinctly announced, after eulogizing the President very highly for this message, that the interpretation of it was simply saying to the Border slave State men, 'Gentlemen, if you do not take this, we will take your negroes anyhow.'" — "I am," said Mr. Latham (Dem.) of California, "very free to say, that I believe the motive which prompted the sending of this resolution by the President to Congress to be a proper and patriotic one; . . . but I am not prepared, as a representative of one of the States on the Pacific coast, to pledge the people thereof to submit to any kind of taxation that the Government may see fit to impose in a general scheme of emancipation." — "I am," said Mr. Morrill (Rep.) of Maine, "greatly surprised at the course of this debate. I had supposed it was possible for somebody in some way to allude to the subject of slavery, without eliciting indignation, or without rendering it a subject for discussion, for latitudinarian discussion, for discussion in various directions, for discussion in which gentlemen must think it necessary to define their positions. . . . I cannot conceive that such a proposition as that is offensive, or can possibly be offensive, to any man or any class of men who have not made up their minds, that, above all things, — Constitution, country, every thing, — they hold slavery to be supreme. They will stand on that, no matter what becomes of the country. They will not only resist all legislation on the subject, but they will treat with scorn and contempt every invitation to consider the subject. That is the attitude in which senators place themselves here. They are indignant that the President of the United States proposes that these States in their own way shall consider whether it is not expedient to get rid in the future of the cause of our present troubles." The question was taken on Mr. Davis's amendment by yeas and nays, — yeas 4, nays 34.

On the 27th, Mr. Henderson (Union) of Missouri offered an amendment, to insert at the end of the resolution the following proviso : " That nothing herein contained shall be construed to imply a willingness on the part of Congress that any of the States now composing the Union shall be permitted to withdraw permanently their allegiance to the Government; but it is hereby declared to be the duty of the country to prosecute the war until the Constitution shall have been restored over every State professing to have seceded." Mr. Henderson advocated his amendment, and avowed his intention to vote for the resolution. "I regard it," he said, "as no insult to the people of my State; I regard it as no threat: but I regard it as a measure that is conciliatory, and looks to the future peace and harmony of the country, and to the early restoration of the Union. If this spirit had been more largely cultivated in days gone by, we would not this day be forced to witness a ruined South and a deeply oppressed North. Why, sir, ninety-six days of this war would pay for every slave, at full value, in the States of Kentucky, Missouri, Maryland, Delaware, and the District of

Columbia." Mr. Henderson's amendment was rejected.

Mr. Sherman, on the 2d of April, made an elaborate speech in favor of the joint resolution, and of the abolition of slavery in the District of Columbia, and in favor of enacting "the most rigid law of confiscation against the leaders of the Rebellion."

The joint resolution was ordered to a third reading; and was read the third time, at length, as follows: "*Resolved*, &c., That the United States ought to co-operate with any State which may adopt the gradual abolishment of slavery; giving to such State pecuniary aid, to be used by such State in its discretion, to compensate for the inconveniences, public and private, produced by such change of system."

Mr. Saulsbury called for the yeas and nays on the passage of the resolution, and they were ordered; and, being taken, resulted — yeas 32, nays 10 — as follows: —

YEAS. — Messrs. Anthony, Browning, Chandler, Clark, Collamer, Davis, Dixon, Doolittle, Fessenden, Foot, Foster, Grimes, Hale, Harlan, Henderson, Howard, Howe, King, Lane of Indiana, Lane of Kansas, Morrill, Pomeroy, Sherman, Sumner, Ten Eyck, Thomson, Trumbull, Wade, Wilkinson, Willey, Wilmot, and Wilson of Massachusetts, — 32.

NAYS. — Messrs. Bayard, Carlile, Kennedy, Latham, Nesmith, Powell, Saulsbury, Stark, Wilson of Missouri, and Wright, — 10.

So the joint resolution was passed in the Senate, and received the approval of the President on the 10th of April, 1862.

CHAPTER V.

THE PROHIBITION OF SLAVERY IN THE TERRITORIES.

MR. ARNOLD'S BILL. — MR. LOVEJOY'S REPORT. — MOTION TO LAY THE BILL ON THE TABLE. — MR. LOVEJOY'S SUBSTITUTE. — REMARKS OF MR. COX. — MR. DIVEN. — MR. OLIN. — MR. CRISFIELD. — MR. KELLEY. — MR. SHEFFIELD. — MR. STEVENS. — MR. THOMAS. — MR. BINGHAM. — MR. FISHER. — PASSAGE OF THE BILL IN THE HOUSE. — IN THE SENATE. — MR. BROWNING'S REPORT. — MR. BROWNING'S AMENDMENT. — MR. CARLILE'S SPEECH. — MR. WADE'S SPEECH — PASSAGE OF THE BILL AS AMENDED. — AMENDMENT OF THE SENATE CONCURRED IN.

NO question during the existence of the Republic of the United States has excited so intense and profound an interest as the question, whether freedom or slavery should predominate in the Territories. The vast extent of the territorial possessions of the United States, the power of the rising commonwealths upon the destinies of the nation, made their territorial condition one of intense solicitude alike to the friends and enemies of slavery. Freedom and slavery have often contended for ascendency in the Territories. In these oft-repeated contests, the sentiments and opinions, the interests and passions, of vast sections have been deeply aroused, and the whole nation stirred to its profoundest depths. In these struggles, the slaveholding interests were accustomed to win decisive victories; but, in 1860, the advocates of the freedom of the Territories achieved a national triumph in the election of a President fully and unreservedly pledged to their policy.

In the House of Representatives, on the 24th of March, 1862, Mr. Arnold (Rep.) of Illinois introduced a bill to render freedom national, and slavery sectional; which was read, and referred to the Committee on Territories. On the 1st of May, Mr. Lovejoy (Rep.) of Illinois reported from the Committee on Territories Mr. Arnold's bill to make freedom national, and slavery sectional; which was read, recommitted to the Committee on Territories, and ordered to be printed.

Mr. Lovejoy, on the 8th of May, from the Committee on Territories, reported it back, with an amendment to the title, and with the recommendation that it pass the bill of the House, to render freedom national, and slavery sectional; and moved the previous question upon its engrossment and third reading. It provided, that to the end that freedom may be, and remain for ever, the fundamental law of the land in all places whatsoever, so far as it lies within the powers or depends upon the action of the Government of the United States to make it so, slavery and involuntary servitude, in all cases whatsoever, shall henceforth cease, and be prohibited for ever, in all the following places: 1. In all the Territories of the United States now existing, or hereafter to be formed or acquired in any way. 2. In all places purchased or to be purchased by the United States, with the consent of the Legislatures of the several States, for the erection of forts, magazines, arsenals, dockyards, and other needful buildings. 3. In all vessels on the high seas, and on all national highways, beyond the territory and jurisdiction of each of the several States from which or to which the said vessels may be going. 4. In all places whatsoever where the National Government is supreme, or has exclusive jurisdiction or power. The bill further provided, that any person now held, or attempted to be held hereafter, as a slave in any of the places above named, is hereby declared to be free; and that the right to freedom hereby declared may be asserted in any of the courts of the United States or of the several States, in behalf of the party, or his or her posterity, after any lapse of time, upon the principle that a party once free is always free. Mr. Cox (Dem.) of Ohio moved that the bill be laid upon the table; upon which motion Mr. Washburn (Rep.) of Illinois demanded the yeas and nays, and they were ordered, — yeas 50, nays 64. On motion of Mr. M·Knight (Rep.) of Pennsylvania, the House adjourned.

On the 9th of May, the Speaker announced as the special order of the day, the bill prohibiting slavery in the Territories. Mr. Lovejoy withdrew his demand for the previous question, and offered a substitute for the pending bill. The bill provided that slavery, in all cases whatsoever, shall henceforth cease, and be prohibited for ever, in all the following places; namely, First, In all the Territories of the United States now existing, or hereafter to be formed or acquired in any way. Second, In all places purchased or to be purchased by the United States, with the consent of the Legislatures of the several States, for the erection of forts, magazines, arsenals, dock-yards, and other needful buildings, and in which the United States have or shall have exclusive legislative jurisdiction. Third, In all vessels on the high seas beyond the territory and jurisdiction of of each of the several States from which or to which the said vessels may be going. Fourth, In all places whatsoever where the National Government has exclusive jurisdiction. That any person now held, or attempted to be held hereafter, as a slave in any of the places above named, is declared to be free; and the right to freedom may be asserted in any of the courts of the United States or of the several States, in behalf of the party, or his or her posterity, after any lapse of time. Mr. Allen (Dem.) of Illinois moved that the bill be laid upon the table, — yeas 50, nays 65.

Mr. Olin (Rep.) of New York desired to amend and debate it. Mr. Lovejoy withdrew the demand for the previous question, and moved to amend his substitute by striking out these words, "and all national highways." "That," he said, "relieves the bill from some of the objections which have been brought against it by some gentlemen who are friends of the bill." Mr. Lovejoy moved the previous question, to test the sense of the House, whether the bill should be discussed or not. The House decided, — ayes 42, noes 61. Mr. Lovejoy then moved to recommit the bill. "I do not," he said, "propose at present to enter at any length into the discussion of this bill. It is in accordance with the uniform policy of the Government on its organization to prohibit the crime of slavery in the Territories. From the result of the vote just taken, I suppose there are gentlemen here who wish to discuss it; and reserving to myself the right, if I shall think it necessary, to resume the floor before the debate shall close, I now give way to any one who may desire it." — "I move," said Mr. Cox of Ohio, "to add to the motion to recommit instructions, that neither this bill nor any similar bill shall be reported back to the House. I believe it

to be a suicidal bill, — a bill for the benefit of secession
and Jeff. Davis. The army and the people are against
all such aids to the enemy of the country. The conservative men of the House have the power, and ought
to 'squelch' out the whole negro business. They are
responsible for this continuous agitation. From the
very commencement of the session, we have had these
bills before us in one shape or another, postponed from
time to time, and delayed by dilatory motions and
adjournments. Now, I want to see the conservative
element of the House, if there is any such thing left
here, come up and vote this thing right down. I therefore hope the House will send this back to the committee; and, in sending it back to the committee, let us
give it such a death-blow as will destroy all similar
measures." Mr. Wickliffe (Dem.) of Kentucky suggested to Mr. Cox to recommit, with instructions "not
to report it back until the next session, during the cold
weather." Mr. Cox moved to recommit the bill, with
instructions "to report it back at the next session, on
the very last day." Mr. Diven (Rep.) of New York
" wanted Congress to exhaust the last power it has
over this institution, whenever and wherever it can be
done." Mr. Wickliffe quoted at length "the decision
of Justice Story on the rights of slavery, for the benefit of the country people." Mr. Diven was of opinion,
that "when we acquire land for the purpose of a navy-
yard, and exclude the States ceding that land from any
civil jurisdiction over it, we take it with the right to
control it as we please." Mr. Thomas (Opp.) of Massachusetts called the attention of Mr. Diven to the law
of 1795, by which the civil jurisdiction is given to the

States over cessions made to the General Government. Mr. Diven wanted to free the bill of all ambiguity, "and let the operation of the law extend nowhere except where slavery may exist by virtue of the Constitution and laws of the United States; and I repeat, as I have so often done already, but I wish to be emphatic, that, if such a spot exists upon the broad earth, let us exercise the power to abolish slavery." Mr. Cox modified his motion by moving to postpone the bill till the first day of the next session, instead of the last. Mr. Arnold of Illinois advocated the bill and all its provisions. Mr. Olin of New York and Mr. Kellogg (Rep.) of Illinois objected to portions of the bill concerning the prohibition of slavery in the dockyards, arsenals, and forts. Mr. Olin would "be as glad as any one to see the institution of slavery at least so crippled, that it will never henceforward be a disturbing cause in the administration of the Government. I, for one, will not consent to step an inch beyond the plain guaranties of the Constitution to accomplish even that purpose. Our only justification in the eyes of the civilized world for this warfare going on in our midst is, that we stand here, in obedience to law, in defence of the Constitution and law; and the moment we lay aside that shield of protection, and prosecute this war for other purposes, whatever result may be wrought out by the prosecution of the war, it would be a wicked war. It would be, on every principle of Christianity, an unjustifiable war. Our only defence before God, posterity, and the world, is that we fight in defence of the laws, not for their subversion. The wickedness of this Rebellion consists not in the fact that it is treason, always held to be a crime all the world over. Its chief enormity consists in the fact, that it is treason against such a Government as this, based on the common consent of the governed, with provision in the fundamental law to alter, change, or modify that Government in a peaceful way and by forms of law. If such a Government can be overthrown by force and violence, there is an end to all government except that of despotism and the sword. Hence it is, that rebellion against such a Government as this is of a deeper and more damnable dye than any other that has yet stained the annals of history."

"I denounce this bill," said Mr. Crisfield (Opp.) of Maryland, "as a palpable violation of the rights of States, and an unwarrantable interference with the rights of private property. I denounce it as a fraud upon the States which have made cessions of land to this Government, a violation of the Constitution, and a breach of the pledges which brought the dominant party into power. I denounce it as an usurpation and a tyrannical exercise of power, destructive of the peace of the country. Sir, I denounce it in this House, and to the American people. I denounce it before the civilized world. I declare that those who seek to accomplish the great wrong this bill perpetrates seek the ruin of all constitutional government on this continent, and are the foes of regulated liberty everywhere."—" What is this institution of slavery," asked Mr. Kelley (Rep.) of Pennsylvania, "that it should claim our special regard and care? How has it blessed us, and what measure of gratitude do we owe it? Sir, it is saturating every acre of Southern land with the best blood of the North. It is filling our villages and towns with widows and orphans. The names of the marshes and barren fields of the slave States are sanctified to tens of thousands of Northern mothers and wives as the places of the rude burial of the torn and mangled remains of their loved ones. Tens of thousands of those, who, approaching manhood, were warmed by generous hope and just ambition, and upon whom widowed mothers or aged fathers hoped to lean in their declining years, will move through our streets the mutilated victims of the system of slavery. The scars and wounds of these brave youth will bear honorable testimony to their devotion to constitutional law, and proclaim to the coming generation the character and the cause of the war in which they were received. The Rebellion is the result of slavery, and follows naturally enough a defeated attempt to overthrow by enigmatical legislation and judicial chicanery the well and long settled laws, principles, and habits of the land. I say, therefore, that in the interest of future peace, and in the interest of freedom and justice, we are called upon to pass this bill. The Constitution does not create it; the Constitution does not in terms recognize it: it only tolerates it; and this law does not propose to interfere with that toleration. It does not propose to abolish slavery anywhere. It only proposes to say to the slave-owner, 'Keep your slaves out of these places as *employés:* do not interfere with the system of free labor, and attempt to force the free mechanic into companionship with your slaves, or we will protect his dignity and interests by making freemen of your instruments.'" Mr. Fessenden (Rep.) of

Maine declared, that, "when this Union is restored, we want to see the rights of the North guaranteed to us as well as the rights of the South guaranteed to them." Mr. Sheffield (Dem.) of Rhode Island had no tenderness with reference to this matter of slavery. "I say here, now, and always, I hate that institution. I think that freedom is the common law of the Territories, and that nothing but positive law can carry slavery there; and we might as well here undertake to re-enact the Decalogue as to enact this law."

Mr. Stevens (Rep.) of Pennsylvania said, "This bill proposes that there shall be no slavery hereafter in the navy and dock yards of the United States, or in any other places where the United States have exclusive jurisdiction. Now, every argument which can be used against this bill would apply with equal force against the bill which we have lately passed, and which has received the sanction of the Executive, abolishing slavery in the District of Columbia. I cannot possibly see how any gentleman, who could not possibly see a constitutional objection in the one case, can see it in the other." Mr. Thomas of Massachusetts asked Mr. Stevens "to call to mind the fact, that the bill for emancipation in the District of Columbia provided a reasonable compensation, while this bill provides none whatever."— "I did not," replied Mr. Stevens, "suppose, indeed I have hardly heard, that anybody doubted the power of Congress to abolish slavery in the District of Columbia, without compensation." Mr. Thomas called the attention of Mr. Stevens "to the fifth of the amendments to the Constitution, which provides that private property shall not be taken for public use, without just compensation." Mr. Stevens did not know "that the gentleman held that doctrine. It is so rare a doctrine in the free States, that I did not know that any one from that quarter held it. I supposed, in reference to the question of slavery, that, wherever the Government had exclusive power, they had the right to do with it as the States did with it, — abolish it, without compensation. Does any man doubt that the States have that right?" — "Yes, sir," replied Mr. Thomas. "Then," said Mr. Stevens, "there is one doubter that will not be damned for that." Mr. Wickliffe asked, "Where has slavery been abolished without compensation?" Mr. Stevens answered, "In Pennsylvania, in New York; and he thought Massachusetts had never made any compensation. . . . I do not believe," he said, "there is any man from the free States, except the gentleman from the Boston district, who ever doubted that the legislative power of any locality, where they have the exclusive jurisdiction, have the right to abolish slavery, without compensation: and this is the first time I ever heard the opposite idea suggested by a man from a free State, and I trust in God it is the last; for it is no credit to a free State to entertain such an idea." — "To whom," asked Mr. Hooper (Rep.) of Massachusetts, "does the gentleman refer as 'from the Boston district'?" Mr. Stevens replied, "I carried him as near Boston as I could; for I did not like to say from the Quincy district, for that would seem such a humiliation!" Mr. Thomas said, "The gentleman need not trouble himself about that. The position is this: that if the law of this District, as it existed at the time of the passage of that bill, recognized a right in a person which was capable of valuation, then the provision of the Constitution to which I have referred applies; and you could not have taken that property, if it is property, or that right which is capable of computation, without furnishing that just compensation."

Mr. Bingham (Rep.) of Ohio said that the bill abolishing slavery in the District " showed conclusively upon its face that it was a matter of pure election upon the part of the United States what compensation they should give, or whether they should give any at all; and for this reason it was that Congress gave a gratuity, graduating the amount so that it should not exceed in the aggregate three hundred dollars each. No one knows better than the learned gentleman from Massachusetts, that such legislation as that, under the general provision of the Constitution which protects property, is absolutely inadmissible. The Congress of the United States cannot be the judge of the value under that clause of the Constitution at all, and it never was." Mr. Stevens declared " that the liberation of slaves in any locality where any legislature has exclusive jurisdiction is a political question, and it is a question of the organization of society, and in no sense of the word the taking of private property. It is a police and a political question, which the supreme legislature of any locality has a right to decide as it chooses; and to say that that is not constitutional, is to inaugurate a new, a strange, and an awful doctrine, especially to come from the district of the sage of Quincy." — " Will the gentleman allow me," said Mr. Thomas, "to say that the sage of Quincy to whom he alludes, and for whom his respect is not more profound than mine, affirmed, when he was at Ghent negotiating the treaty of peace, in his correspondence with the British commissioners, not only that there was property in slaves, but that the effort of the British officers and soldiers to seduce slaves from their masters was in violation of the laws of nations? And I will say further, that Mr. Adams never voted for the emancipation of slaves in the District of Columbia, though his very humble successor felt it his duty to do so." — "'The sage of Quincy,'" replied Mr. Stevens, "has declared more than twenty times, and half that number of times within my hearing, the entire competency of Congress to abolish slavery, wherever Congress has exclusive jurisdiction, without compensation." — "Within your hearing?" inquired Mr. Thomas. "I have often," replied Mr. Stevens, "heard him make the declaration; and I have heard Henry Clay make the same declaration." — "I can only," said Mr. Thomas, "say that Mr. Adams's entire public record is to the contrary."

Mr. Roscoe Conkling (Rep.) of New York remarked, that, "about a week ago, this House, with great unanimity so far as this side of the House is concerned, upon deliberation, raised a select committee, and to that committee committed this very subject, — this whole subject of confiscation and emancipation everywhere within the jurisdiction of the United States. I understand that committee is now ready to report. My suggestion is, that, that committee being nearly ready to give an account to the House of its stewardship, — quite ready, some gentleman says, — it would be well, perhaps courtesy toward them, to commit this bill to that committee, and let it re-appear, if it is to appear at all, when they shall have given us their work, and we have an opportunity to see whether this present purpose is within the scope of the two bills which I understand they mean to report." Mr. Fisher (Union) of Delaware took the floor, and the House adjourned to Monday, the 12th of May, when it resumed the consideration of the bill. Mr. Fisher said, "I am sure there is no man in this House who can possibly desire more than I do to see our country rid of the great curse of slavery. No man is more profoundly penetrated with the conviction, that it would have been far better for the harmony of our Union, as well as for the welfare and prosperity of the States, if slavery had never been known among us. It is hardly necessary at this day to discuss these points. The terrible and exhausting civil war in which we are now engaged will tell to future generations the sorrowful story of the effect of the institution upon the peace and harmony of our Union. Sad and satisfactory proof may also be found in the debates even of the Continental Congress, which declared the independence of the United Colonies, that the great and almost the only trouble the patriots of that immortal body had to meet was just such an one as we, their descendants, are engaged in discussing here from day to day. The ink with which the Declaration of Independence was written had scarcely dried, when, upon the question as to how the taxes necessary to maintain it should be levied, the subject of slavery came up to trouble and distract the national councils. It stood with defiant boldness upon the very threshold of the hall in which was debated and adopted the old Articles of Confederation in 1783; and again in 1787, when the framers of our present form of government, intended for a more perfect Union of the States, assembled at Annapolis, its ghastly form again stalked in to disturb and distract the deliberations of those good and great men; and, from that day to the present, this evil genius of our destiny has from time to time returned to embarrass and impede our onward progress in power, and to position among the nations of the earth, until now it has culminated in the production, in the freest and best Government the world ever knew, of the most gigantic, causeless, and wicked Rebellion of which history furnishes any record."

Mr. Lovejoy modified his substitute, so that it read, —

"To the end that freedom may be and remain for ever the fundamental law of the land in all places whatsoever, so far as it lies within the powers or depends upon the action of the Government of the United States to make it so, therefore —

"*Be it enacted by the Senate and House of Representatives of the United States of America in Congress assembled,* That slavery or involuntary servitude, in all cases whatsoever (other than in the punishment of crime, whereof the party shall have been duly convicted), shall henceforth cease, and be prohibited for ever, in all the Territories of the United States now existing, or hereafter to be formed or acquired in any way."

Mr. Cox moved to lay the bill on the table. Mr. Lovejoy demanded the yeas and nays; and they were ordered, — yeas 49, nays 81. The substitute was then agreed to. Mr. Lovejoy moved to amend by striking out the preamble, on which he called the previous question. Mr. Cox "would like to amend that by inserting the words, 'to carry out the Chicago Platform, and to dissolve the Union.'" The amendment striking out the preamble was agreed to; and the bill was ordered to be engrossed, and read a third time. Mr. Lovejoy moved the previous question on the passage of the bill; and it was ordered. Mr. Allen of Illinois demanded the yeas and nays on the passage of the bill. The question was taken; and it was decided in the affirmative, — yeas 85, nays 50, — as follows: —

YEAS. — Messrs. Aldrich, Alley, Arnold, Ashley, Babbitt, Baker, Baxter, Beaman, Bingham, Francis P. Blair, Samuel S. Blair, Blake, Buffinton, Campbell, Chamberlin, Clark, Colfax, Frederick A. Conkling, Roscoe Conkling, Cutler, Davis, Dawes, Delano, Diven, Duell, Dunn, Edgerton, Edwards, Eliot, Ely, Fenton, Fessenden, Franchot, Frank, Gooch, Granger, Hale, Harrison, Hickman, Hooper, Horton, Hutchins, Julian, Kelley, William Kellogg, Lansing, Loomis, Lovejoy, M'Knight, M'Pherson, Mitchell, Moorhead, Anson P. Morrill, Justin S. Morrill, Olin, Pike, Porter, Potter, Alexander H. Rice, John H. Rice, Riddle, Edward H. Rollins, Sargent, Sedgwick, Shanks, Sheffield, Shellabarger, Stevens, Stratton, Benjamin F. Thomas, Train, Trimble, Trowbridge, Van Horn, Verree, Wall, Wallace, Charles W. Walton, E. P. Walton, Washburne, Wheeler, Albert S. White, Wilson, Windom, and Worcester, — 85.

NAYS. — Messrs. Allen, Ancona, Joseph Baily, Biddle, Jacob B. Blair, George H. Browne, William G. Brown, Calvert, Casey, Clements, Cobb, Cox, Cravens, Crisfield, Crittenden, Dunlap, English, Grider, Haight, Hall, Harding, Holman, Johnson, Kerrigan, Knapp, Law, Lazear, Leary, Lehman, Mallory, Maynard, Menzies, Morris, Noell, Odell, Perry, John S. Phelps, Richardson, Robinson, Segar, John B. Steele, William G. Steele, Francis Thomas, Vibbard, Voorhees, Wadsworth, Ward, Webster, Wickliffe, and Woodruff, — 50.

So the bill was passed by the House of Representatives. Mr. Lovejoy moved to amend the title by striking it out, and inserting in lieu thereof as follows: "An act to secure freedom to all persons within the Territories of the United States;" and this amendment was agreed to.

In the Senate, on the 15th of May, Mr. Browning (Rep.) of Illinois, from the Committee on Territories, to whom was referred the bill to secure freedom to all persons within the Territories of the United States, reported it with an amendment.

On the ninth day of June, Mr. Wade (Rep.) of Ohio moved to take up the bill from the House prohibiting slavery in the Territories. Mr. M'Dougall (Dem.) of California demanded the yeas and nays, — yeas 20, nays 15. So the motion was agreed to; and the Senate, as in Committee of the Whole, proceeded to consider the bill to secure freedom to all persons within the Territories of the United States. The Committee on Territories reported the bill with an amendment, to strike out all after the enacting clause, and to insert the following in lieu thereof: "That, from and after the passage of this act, there shall be neither slavery nor involuntary servitude in any of the Territories of the United States now existing, or which may at any time hereafter be formed or acquired by the United States, otherwise than in punishment of crimes, whereof the party shall have been duly convicted." The amendment was agreed to, the bill was reported to the Senate as amended, and the amendment was concurred in. Mr. Carlile said, "I should like to make an inquiry of those who have this bill in charge, whether this bill will interfere with the right of the Indians in the Indian Territory to their slaves. I have been looking into the treaty stipulations with the Choctaws and Seminoles and other tribes that are settled now in what we call the Indian Territory, and those treaties expressly secure to the Indians the entire legislative control of that country. I suppose it is not the intention of the Senate to violate any treaty stipulations with the Indian tribes." Mr. Wade did " not intend to say that it would interfere with an unorganized Territory belonging to the United States. It does not interfere with them now; but whenever a Territory of the United States is organized there, then I have no doubt this bill, if it should become a law, would prohibit slavery in that Territory. In my judgment, it would not interfere with any of their rights there now." The amendment was ordered to be engrossed, and the bill to be read a third time. It was read a third time; and on the question, " Shall the bill pass?" Mr. Carlile called for the yeas and nays, and they were ordered; and, being taken, resulted — yeas 28, nays 10 — as follows: —

YEAS. — Messrs. Anthony, Browning, Chandler, Clark, Collamer, Cowan, Dixon, Fessenden, Foot, Foster, Grimes, Hale, Harlan, Harris, Howard, Howe, King, Lane of Indiana, Pomeroy, Rice, Simmons, Sumner, Ten Eyck, Trumbull, Wade, Wilkinson, Wilmot, and Wilson of Massachusetts, — 28.

NAYS. — Messrs. Carlile, Davis, Kennedy, Latham, M'Dougall, Nesmith, Powell, Saulsbury, Stark, and Wright, — 10.

So the bill was passed in the Senate.

In the House of Representatives, on the 17th of June, the bill was taken up, and Mr. Lovejoy moved the previous question on concurring in the amendment of the Senate. The previous question was seconded, and the yeas and nays ordered on motion of Mr. Phelps (Dem.) of Missouri. The question was taken on concurring in the Senate amendment, — yeas 72, nays 38. So the Senate amendment, reported by Mr. Browning from the Committee on Territories to the House bill originally introduced by Mr. Arnold, and reported with amendments by Mr. Lovejoy from the Committee on Territories, was concurred in. The bill passed, and was approved by the President on the 19th of June, 1862. This act prohibits for ever slavery in all the territory of the United States now existing, or that may hereafter be acquired; thus closing for ever the long contest betwen freedom and slavery for the vast Territories now in possession of the United States.

CHAPTER VI.

CERTAIN SLAVES TO BE MADE FREE.

MR. POMEROY'S BILL. — MR. TRUMBULL'S BILL. — MR. MORRILL'S JOINT RESOLUTION. — REPORT OF THE JUDICIARY COMMITTEE. — MR. SUMNER'S AMENDMENT. — MR. SHERMAN'S AMENDMENT. — REMARKS OF MR. WILLEY. — MR. HALE'S REPLY. — MR. HARRIS'S AMENDMENT. — REMARKS OF MR. HOWARD. — MR. COLLAMER'S AMENDMENT. — MOTION TO REFER TO A SELECT COMMITTEE. — REMARKS OF MR. WILMOT. — MR. WILSON'S AMENDMENT. — MR. COLLAMER. — MOTION TO REFER TO A SELECT COMMITTEE BY MR. CLARK. — REMARKS OF MR. HALE. — MR. WILSON'S REPLY. — SELECT COMMITTEE. — MR. CLARK'S REPORT. — MR. SUMNER'S AMENDMENT. — MR. DAVIS'S AMENDMENT. — MR. SAULSBURY'S AMENDMENT. — MR. WILSON'S AMENDMENT. — MR. CLARK'S AMENDMENT. — MR. SUMNER'S AMENDMENT. — PASSAGE OF THE BILL. — HOUSE. — MR. ELIOT'S RESOLUTION. — MR. ROSCOE CONKLING'S AMENDMENT. — MR. CAMPBELL'S RESOLUTION. — MR. STEVENS'S RESOLUTION. — MR. CONWAY'S RESOLUTION. — BILLS REFERRED TO JUDICIARY COMMITTEE. — MR. HICKMAN'S REPORT. — MR. BINGHAM'S SUBSTITUTE. — MR. PORTER'S AMENDMENT. — MR. ELIOT'S REPORT. — BILL DEFEATED. — RECONSIDERATION. — RECOMMITTED ON MOTION OF MR. PORTER. — REPORTED BACK BY MR. ELIOT. — MR. CLARK'S AMENDMENT. — SENATE AMENDMENT LOST IN THE HOUSE. — SENATE CONFERENCE COMMITTEE. — HOUSE CONFERENCE COMMITTEE. — REPORT OF CONFERENCE COMMITTEE. — MR. CLARK'S SENATE AMENDMENT ADOPTED.

THE Thirty-seventh Congress assembled on the 4th of July, 1861. In the Senate, on the 16th, Mr. Pomeroy (Rep.) of Kansas introduced a bill " to suppress the Slaveholders' Rebellion." This bill set forth that slavery had culminated in a formidable Rebellion; that it presented to the nation the great question, which it must settle now, and settle for ever, whether American slavery shall die, or American freedom shall live;

that by virtue of the Constitution, and as a great military necessity, it be enacted that there shall be no slavery in any of the States that claim to have seceded from the Government, and are in open and armed resistance to the laws and Constitution of the United States. The bill was read twice, and ordered to lie on the table and be printed.

On the 5th of December, 1861, Mr. Trumbull (Rep.) of Illinois introduced a bill, which provided that the slaves of persons who shall take up arms against the United States, or in any manner aid or abet this Rebellion, shall be discharged from service or labor, and become for ever thereafter free, any law to the contrary notwithstanding. In presenting his bill, Mr. Trumbull said, "The right to free the slaves of rebels would be equally clear with that to confiscate their property generally; for it is as property that they profess to hold them: but, as one of the most efficient means for attaining the end for which the armies of the Union have been called forth, the right to restore to them the God-given liberty of which they have been unjustly deprived is doubly clear. It only remains to inquire, whether, in making use of lawful means to crush this wicked Rebellion, it is policy to confiscate the property of rebels, and take from them the support of unrequited labor. Can there be a question on this point? Who does not know that treason has gained strength by the leniency with which it has been treated? We have dallied with it quite too long already. Instead of being looked upon as the worst of crimes, — as it really is, — it has come to be regarded as a trivial offence, to be atoned for by a promise to do so no more. The despoilers of loyal citizens, the conspirators against the peace of a nation, the plunderers of the public property, the assassins of liberty, when they have fallen into our hands, have been suffered to escape on taking an oath of allegiance which many have not scrupled to violate on the first opportunity.

On the 11th of December, Mr. Morrill (Rep.) of Maine introduced a joint resolution to confiscate the property of rebels, and satisfy the just claims of loyal persons. This joint resolution provided that any and all claim or right of a person, who shall conspire with others to overthrow, put down, or destroy by force, the Government of the United States, to the labor of any other person under the laws of any State or Territory, shall be declared to be annulled, any law or usage of any State or Territory or of the United States to the contrary notwithstanding. Mr. Morrill's resolution was read twice, referred to the Judiciary Committee, and ordered to be printed. Mr. Trumbull, Chairman of the Judiciary Committee, to which the bill he had introduced was referred, reported it back on the 15th of January, 1862. On the 25th of February, the Senate, on motion of Mr. Trumbull, proceeded to its consideration, as in Committee of the Whole. Mr. Pomeroy of Kansas inquired " if the senator from Illinois intended by the third section to commit the Government to the returning of fugitive slaves." — " Unquestionably not," replied Mr. Trumbull; "and I do not think the language of the bill warrants that construction. It says to the commissioners, to the United States judges, to everybody, 'You shall never make an order, under the Fugitive-slave Act, to surrender up a man claimed as a fugitive from service or labor, until it is first proved to your satisfaction that the claimant is and has been loyal to the Government.' That is the intention of the provision." Mr. Pomeroy was opposed to the section favoring the colonization of the emancipated slaves. If that provision was insisted on, he should feel called upon " to offer an amendment for the transportation, colonization, and settlement, in some country beyond the limits of the United States, of such slaveholders as have been engaged in the Rebellion." Mr. Willey (Union) of Virginia thought an immense number of negroes would be enfranchised before the close of the war, and thrown upon the community. He was " in favor of colonization; but where was the money to come from ? " — " I may be in error," said Mr. Ten Eyck (Rep.) of New Jersey; "but, for one, I should be opposed to the second section, which provides for the enlargement or liberation of persons held to service or labor, unless the third section, or a section similar to it, becomes a law also at the same time." — " I concur," said Mr. Sumner (Rep.) of Massachusetts, "with the senator from Kansas in all he has said in relation to the Fugitive-slave Bill. I have never called that a law, or even an act. I regard it simply as a bill; still, a bill having no authority under the Constitution of the United States. There is no fountain in that instrument out of which that enormity can be derived. That is my idea : I believe it is the idea of the senator from Kansas. I therefore propose an amendment which shall remove all such implication or possibility of recognition, on our part, of that bill ; while at the same time I believe it will carry out completely, adequately, in every respect, the idea of the senator from Illinois in the measure which is now under consideration. I propose to strike out all after the word 'before,' in the sixteenth line, down to the word 'that,' in the nineteenth line, being these words, 'Any order for the surrender of the person whose service is claimed, establish not only his title to such service, as now provided by law, but also,' and, instead thereof, insert, 'proceeding with the trial of his claim, satisfactorily prove :' so that the sentence will read, 'He shall in the first instance, and before proceeding with the trial of his claim, satisfactorily prove that he is, and has been during the existing Rebellion, loyal to the Government of the United States." Mr. Trumbull was entirely willing the Senate should adopt it; and it was agreed to.

Mr. M'Dougall (Dem.) of California, on the 3d and 4th of March, addressed the Senate in a speech of great length in opposition to the enactment of the pending bill or any kindred measure. He was followed by Mr. Cowan (Rep.) of Pennsylvania in opposition to the measure. "If it passes," he said, "I think it will be the great historic event of the times, — times which are as fruitful of events as any the world has ever witnessed. Upon the disposition we may make of it, perhaps the fate of the American Republic may depend; and no one surely can overrate the magnitude of any thing which may be attended with such consequences. . . . Pass this bill, and the same messenger who carries it to the South will come back to us with the news of their complete consolidation as one man. We shall then have done that which treason could not do: we ourselves shall then have dissolved the Union; we shall have rent its sacred charter, and extinguished the last vestige of affection for it in the slave States by our blind and passionate folly."

Mr. Morrill of Maine, on the 5th, addressed the Senate earnestly and eloquently in favor of the bill. "The great measure before us," said Mr. Morrill, "and none greater has ever been before the Senate, has been characterized in this debate in earnest, eloquent, indignant, and, I think I am authorized to say, satirical speech, as extraordinary, unconstitutional, oppressive, and inexpedient. . . . If slavery makes war on the nation for any purpose, I maintain the right of the Government, *under the Constitution,* to defend itself, and, in doing so, 'to liberate the slaves' of rebels; and that whenever and howsoever the question arises between 'the existence of the institution' and the Constitution, slavery and the Union, the former must go to the wall, *must perish*, if necessary to preserve the latter; and that this may be done in *the name and in the behalf* of 'American constitutional liberty.' . . . The *right* of slavery to 'exemption from interference within its locality' is lost in its audacious revolt and armed assault on the Government. Its cry 'to be let alone,' amid the cannonading of Sumter, is a shallow pretence to conceal a wicked purpose."

Mr. Browning (Rep.) of Illinois followed, on the 10th, in a lengthy and elaborate speech in opposition to the passage of the bill. He thought legislation of this character dangerous, and maintained that "the war powers of the Government were fully adequate to the needs of the occasion." Mr. Carlile (Dem.) of Virginia followed, on the 11th, in a long and discursive speech in opposition. He declared that "self-preservation would compel the States within which slavery now exists, if the slaves were emancipated, either to expel them from the State, or re-enslave them. If expelled, where would they go? The non-slaveholding States, many of them, exclude them by express constitutional provision; others would do so: for we are told by the advocates of emancipation, that the negro is not to be permitted, when liberated, to come into their States. What follows? — extermination or re-enslavement. Can it be possible that the Christian sentiment of the North, which, it is said, demands the abolition of slavery, desires the extermination of the negro race? The well-being, if not the existence, of the white race, would demand their re-enslavement; and it would be done."

On the 7th of April, on motion of Mr. Trumbull, the Senate resumed the consideration of the bill; and Mr. Trumbull defended it against the assaults made upon it, in an elaborate speech, which he closed by saying, "Such an opportunity to strike a blow for freedom seldom occurs as that now presented to the American Congress. As most of the owners of slaves are engaged in the Rebellion, and will probably continue so for some time, the effect would be, if this bill were speedily enacted into a law, that they would by their own act give freedom to most of the slaves in the country; and thus would be solved in a great measure, through the agency of this wicked Rebellion, the great question, What is to be done with African slavery? — a subject in view of which Jefferson in his day exclaimed, that 'he trembled when he remembered that God was just.' I appeal to senators, as philanthropists, as patriots, as lovers of the Union and of constitutional liberty, not to let pass this opportunity, which a wicked Rebellion presents, of making it the means of giving freedom to millions of the human race, and thereby destroying to a great extent the source and origin of the Rebellion, and the only thing which has ever seriously threatened the peace of the Union."

Mr. Henderson (Union) of Missouri, on the 8th, made a lengthy but eloquent speech against the bill. "It is useless," said Mr. Henderson, "to devise cunning schemes to effect the destruction of slavery. It is worse than useless to violate the least of constitutional safeguards to accomplish it. The shells that passed from rebel batteries to Fort Sumter, twelve months ago, wrote its doom in living letters upon the Southern skies. If they will destroy it themselves, let all the responsibility of evils to spring from this sudden change in the labor and social system of the country rest upon the authors of the war."

Mr. Sherman, on the 10th, moved an amendment in the nature of a substitute. It provided for confiscating the property and freeing the slaves of certain leading classes of rebels. Mr. Willey again spoke in earnest condemnation of the bill and all kindred measures. "What will be," he asked, "the necessary and inevitable result of this policy if it be carried into effect? It will be, that Virginia, by this increase of the free negro population under the operation of this bill, will be driven not only to re-enslave those who may be manumitted under the operation of the present bill, but also to re-enslave the sixty thousand free negroes already there. That will be the policy that my honorable friend from

Kentucky (Mr. Davis) will see take effect in his State; and so it must be in Maryland, and in every State where the operation of this bill will, to any extent, increase the number of the free negro population. . . . You are surrounding us by an impassable barrier of constitutional interdictions against the diffusion of this population; while at the same time you want to manumit our slaves, and throw them broadcast on our community. Sir, the evil will be unendurable; and the result will be the re-enslavement of the slaves thus manumitted, as well as those already free in our State." Mr. Hale replied to Mr. Willey's intimation, that the emancipated slaves would be re-enslaved, in a defiant and effective speech. "I have," he said, "as high regard for the chivalry, bravery, and power of Kentucky, Virginia, and Maryland, and any of these States, as any man has; but I tell them, and I tell the legislature of every State in the Union, that, when they undertake that, they undertake a job that they cannot do: they set themselves in opposition to the moral sentiment of the country and of the world. There is not a monarch to-day on the throne of any of the kingdoms of Europe situated there so firmly, that he dare to set himself in opposition to the moral sentiment of mankind. I take it, sir, that it is neither fanaticism nor superstition to say, that when the Creator of the earth made the earth, and the same Power made colored men, he intended that the colored men he had made should dwell upon the earth that he had made; and that when the broad earth was subjected to the servitude of man, and the fiat went forth that by the sweat of the brow of man should his living be obtained from the earth, it was a universal edict, irrespective of complexion, and that the earth is subject to the servitude of supporting the black man as well as the white. I laugh to scorn all attempts and all threats at re-enslaving this people. I tell you, it cannot be done." " If the honorable gentleman," replied Mr. Willey, "had been better cognizant of my antecedents, humble as they are, on this subject, he certainly would never have conceived it to be his duty to rise here, and rebuke me for having uttered sentiments that were contrary even to his peculiar theories. It is not becoming a man to speak of himself; but, rightfully or wrongfully, I have that consciousness which satisfies my own heart, having devoted nearly half of all I had in setting negroes free. Thousands of dollars out of my poor pittance and estate have been surrendered as attestations of my belief in the doctrine for which the honorable Senator from New Hampshire has thought it necessary to rise up here and rebuke me."

Mr. Harris (Rep.) of New York, on the 14th, submitted a substitute he intended to offer, and addressed the Senate in exposition of his views of the duty demanded by the needs of the country. Of the seventh section of his intended amendment he said, " The seventh section of the substitute, which is in substance the same as the second section of the original bill, relates exclusively to the slave property of rebels. Unlike the provisions of preceding sections, the forfeiture declared is applicable alike to all persons who shall be found engaged in the Rebellion. This is clearly right. All must agree, I think, that slavery is the chief, indeed the sole, producing cause of the Rebellion. It has long been, and, so long as it continues to exist, it will be, the great disturbing element in our political system. Northern politicians, seeking to obtain political power, have cowered before it, and ignominiously yielded to its imperious exactions. In this way, it has been able to hold the reins and control the policy of the Government for most of the time since our history as a nation began, — often, very often, to the serious prejudice of our best interests as a nation. It was because, and only because, this power had been wrested from its hands by an indignant and long-suffering people, that this Rebellion was inaugurated."

Mr. Powell (Dem.) of Kentucky, on the 16th, spoke in opposition to the bill, and in severe denunciation of the antislavery policy of the administration. Mr. Howard (Rep.) of Michigan addressed the Senate in support of the policy of confiscation, and the emancipation of the slaves of rebels, in a speech of great clearness and logical power. He arraigned the slaveholding leaders of the Rebellion for their "deceptive, delusive, and wicked words and deeds." He said, "Sir, even Satan, disguising his horrid form, and —

'Squat like a toad fast by the ear of Eve,'

practised no more deliberate deceit upon the sleeping mother of the race. They alarmed the fears of the timid and unthinking; they aroused the vigilance which ever presides over property; they stirred up the gall and bitterness of the bigot and fanatic, who deduce the right of slavery from the gospel itself; they inflamed the sectional pride of those who mistakenly claim personal and heroic qualities superior to those of Northern men; addressing the rich planter, they scoffed at labor as fit only for slaves; they spoke of the rapid increase of population in the free States as an alarming portent, and sorrowed deeply over the prospect of being compelled to submit to the will of a majority. Finding that, by their own incautious haste in forcing the Northern Democracy to adopt obnoxious measures, they had united the Northern people to resist the further triumphs of their ambition, and had thus lost the balance of power, they invoked eloquently the memories of their former domination, and wept over its decline. At every public gathering, the air was burdened with their impassioned appeals to the masses to rise, and resist the imaginary wrongs threatened by the North, or, as they derisively called the friends of the Government, Yankees. Every court-house, every church, every fairground, was vocal with traitorous eloquence; and God's innocent air was loaded with execrations against a Government, the work of their and our fathers, which never harmed a hair of their heads, and whose only fault — shown in the compromise measures of 1833 — was, that it had loved them, not wisely, but too well. To the aspirant after place and honor, they held out the prospect of a separate Congress, President, separate cabinet ministers, judges, and ambassadors and consuls abroad; to the lovers of adventure and booty, they pointed to the weak and distracted governments of Mexico and the Central-American States, to their mines, their cotton and sugar lands, and the ornaments of their churches. Their ambition grasped Cuba; and that island was soon to undergo a practical verification of the doctrines of the Ostend Conference, which had received the blind adhesion of the President whom their votes had elected in

1856. And at the foundation of this splendid chimera of revolution and dominion, the pivot on which the whole structure was to turn, was the idea, repelled by *all* the accredited teachers of morals and public law, that the black man was born to be a slave, and that it was to defy the decrees of God and Nature to allow him to be free."

Mr. Davis (Opp.) of Kentucky followed, on the 22d and 23d, in a very long and exhaustive speech in opposition. He averred that "neither the Declaration of Independence nor the Constitution was ever intended to embrace slaves, nor any of the negro race, nor any of the Indian race, nor foreigners. It has been attempted in this argument to apply the prohibitions of the Constitution to foreigners. It no more embraces foreigners than it does quadrupeds. It no more embraces Indians or slaves, except one or two prohibitions that are intended to preserve the humanity of our laws, than it does quadrupeds or wild beasts. The only partners to our political partnership were the white men. The negro was no party, and he cannot now constitutionally be any party, to it. He was outside of it at the time the Constitution was formed, and will be for ever, to this fundamental law of our Government."

Mr. Sherman (Rep.) of Ohio spoke in support of his substitute. On the 24th, Mr. Collamer (Rep.) of Vermont addressed the Senate in an elaborate and able and effective speech. "The slaves," he said, "are now in the possession and control of their masters, except so far as our army goes. If they try to get away, especially if they are at any considerable distance from our armies, their masters will not allow them to do it. Of course, the masters are not going to let them get away to join us to shoot them: they will stop them, perhaps kill them in the attempt. If we knew people were going from us to join the enemy and fight us, we should not let them go: neither do they. Now, by this bill, we say to these slaves, if they are ever to learn what we do at all (and, if they do not, it can have no effect), 'You need not run any risk about offending your master: perhaps your master will succeed in the Rebellion; and you will suffer pretty hard if you undertake to run away, and he catches you. You may remain quietly with your master, and not incur the hazard of his displeasure or punishment; but if, after all, your master does not succeed, you shall be free, whether you help us or not.' Is that good policy? That is the bill. It does not seem to me to be a very wise means to the end, if such an end is had in view, as I suppose."

Mr. Sherman withdrew his amendment, to enable the senator from Vermont to submit his substitute; and Mr. Trumbull then addressed the Senate upon the various substitutes proposed. On the 29th, Mr. Cowan moved "that all bills, substitutes, and amendments relating to the punishment of rebels, and the forfeiture and confiscation of their property, be referred to a select committee of seven, to examine and report upon the same."

Mr. Browning addressed the Senate at great length in earnest remonstrance against the policy embodied in these bills. On the 30th, Mr. Wilmot addressed the Senate in earnest advocacy of the bill. He said, "The second section, that providing for the emancipation of the slaves of rebels, I sustain in the whole length and breadth of its provisions. While I shall claim for the

Government full power over the subject of slavery, I would not at this time go beyond the provisions of this bill. I would to-day give freedom to the slaves of every traitor; and, after that, would confidently look for the early adoption of the policy recommended by the President, gradually to work out the great result of universal emancipation. . . . This great revolt against the integrity and sovereignty of the nation has no other foundation than slavery. Democratic government is a perpetual danger to slavery. The government of an oligarchy is demanded as security for its perpetuity and power. Here is the cause of the Rebellion, with its immense sacrifices of life and treasure. Amidst the sacrifices of this hour, this universal wreck of interests, shall the slaveholding traitor grasp securely his human chattel?"

Mr. Wright (Union) of Indiana followed in support of the policy of confiscation. The President stated that the pending question was the motion of Mr. Cowan to commit the bill and all the amendments to a special committee. Mr. Wilkinson, Mr. Wade, Mr. Hale, and Mr. Trumbull, earnestly opposed the motion; and Mr. Cowan made an equally earnest appeal for reference. Mr. Howard moved to submit an amendment to the pending resolution, in the following words: —

"With instructions to bring in a bill for the confiscation of all the property of the leading insurgents, and the emancipation of the slaves of all persons who have taken up arms against the United States during the present insurrection."

Mr. Davis moved to strike out the words, " and the emancipation of the slaves of all persons." The question being taken by yeas and nays, resulted — yeas 11, nays 29 : so the amendment to the amendment was rejected.

Mr. Howard then withdrew his amendment. The question was taken on Mr. Cowan's motion to refer all the bills and amendments to a special committee,—yeas 18, nays 22.

On the 1st of May, the Senate resumed the consideration of the bill; the pending question being Mr. Collamer's substitute. Mr. Wilson (Rep.) of Massachusetts moved to strike out the sixth section of the amendment proposed by Mr. Collamer, and to substitute in lieu of it, "That, in any State in which the inhabitants have by the President been heretofore declared in a state of insurrection, the President is required, for the speedy and more effectual suppression of said insurrection, within thirty days after the passage of this act, to appoint a day when all persons holden to service in any such State, whose service is by the law of said State due to one, who, after the passage of this act, shall levy war or participate in insurrection against the United States, or give aid to the same, shall be for ever free, any law to the contrary notwithstanding." In support of this amendment, Mr. Wilson said, "I am free to confess that the provision emancipating the slaves of rebels is, with me, the chief object of solicitude. I do not expect that we shall realize any large amount of property by any confiscation bill that we shall pass. After the conflict, when the din of battle has ceased, the humane and kindly and charitable feelings of the country and of the world will require us to deal gently with the masses of the people who are engaged in this Rebellion. It will be pleaded, that wives and children will suffer for the crimes of husbands and fathers; and such appeals will have more or less effect upon the future policy of the Government.

But, sir, take from rebel masters their bondmen, and from the hour you do so until the end of the world, to 'the last syllable of recorded time,' the judgment of the country and the judgment of the world will sanction the act.... Slavery is the great rebel, the giant criminal, the murderer striving with bloody hands to throttle our Government and destroy our country. Senators may talk round it, if they please; they may scold at its agents, and denounce its tools: I care little about its agents or its tools. I think not of Davis and his compeers in crime: I look at the thing itself, — to the great rebel with hands dripping with the blood of my murdered countrymen. I give the criminal no quarter. If I, with the light I have, could utter a word or give a vote to continue for one moment the life of the great rebel that is now striking at the vitals of my country, I should feel that I was a traitor to my native land, and deserved a traitor's doom.... While I would not take the lives of many, if any; while I would not take the property of more than the leaders, — I would take the bondmen from every rebel on the continent; and, in doing it, I should have the sanction of my own judgment, the sanction of the enlightened world, the sanction of the coming ages, and the blessing of Almighty God. Every day, while the world stands, the act will be approved and applauded by the human heart all over the globe.... When slavery is stricken down, they will come back again, and offer their hands, red though they be with the blood of our brethren; and we shall forgive the past, take them to our bosoms, and be again one people. But, senators, keep slavery; let it stand; shrink from duty; let men whose hands are stained with the blood of our countrymen, whose hearts are disloyal to our country, hold fast to the chains that bind three millions of men in bondage,—and we shall have an enemy to hate us, ready to seize on all fit opportunities to smite down all that we love, and again to raise their disloyal hands against the perpetuity of the Republic. Sir, I believe this to be as true as the holy evangelists of Almighty God; and nothing but the prejudices of association on the one side, or timidity on the other, can hold us back from doing the duty we owe to our country in this crisis." Mr. Morrill made an effective reply to Mr. Cowan and Mr. Collamer, and an earnest appeal for the bill. Mr. Howe (Rep.) of Wisconsin expressed his doubts. Mr. Davis again addressed the Senate. He asked "that slaves should have the same fate with other property." He did "not object to confiscating slaves with other property, upon condition that the proceeds should go into the treasury." Mr. Clark (Rep.) of New Hampshire would not sell the confiscated slaves. "You take," he said, "a negro from a rebel, as the senator proposes. He belongs to the United States. The senator contends that you must sell him. You sell him. Who buys him? Where do you sell him? Where do you find your market? Not in a free State, but in a slave State. You sell him to one of these slaveholders; and the rebels come and seize him, and have him engaged on fortifications in a week."

On the 2d of May, Mr. Doolittle (Rep.) of Wisconsin addressed the Senate. Mr. Wade made an emphatic speech in favor of action. He declared, that "if every man in this Senate, if every man in this Congress, stood forth as an advocate for perpetual and eternal slavery, it would only be the poor instrumentalities of man fighting against God. God and Nature have determined the question, and we shall not affect it much either way. But I throw out these hints to those gentlemen who seem to believe that the world will not go round when slavery is abolished. As the Almighty sometimes overrules the wickedness of man to perfect a glorious end, so the hand of God was never more obvious than in this Rebellion. Slavery might have staggered along against the improvement of the age, against the common consent of mankind, a scoff and a byword on the tongue of all civilized nations, for a great many years; but this Rebellion has sealed its fate, and antedated the time when it becomes impossible. You cannot escape from this war, without the emancipation of your negroes. It will not be because I am going to preach it; it will not be because I am going to move any thing in that direction: but it is because I see the hand of God taking hold of your own delinquency to overrule for good what your rulers meant for evil. Proslavery men seem to suppose that the Ruler of the universe is a proslavery Being; but, if I have not mistaken him greatly, he is at least a gradual emancipationist." Mr. Collamer followed in reply to Mr. Wade, and in support of his amendment. He declared that "our legislation should be consecutive and in certain progress, rising from step to step, as the necessities of the occasion may require;" and he "had attempted to frame his bill on that principle." The sixth section provided, when the insurrection has existed six months, "then, in that case, the President is authorized, if in his opinion it is necessary to the successful suppression of said insurrection, by proclamation to fix and appoint a day when all persons holden to service or labor in any such State, or part thereof, as he shall declare, whose service or labor is by the law or custom of said State due to any person or persons, who, after the day so fixed by said proclamation, shall levy war or participate in insurrection, shall be free."—"It is proposed," he said, "by the senator from Massachusetts, that the section shall be entirely changed. By this amendment, the proclamation is made a matter of no consequence at all. The President is left no discretion about it. It is a simple declaration, that, in thirty days, the President shall issue a proclamation, fixing a day when the slaves shall be free, — the slaves of any person who shall be engaged in rebellion after the passage of the act, not after the time fixed by proclamation. . . . The honorable senator from Massachusetts, and the honorable senator from Ohio, seem never to have understood the explanation which I gave before, and I do not know that they ever will. Perhaps it is because they do not want to understand it. The honorable senator from Massachusetts especially, in offering his amendment and in speaking upon it yesterday, seemed to be set upon the idea, — he entertains it strongly, and he expresses it strongly, as belongs to him, — that the existence of slavery and the existence of this country under the General Government are incompatible. I shall not misrepresent him: I may have misunderstood him; but, if I did understand him, that is his belief. He thinks slavery is the origin of all the difficulty, and that the trouble will continue as long as it exists; and he comes in with this amendment, to effect — what? That purpose, of course." Mr. Saulsbury (Dem.) of Delaware predicted "that in 1870, let this war terminate as it may, whether you conquer the seceded States or not, if local State governments are preserved in this country, there will then be more slaves in the United States than there were in 1860. . . . I presume that local State governments will be preserved. If they are, if the people have a right to make their own laws and to govern themselves, — and I presume that even my friend from Massachusetts will not object to that, — they will not only re-enslave every person that you attempt to set free, but they will re-enslave the whole race. I do not mean to suggest a thing that I will not favor: I take all the responsibility of the utterance in my own person. I say to you, sir, and I say to the country, that if you send five thousand slaves into the State of Delaware, — we have got about two thousand slaves now, and we have about twenty thousand free negroes, — if you send five thousand more of that class of people among us, contrary to our law, contrary to our will, I avow upon the floor of the American Senate, that I will go before my people for enslaving the whole race, because I say that this country is the white man's country. God, nature, every thing, has made a distinction between the white man and the negro; and by your legislation you cannot bring up a filthy negro to the elevation of the white man, if you try to put him upon that platform."

The Senate, on the 5th of May, resumed the consideration of the bill; and Mr. Howe of Wisconsin spoke in opposition to it, and in reply to several senators. Mr. Foster (Rep.) of Connecticut followed in a review of the bill and amendments, and in support of Mr. Collamer's substitute.

On the 6th, the Senate having resumed the consideration of the bill, Mr. Wilson withdrew his amendment to the sixth section of Mr. Collamer's amendment, and moved an amendment in eight sections as a substitute for Mr. Collamer's substitute for the original bill. Mr. Wilson, in explanation of the sixth section relating to slavery, said, that "the amendment of the senator from Vermont provides for discharging the slaves of persons under certain conditions; that is, that the President may do it if he deems it necessary for the suppression of the Rebellion. He puts it in the discretion of the President. My amendment makes it imperative upon the President to issue his proclamation, immediately after the passage of the act, to fix a day, not more than thirty days after the act is passed, when the slaves of all persons who engage in insurrection or rebellion after they have had the warning of thirty days, after the time is fixed, shall be made free." Mr. Clark said, "The amendment proposed by the senator from Massachusetts, it strikes me, is an important one. I think it goes a good way towards harmonizing some of the differences in the minds of senators. If there could be time for considering it further, or for maturing it, or if it were sent to a committee to perfect it, it seems to me the Senate might readily come to some conclusion that would be satisfactory. I will move that the whole subject, this amendment and all the other bills, be committed to a select committee of five, for the purpose of being perfected." Mr. Sumner (Rep.) of Massachusetts suggested that the committee should consist of seven members; and Mr. Clark accepted that suggestion. Mr. Hale said, "There is a difficulty in my mind in regard to the amendment of the senator from Massachusetts. I think I have been as anxious and as earnest as anybody to advance the cause of free principles, so far as might be done consistently with the rights we owe under the Constitution; but it seems to me the machinery of the sixth section of the amendment of the senator from Massachusetts is objectionable to the exception that it is not in accordance with the Constitution." Mr. Wilson said, in response to Mr. Hale, "Slavery has made this Rebellion, and alone is responsible for it; and yet such has been the overshadowing power of slavery, so omnipotent has it been in these halls and over this Government, that when we, who are the children of democratic institutions, who have in our blood, in our being, in our very souls, love of liberty, and hatred of oppression, are called upon to act; when our brethren have been foully murdered, and wives and children and fathers are bowed in agony of soul all over the country; when the existence of this nation is threatened by this system of slavery, — when we, under all these circumstances, are called upon to deal with it, such is its lingering power over even us, that we can take rebel lives, take rebel property, take any thing and every thing, but are reluctant to touch slavery, the cause of all. Sir, if the Congress of the United States shall fail to free the slaves of rebel masters, the men who are endeavoring to destroy the national life, I believe Congress will fail to do the duties of the hour, — the duties that the nation and God require at their hands. I feel deeply upon this question. The conviction is upon me, that this is the path of duty to my country, and that the future peace of the nation requires that this slave interest shall be broken down; and now is the opportunity, — an opportunity that only comes to nations once in ages. It comes to us now. Let us hail and improve it." Mr. Hale said, in reply, "I am willing to go as far as anybody, within the limits of the Constitution, to cripple slavery; and I think the Government ought to make use of that as a physical agency in suppressing the Rebellion, when it is brought in contact against it. All that I suggested to the senator was, that I did not think the machinery he had prescribed in this sixth section was precisely the mode and manner of doing the thing; because it does not look like a war measure, and it does not look like availing ourselves of the physical assistance of that body of men, but it is simply in the form of a judicial trial for crime, and pronounces, as a punishment for crime, the liberation of the slaves. Sir, this new Republican party came into power upon the destruction of two parties that had been false on this subject; and now, whatever party may succeed this Republican party, — and God only knows what it will be, — I hope that they may not write on our tombstones that we split on the rock on which our predecessors did; and that is in want of fidelity to our declared principles. If there is one principle that we have declared often, early, and long, it is fidelity to the Constitution, — to its requirements and its restrictions. The mourners go about the streets in all the places that used to be the high places of power of those two old parties, mourning over their derelictions; and I trust that will not be left to us. No, sir: let us, under the flag, — the old flag, — under the Constitution, — the old

Constitution, — carry on the warfare in which we are engaged; and, if we fail, we shall not fail because the Constitution does not give us power enough, but because we are recreant, and do not use the power that it does give us."

Mr. Harris would vote for the proposition of Mr. Clark to commit all the bills and amendments to a special committee. "The recommittal," said Mr. Wade, " of this bill, after it has been for four months under our consideration, and at a period which I hope is towards the end of this session, will be a proclamation to the people that will fill them with more despondency for your Government than the loss of half a dozen battles; and it will be viewed with as much regret by all the loyal people in the seceded States as by those in the Northern States." — " The senator from Ohio knows well," said Mr. Sumner, " that I always differ from him with regret; he knows also that I differ from him very rarely; but I do differ from him to-day. I shall not follow him in what he has said on the constitutional question; nor shall I follow the senator from New Hampshire in what he has said on that question. The precise point on which we are to vote, as I understand it, has been stated by the senator from New York. It is, Shall the pending bill and all the associate propositions and amendments be referred to a select committee, with instructions to report forthwith? Sir, it seems to me, in the present stage of this discussion, the time has arrived for such a motion." Mr. Trumbull was opposed to recommitting the bill to a special committee; but " senators favorable to the bill insist upon it: I can only acquiesce; and that I desire to do gracefully." Explanatory speeches were then made by Messrs. Ten Eyck, Foster, Wade, Collamer, Fessenden, and Cowan. Mr. Wilson moved to amend Mr. Clark's motion, so that the committee should consist of nine members; and Mr. Clark accepted the amendment. Mr. Foster called for the yeas and nays, and they were ordered; and, being taken, resulted — yeas 24, nays 14. The President appointed as the committee, — Mr. Clark, chairman; Mr. Collamer, Mr. Trumbull, Mr. Cowan, Mr. Wilson of Massachusetts, Mr. Harris, Mr. Sherman, Mr. Henderson, and Mr. Willey. Mr. Trumbull, at his own request, was excused; and Mr. Harlan was appointed in his place.

Mr. Clark, Chairman of the Select Committee, reported " a bill to suppress insurrection, and punish treason and rebellion; " and asked to be discharged from the further consideration of the several bills referred to the committee. On the 16th, on motion of Mr. Clark, the Senate, by a vote of 23 to 19, took it up for consideration. The bill provided, that at any time, after the passage of the act, the President might issue his proclamation, proclaiming that the slaves of persons found, thirty days after the issuing of the proclamation, in arms against the Government, will be free, any law or custom to the contrary; that no slave escaping from his master shall be given up, unless the claimant proves he has not given aid or comfort to the Rebellion; and that the President shall be authorized to employ persons of African descent for the suppression of the Rebellion. Mr. Davis moved to amend the bill by striking out the words, " and all his slaves, if any shall be declared and made free." —

"Then," remarked Mr. Clark, "as I understand it, the objection is, not that we take the negro from the master by way of punishment, but that we do not give him to somebody else, or put him into the public treasury."— "Yes, sir," replied Mr. Davis, "that is the objection; that you do not sell the negro, — do not appropriate the negro as you would other property." The question was taken on Mr. Davis's motion, — yeas 7, nays 31. Mr. Sumner moved to amend the bill by striking out all after the enacting clause of the original bill, and inserting an amendment in the form of a new bill. He then addressed the Senate in an elaborate, exhaustive, and eloquent speech. "There is a saying," said Mr. Sumner, "often repeated by statesmen, and often recorded by publicists, which embodies the direct object of the war which we are now unhappily compelled to wage, —an object sometimes avowed in European wars, and more than once made a watchword in our own country, —'indemnity for the past, and security for the future.' Such should be our comprehensive aim; nor more, nor less. Without indemnity for the past, this war will have been waged at our cost. Without security for the future, this war will have been waged in vain. Treasure and blood will have been lavished for nothing. But indemnity and security are both means to an end; and that end is the national unity under the Constitution of the United States. It is not enough if we preserve the Constitution at the expense of the national unity; nor is it enough if we enforce the national unity at the expense of the Constitution. Both must be maintained. Both will be maintained, if we do not fail to take counsel of that prudent courage which is never so much needed as at a moment like the present. In declaring the slaves free, you will at once do more than in any other way, whether to conquer, to pacify, to punish, or to bless: you will take from the Rebellion its mainspring of activity and strength; you will stop its chief source of provisions and supplies; you will remove a motive and temptation to prolonged resistance; and you will destroy for ever that disturbing influence, which, so long as it is allowed to exist, will keep this land a volcano, ever ready to break forth anew. But, while accomplishing this work, you will at the same time do an act of wise economy, giving new value to all the lands of slavery, and opening untold springs of wealth; and you will also do an act of justice, destined to raise our national name more than any triumph of war or any skill in peace. God, in his beneficence, offers to nations, as to individuals, opportunity, *opportunity*, OPPORTUNITY, which, of all things, is most to be desired. Never before in history has he offered such as is now ours. Do not fail to seize it. The blow with which we smite an accursed rebellion will at the same time enrich and bless; nor is there any prosperity or happiness which it will not scatter abundantly throughout the land. And such an act will be an epoch marking the change from barbarism to civilization. By the old rights of war, still prevalent in Africa, freemen were made slaves; but by the rights of war, which I ask you to declare, slaves will be made freemen."

Mr. Davis said, "I have an amendment to offer, to come in at the close of the bill,—that no slave shall be emancipated under this act until such slave shall be taken into the possession of some agent of the United

States, and be *in transitu*, to be colonized without the United States of America," — yeas 6, nays 30. Mr. Saulsbury moved to strike out the ninth section of the bill. Mr. Trumbull would vote with the senator from Delaware to strike out the section. He hoped the friends of a really efficient measure would vote to strike it out. "I would," he said, "free the slaves of all who shall continue in arms after the passage of the act. That would be my proposition; and I cannot conceive how it is, when these men are with arms in their hands, as the senator from New Hampshire said, shooting our brothers and our sons, that we can insist upon holding their negroes in their possession to enable them to shoot our sons and our brothers." Mr. Wilson said, "The motion that has been made, and what has been said upon it, impose upon me the necessity of making now a motion that I intended to make at some time; and that is, to strike out in the ninth section the words 'at any time,' in the first line, and insert 'immediately;' and to strike out the word 'whenever,' in the second line; and, in the third and fourth lines, to strike out 'shall deem it necessary for the suppression of this Rebellion, he:' so that the section, if amended as I propose, will read, 'That, immediately after the passage of this act, the President of the United States shall issue his proclamation, commanding all persons immediately to lay down their arms,' making it imperative. I think, that, since this bill was reported, there are reasons why I shall vote that way." Mr. Clark said, "The Senate, perhaps, will pardon me for saying, that, in the committee, the original proposition stood as the senator from Massachusetts proposes now to have it: but we found that the measure now reported was the measure upon which we could agree, and that we could not agree upon any other measure; and therefore it was reported as it stands here. I shall vote for the proposition as it stands in the bill, for that reason." — "I shall," said Mr. Cowan, "oppose the amendment of the senator from Massachusetts, and I believe that I shall vote to strike out the section: and I shall do so for a very simple reason; and that is, that it is utterly valueless in the bill." He thought "the President and his generals, under the war power, clothed with ample authority." Mr. Sumner was "very glad to hear the senator make that declaration, that Gen. Hunter, in his opinion, has the power." "If," said Mr. Cowan, "the senator from Massachusetts wants an exceedingly fine point to stand upon, I will allow him the benefit of it. I hope he understands me; and I hope, too, that he is honorable and manly enough to understand what I say in its true sense. I do not mean to say that Gen. Hunter has the power as against the will of the President, his superior; but I mean to say that the President, the commander-in-chief of the army, and the generals of the army, acting in obedience to that superior authority, have the power."

Mr. Fessenden (Rep.) of Maine supported the bill reported by the Select Committee. Mr. Wade said, "I do not know that we shall get any thing; but, if we only get this bill, we shall get next to nothing." Mr. Willey opposed the emancipation of the slaves of rebels by proclamations. On the 20th, the Senate resumed the consideration of the bill; and Mr. Davis addressed the Senate in a very lengthy speech, consuming the day, in opposition to the measure.

In the House of Representatives, on the 2d of December, 1861, Mr. Eliot (Rep.) of Massachusetts introduced, on leave, a joint resolution, setting forth, that while we disclaim all power under the Constitution to interfere by ordinary legislation with the institutions of the States, yet the war now existing must be conducted according to the usages and rights of military service: "That therefore we do hereby declare the President, as the commander-in-chief of our army, and the officers in command under him, have the right to emancipate all persons held as slaves in any military district in a state of insurrection against the National Government; and that we respectfully advise that such order of emancipation be issued, whenever the same will avail to weaken the power of the rebels in arms, or to strengthen the military power of the loyal forces." Mr. Dunn (Rep.) of Indiana moved to lay the resolution on the table. Mr. Vallandigham (Dem.) of Ohio demanded the yeas and nays; and they were ordered, — yeas 56, nays 70. Mr. Roscoe Conkling (Rep.) of New York moved to amend the resolution so as to confine it to slaves held by disloyal persons. Mr. Stevens (Rep.) of Pennsylvania moved the postponement of the resolution to the 10th; and his motion was agreed to. Mr. Campbell (Rep.) of Pennsylvania introduced a resolution declaring that Congress should confiscate the property, slaves included, of all rebels; and, on his motion, it was postponed to the 10th. Mr. Stevens of Pennsylvania offered a resolution setting forth that slavery has caused the Rebellion; that there can be no solid and permanent peace and union so long as it exists; that slaves are used as an essential means of supporting the war; that, by the law of nations, it is right to liberate the slaves of an enemy to weaken his power; and that the President be requested to declare free, and to direct all our generals to order freedom to, all slaves who shall leave their masters, or who shall aid in quelling the Rebellion. The resolution of Mr. Stevens was postponed to the 10th, — the day fixed for the consideration of the resolutions introduced by Mr. Eliot and Mr. Campbell.

On the 3d, Mr. Gurley (Rep.) of Ohio gave notice of his intention to introduce a bill to confiscate the property and make free the slaves of persons engaged in the Rebellion. Mr. Conway (Rep.) of Kansas, on the 4th, introduced a resolution touching the treatment of slaves in the seceded States; and it was postponed to the 10th for consideration. Mr. Bingham (Rep.) of Ohio introduced a bill to confiscate the property and free the slaves of rebels; and, on his motion, it was referred to the Judiciary Committee, of which he was a member. On the 12th of December, the House proceeded to the consideration of the resolution introduced by Mr. Eliot the first day of the session. Mr. Eliot addressed the House in an earnest speech in favor of expressing, at the earliest moment, the judgment of the House and the people. "It is no time," he said, "for set speech. The times themselves are not set. Speech is demanded, but such as shall crystallize into acts and deeds. Thoughts of men go beyond the form of words into the realities of things." Mr. Eliot deplored the modification of Frémont's proclamation. The slaves stood "with arms stretched out to us, yearning to help us. The shackles have fallen from their limbs; and, as they work for the

Government, it does not need that I should say to you, that thenceforth and for evermore they become free men." Mr. Steele (Dem.) of New York denied the proposition that slavery was the cause of this war. "I declare," he said, "that the unnecessary agitation of the slavery question was the cause of the war." Mr. Conway, (Rep.) of Kansas followed Mr. Steele in a speech of rare eloquence and power. He declared that "the inexorable and eternal condition of the life of slavery is, that it must not only hold its own, but it must get more. Such is the unchangeable law, developed from the conflict of slavery with the order of justice; and no one is competent to render a judgment in the case who does not recognize it. Sir, we cannot afford to despise the opinion of the civilized world in this matter. Our present policy narrows our cause down to an ignoble struggle for mere physical supremacy; and for this the world can have no genuine respect. Our claim of authority, based on a trivial technicality about the proper distinction between a Federal Government and a mere confederacy, amounts to nothing. The human mind has outgrown that superstitious reverence for government of any kind which makes rebellion a crime *per se;* and right of secession, or no right of secession, what the world demands to know in the case is, upon which side does the morality of the question lie? As a bloody and brutal encounter between slaveholders for dominion, it is justly offensive to the enlightened and Christian sentiment of the age. Yet the fate of nations, no less than that of individuals, is moulded by the actions, and these by the opinions, of mankind. So that public opinion is the real sovereign, after all; and no policy can be permanently successful which defies or disregards it. The human mind, wherever found, however limited in development or rude in culture, is essentially logical; the heart, however hardened by selfishness or sin, has a chord to be touched in sympathy with suffering; and the conscience has its 'still small voice,' which never dies, to whisper to both heart and understanding of eternal justice. Therefore, in an age of free thought and free expression, the brain and heart and conscience of mankind are the lords who rule the rulers of the world; and no mean attribute of statesmanship is quickness to discern and promptness to interpret and improve the admonitions of this august trinity."

Mr. Harding (Opp.) of Kentucky, on the 17th, spoke earnestly against the resolution, and the policy of emancipating the slaves of rebels. He emphatically asserted that "a war upon the institution of slavery would be not only unconstitutional and revolutionary, not only a criminal violation of the plighted faith of Congress and of the Administration, but utterly at war with every principle of sound policy. Whoever lives to see that fearful and mad policy inaugurated, will see the sun of American liberty go down in clouds and darkness, to rise no more. The last hope of a restoration of the Union — the last hope of free government upon this continent — will then sink, and utterly perish. If the war, righteously begun for the preservation of the Constitution and the Union, should be changed to an anti-slavery war, then Kentucky will unitedly make war upon that war; and, if an army from the North should move toward Kentucky to visit upon her the horrors of a war for emancipation, then Kentucky will meet that army at the threshold, dispute every inch of ground, burn every blade of grass, and resist to the last extremity." Mr. Kellogg (Rep.) of Illinois moved to refer the resolution of Mr. Eliot and all other kindred propositions to the Judiciary Committee, — yeas 77, nays 57.

Mr. Hickman (Rep.) of Pennsylvania, Chairman of the Committee on the Judiciary, on the 20th of March reported back the resolutions and bills referred to the committee, with a recommendation that they do not pass. Mr. Bingham submitted a minority report, as a substitute for the bill he had introduced early in the session. This substitute declared free, and for ever released from servitude, the slaves of persons giving aid to the Rebellion. Mr. Porter (Rep.) of Indiana moved to amend the substitute by striking it out, and inserting the bill proposed by Mr. Sherman of Ohio in the Senate. Mr. Porter said that "the gentleman from Ohio (Mr. Bingham), out of his honest and implacable hatred of slavery, desires, through the provisions of his amendment, to give it a stunning blow. While my amendment is aimed only at weakening the Rebellion, it will go, perhaps, very far towards the end which the gentleman desires to see accomplished. The slaveholders in the rebel service are chiefly among the officers. Few privates own slaves." Mr. Porter then moved to recommit the bill, with instructions to report the bill he had offered as a substitute. Mr. Walton (Rep.) of Vermont moved to amend the instructions, so that the committee shall be instructed to report back Mr. Collamer's bill, — yeas 33, nays 69. On Mr. Porter's motion, the yeas were 25; the nays, 73.

On the 23d of April, Mr. Sheffield of Rhode Island moved to lay Mr. Bingham's amendment on the table, — yeas 54, nays 49. Mr. Olin (Rep.) of New York moved to refer the bills and resolutions reported back by the Committee on the Judiciary to a special committee of seven. Mr. Colfax (Rep.) of Indiana " pleaded only for action." He would cheerfully support Mr. Trumbull's bill, or the bill of Mr. Sherman. "I can vote," he declared, "for nearly any one of them, variant as their provisions are." Mr. Dunn of Indiana would "adopt a moderate but steadfast policy." Mr. Bingham eloquently appealed for such legislation as should punish treason, and give security and repose to the country. "I beg gentlemen to consider that whoever lays violent hands upon the fabric of just civil government, for the purpose of its overthrow, lays violent hands upon the very ark of the covenant of the living God, and forfeits and should be deprived at once of property and life. Why, sir, there is no interest visible to the eye of man this side of the grave more important to all classes, old and young, to the innocent and guilty alike, than a wise and just government. That is precisely the instrumentality through which it comes to be that men live apart, and separate in families. That is the precise instrumentality through which it comes to be that mothers and daughters are respected and protected in the land, and are not owned and sold as slaves. That is the precise instrumentality through which it comes to be that little children are secure and protected by the hearthstone. The gentleman knows that never, since the morning stars sang together, have any people upon this planet come up out of the darkness of savage life to the beautiful and brilliant light of civilization, save under the shelter, care, and protection of civil government; and yet, when these armed traitors strike at this most beneficent and wisest of all governments ever given to the children of men, and we propose to disarm them by taking from them the means by which and through which they would accomplish their destructive purposes, the gentleman rises, and talks about the inhumanity of such legislation."

Mr. Duell (Rep.) of New York said, "In view of these things, it becomes a question of no small moment, What ought the Government to do with slavery now? What policy, if any, should the loyal men of the country adopt respecting the future treatment of this cancer upon the body politic? The reply which ought, in my judgment, to be made to these questions, is this: '*Since slavery made the war, let slavery feel the war.*'"

Mr. Patton (Rep.) of Pennsylvania urged action; and Mr. Hickman opposed the bills, "because the President had all power now." Mr. Crittenden thought these bills tended to create the idea, "that our whole aim is to make the war an abolition measure." Mr. Lovejoy (Rep.) of Illinois resumed the discussion on the 24th of April. "I am for the Union entire," declared Mr. Lovejoy; "but I am not for the return of the domination and tyranny of slavery, which has not allowed me for the last quarter of a century to tread the soil of more than one-half of the Territories of these United States. . . . I insist, therefore, that slavery must perish, in order that American citizens may have the enjoyment of all their rights. I desire the seceded States to come back, but to come in such manner that I can enjoy the privileges of an American citizen within their limits. I have been excluded long enough. In other words, I want them to come back free, and not slave States. Long enough have American citizens been subjected to the cord and knife, and last, and worst of all, the terrible indignity of the scourge, for no other cause than holding and uttering principles in favor of freedom, impartial and universal. . . . The gentleman from Kentucky says he has a niche for Abraham Lincoln. Where is it? He pointed upward. But, sir, should the President follow the counsels of that gentleman, and become the defender and perpetuator of human slavery, he should point downward to some dungeon in the temple of Moloch, who feeds on human blood, and is surrounded with fires, where are forged manacles and chains for human limbs; in the crypts and recesses of whose temple, woman is scourged and man tortured, and outside the walls are lying dogs gorged with human flesh, as Byron describes them stretched around Stamboul. That is a suitable place for the statue of one who would defend and perpetuate human slavery. . . . I, too, have a niche for Abraham Lincoln; but it is in Freedom's holy fane, and not in the blood-besmeared temple of human bondage; not surrounded by slaves, fetters, and chains, but with the symbols of freedom; not dark with bondage, but radiant with the light of liberty. In that niche he shall stand proudly, nobly, gloriously, with shattered fetters and broken chains and slave-whips beneath his feet. If Abraham Lincoln pursues the path evidently pointed out for him in the providence of God, as I believe he will, then he will occupy the proud position I have indicated. That is a fame worth living for;

ay, more, that is a fame worth dying for, though that death lead through the blood of Gethsemane and the agony of the accursed tree. That is a fame which has glory and honor and immortality and eternal life. Let Abraham Lincoln make himself, as I trust he will, the emancipator, the liberator, as he has the opportunity of doing, and his name shall not only be enrolled in this earthly temple, but it will be traced on the living stones of that temple which rears itself amid the thrones and hierarchies of heaven, whose top stone is to be brought in with shouting of ' Grace, grace unto it!'"

Mr. Roscoe Conkling demanded the previous question on Mr. Olin's resolution to refer the resolutions and bills to a select committee, — yeas 71, nays 47. The question recurring on the adoption of the resolution, Mr. Vallandigham demanded the yeas and nays, and they were ordered, — yeas 90, nays 31; and the Speaker announced, on the 28th, the following as the committee, — Abraham B. Olin of New York, Thomas D. Eliot of Massachusetts, John W. Noell of Missouri, John Hutchins of Ohio, Robert Mallory of Kentucky, Fernando C. Beaman of Michigan, and George T. Cobb of New Jersey. Mr. Olin, at his own request, was excused from serving on the committee; and Mr. Sedgwick (Rep.) of New York was appointed.

On the 30th, Mr. Eliot, by unanimous consent, introduced two bills, which were severally read a first and second time, referred to the special committee on the confiscation of rebel property, and ordered to be printed: "A bill to confiscate the property of rebels for the payment of the expenses of the present Rebellion, and for other purposes;' and "A bill to free from servitude the slaves of rebels engaged in abetting the existing Rebellion against the Government of the United States." On the 14th of May, Mr. Eliot reported back these bills by the direction of the committee; and, on the 20th, the House proceeded to their consideration. The debate ran through several days, and was participated in by several members.

Mr. Eliot (Rep.) of Massachusetts opened the debate in support of these twin measures of confiscation and emancipation, and closed by saying, "The strength of our Government, the resources of its loyal citizens, the young men of our homes, the hope and the pride of our life, have been offered up a free sacrifice upon the altar of their country. The war yet continues. Hundreds of thousands of rebel soldiers compose their armies, led on in the field, and sustained in council and in Congress, by traitors, whose property, employed for your destruction, this bill will confiscate, and whose slaves your rightful action will set free. My friends, let there be no hesitation here. The time has come. Your country demands your intervention. By your allegiance to the Constitution you have sworn to protect, and the free institutions our fathers established, I invoke you to consummate quickly this needful legislation, which shall crush out this foul Rebellion, and insure domestic tranquillity for evermore."

Mr. Noel (Union) of Missouri supported these bills, "as the only means by which our loyal people can be protected."—"I would set free," said Mr. Riddle (Rep.) of Ohio, " the slaves of every man and woman engaged in this Rebellion. The guilt of the master should inure at least to the benefit of the slave, and from this huge crime should spring a greater beneficence."—" It is slavery," said Mr. Windom (Rep.) of Minnesota, "that vitiated the conscience, destroyed the morals, brutalized the soul, and, in its own foul fens, generated these monsters of wickedness, whose mad attempts to destroy the Republic are characterized by the frightful excesses to which I have referred. All the want, misery, strife, treachery, bloodshed, barbarity, and desolation, which now stalks through this once-happy country, have their origin in the fell system of human bondage which it has nourished and protected." Mr. Voorhees (Dem.) of Indiana addressed the House in condemnation of the policy of the Government. Mr. Lansing (Rep.) of New York, in an earnest speech, said, "As my abhorrence of slavery could not be increased by its abuses, if it is capable of them; so no mitigation of the system, if it is capable of mitigation, could lessen that abhorrence. No matter to me whether every slaveholder were either a Legree or a St. Clair: my detestation of the system would be the same in either case; for, sooner or later, it will involve in itself every other crime." Mr. Mallory (Dem.) of Kentucky followed Mr. Lansing in an elaborate speech. He "entered his solemn protest" against the charge, that slavery was the cause of the war. "I am no propagandist of slavery," he avowed. " I am the owner of slaves, and the descendant of men, who, as far back as I can trace them in America, were the owners of slaves; and I have made the declaration upon this floor, that the condition of slavery is the very best condition in which you can place the African race. That is my deliberate conviction. I mean here in the United

States of America, and in those States where slavery exists." Mr. Wallace (Rep.) of Pennsylvania spoke for the adoption of these measures, and Mr. Phelps (Dem.) of Missouri followed in opposition. "We have held back," said Mr. Blair (Rep.) of Pennsylvania, "these powerful engines of military policy, in the hope that the enemies of the nation would return to reason and repentance. At all events, it is time for us to try what virtue there is in downright earnestness of purpose. I have not a fear of its results, either upon the war, or upon the welfare of the people South or North. I believe that even this generation will realize the blessings which will flow from such a policy. It will teach the world two things better than they have ever been taught before, — the unity of this nation, and the unity of the human family. When Peace shall come again, she will not tarry with us as a wayfarer, but will dwell with us. The nation, with all cause of fraternal strife banished, will be fitted for a better life; and, wherever its flag shall float, it will command the respect and the honor and the love of men." Mr. Rollins (Rep.) of New Hampshire earnestly advocated the measures. "The path of duty," he said, "never shone so bright for a people as it does for us to-day. As we advance, it grows brighter. The President's message recommending emancipation was the rending of the veil. The gift of freedom to a few poor, but oh! how grateful recipients, has returned to bless the hearts of millions who bestowed it. A deed more rich in virtue, more fruitful in the approving of conscience, more blessed with the smiles of Almighty God, stands not on the records of this nation." Mr. Kerrigan (Dem.) of

New York spoke next in opposition to these bills, because they tended "to create distrust in the public mind." Mr. Menzies (Opp.) of Kentucky opposed any legislation, but declared that "we are not bound to prevent the escape of the slaves of rebels, if they are in the way of our armies. We are not bound to prevent our soldiers from using them, when they can be turned to our advantage. We make no war upon slavery in the States. We are fighting for the Constitution. If slavery is necessarily and incidentally injured in the progress of the war, set the injury down to the account of the Rebellion. They would have it. The rebels must attempt the destruction of their bulwark, the Constitution: we must defend it. Their slaves may take advantage of the conflict and confusion to desert such silly masters. Such injury is chargeable to those who make war upon the Government." Mr. S. C. Fessenden (Rep.) of Maine thought " the early antislavery men have lived to see that 'he who has God on his side is always in the majority.' We learned the lesson at their feet, and from their success to rely upon the merits of our cause and upon God, who to the right will give the victory." Mr. Grider (Opp.) of Kentucky was now opposed to confiscation and emancipation. Mr. Babbitt (Rep.) of Pennsylvania was compelled by his settled convictions to say, that, in his opinion, "one of the most efficient means of speedily crushing out the Rebellion and preserving the Union would be the adoption of measures upon the basis indicated in the bill before us for freeing from servitude the slaves of persistent rebel masters." Mr. Sheffield (Dem.) of Rhode Island earnestly opposed the policy of confiscation and emancipation embodied in these bills, as unauthorized by the Constitution.

Mr. Sedgwick (Rep.) of New York offered an amendment to the bill. "The recital of that amendment avers," said Mr. Sedgwick, "that eleven States formerly of the Union, combined together under the title of 'The Confederate States of America,' have *made war upon* and rebelled against the Government of the United States, and continue in *such war* and rebellion. Upon that fact I propose to base an enactment, by which it shall be the duty of every commanding officer of a naval or military department, within any portion of those States, in some way, by proclamation or otherwise, to invite all loyal persons — and I mean to include in that slaves — to come within the lines, and be enrolled in the service of the United States; and I mean by that any service which they can render, civil or military: and that it shall be the duty of such commanding officers to enroll every such person, and employ such of them as may be necessary in the service of the United States; and the reward for that service I propose to make FREEDOM to them and their descendants for ever. I include in that the slaves not only of rebels, but of persons claiming to be loyal; but I propose for these compensation, and I also propose compensation for the services of all such as may be claimed by widows and minors. I claim the right to this enactment under the war power; and I shall attempt to show that it exists, and that it is within the power of Congress to legislate in regard to it. I will have no disguise of my opinions or intentions. My stand upon the subject is open to all observation. *I am for destroying this hostile institution in every State that has made war upon this Government:* and, if we have military strength enough to reduce them to possession, I propose to leave not one slave in the wake of our advancing armies; not one." — "I believe," declared Mr. F. P. Blair, jun. (Rep.), of Missouri, "that, as long as the negro race remains here, there is no hope, no possibility, nor is it in any aspect desirable, that they should have any share in the political power of the country. I think that the Almighty intended them for the tropics, or that the tropics were intended for them: one or the other is true. Every attempt on the part of the human race to frustrate that intention has brought destruction on the men who attempted it." — "Are we," inquired Mr. Spaulding (Rep.) of New York, "to be struck hard at every opportunity, without giving hard blows in return? I trust not. War means to strike often, and strike hard on both sides, — 'an eye for an eye, and a tooth for a tooth.' War teaches us to use all the means within our power to strengthen ourselves and to weaken our enemy. Let us weaken him in every possible way within the rules of civilized warfare. We should strike him personally, strip him of his property, and strike the shackles from every slave, that, by his labor and services, gives him support. These are the rights of war; and I am prepared to see them fully enforced." Mr. Sargent (Rep.) of California desired "to see this Rebellion utterly overthrown; and therefore I vote for these measures." Mr. Loomis (Rep.) of Connecticut said, "We are told that the Constitution is in the way. But I remember how the Constitution has been perverted from the first in aid of these conspirators against the life of the nation. It has been like a jug, with the handle on the rebel side. Every single step which the National Government has taken in the assertion of its rightful prerogatives has been met with the same cry, — 'Stop! you are violating the Constitution!' At the commencement of the Rebellion, the Constitution had become so perverted in its construction, as to become like Milton's bridge, that led —

'Smooth, easy, inoffensive, down to hell.'

As we look backward through the history of the usurpations of the slave power in our land, it seems to have been a deliberate purpose so to emasculate our organic law as to make secession easy. The Constitution was all bristling with vitality and power to guarantee, protect, and extend slavery, although slavery was nowhere named in that sacred instrument; while liberty, though everywhere guarded by the most explicit guaranties, has had no more meaning for many years past, in the estimation of proslavery commentators, than it had in the old French dictionary, where it was defined only as 'a word of three syllables.'"

Mr. Holman (war Dem.) of Indiana made an earnest and eloquent speech against the policy of emancipation, because it would "divide your councils, and weaken the strength of your armies." "As one of the representatives of Indiana," he said, "I have supported, sir, and will still support, every just measure of this Administration to restore the Union. No partisan interest shall control me when the Republic is in danger. I place the interest of my country far above every other interest. I will make any sacrifice to uphold the Government; but I will not be deterred from condemning, at this time, this or any other series of measures — the offspring of misguided zeal and passion, or the want of faith in our people — which tends to defeat the hope of a restoration of the Union. The citizen soldier, stricken down in battle or worn out by the weary march, falls a willing sacrifice for the Constitution of his country, and his dying eyes light up with hope as they catch the gleam of its starry symbol, while we deliberate on measures which would overthrow the one, and blot out the stars from the other."

Mr. Julian (Rep.) of Indiana made a vigorous and eloquent speech in favor of the extinction of slavery in the rebel States. "This clamor for the Union as it was," he said, "comes from men who believe in the divinity of slavery. It comes from those who would restore slavery in this district if they dared ; who would put back the chains upon every slave made free by our army ; who would completely re-establish the slave power over the National Government, as in the evil days of the past, which have culminated at last in the present bloody strife ; and who are now exhorting us to 'leave off agitating the negro question, and attend to the work of putting down the Rebellion.' Sir, the people of the loyal States understand this question. They know that slavery lies at the bottom of all our troubles. They know, that, but for this curse, this horrid revolt against liberty and law would not have occurred. They know that all the unutterable agonies of our many battle-fields, all the terrible sorrows which rend so many thousands of loving hearts, all the ravages and desolation of this stupendous conflict, are to be charged to slavery. They know that its barbarism has moulded the leaders of this Rebellion into the most atrocious scoundrels of the nineteenth century, or of any century or age of the world. They know that it gives arsenic to our soldiers, mocks at the agonies of wounded enemies, fires on defenceless women and children, plants torpedoes and infernal machines in its path, boils the dead bodies of our soldiers in caldrons, so that it may make drinking-cups of their skulls, spurs of their jaw-bones and finger joints as holiday presents for 'the first families of Virginia' and the 'descendants of the daughter of Pocahontas.' They know that it has originated whole broods of crimes never enacted in all the ages of the past; and that, were it possible, Satan himself would now be ashamed of his achievements, and seek a change of occupation. They know that it hatches into life, under its infernal incubation, the very scum of all the villanies and abominations that ever defied God or cursed his footstool; and they know that it is just as impossible for them to pass through the fiery trials of this war, without feeling that slavery is their grand antagonist, as it is for a man to hold his breath, and live."

Mr. Arnold (Rep.) of Illinois eloquently said, "The cause which bore the cross in 1850 wears the crown to-day. 'No power can die that ever wrought for truth,' while the political graves of recreant statesmen are eloquent with warnings against their mistakes. Where are those Northern statesmen who betrayed liberty in 1820? They are already forgotten, or remembered only in their dishonor. Who now believes that any fresh laurels were won in 1850 by the great men who sought to gag the people of the free States, and lay the slab of silence on those truths which to-day write themselves down, along with the guilt of slavery, in the flames of civil war? Has any man in the whole history of American politics, however deeply rooted his reputation or godlike his gifts, been able to hold dalliance with slavery, and live? I believe the spirit of liberty is the spirit of God; and, if the giants of a past generation were not strong enough to wrestle with it, can the pigmies of the present? It has been beautifully said of Wilberforce, that he 'ascended to the throne of God with a million of broken shackles in his hands as the evidence of a life well spent.' History will take care of his memory; and when our own bleeding country shall again put on the robes of peace, and Freedom shall have leave to gather up her jewels, she will not search for them among the political fossils who are now seeking to spare the rebels by pettifogging their cause in the name of the Constitution, while the slave power is feeling for the nation's throat."

Mr. Harding (Opp.) of Kentucky pronounced the policy of emancipating the slaves of rebels "the weakest and most disastrous policy ever thought of." Mr. Richardson (Dem.) of Illinois said, "The bills now under consideration propose to violate not only your pledges, but, at the same time, the Constitution. You forget your promises : you advocate these bills, and urge their passage through this House." — "Pass these bills under consideration," said Mr. Dunlap (Opp.) of Kentucky, "and we enter upon a new life. A new stage is erected before us; and upon it, for weal or for woe, we shall have to encounter the realities of an untried experiment." Mr. Clements (Union) of Tennessee opposed the bills. Mr. Noel of Missouri earnestly advocated the bills. He said, "Perhaps, sir, in standing up here for the safety and security of the loyal people there, I may be signing my political death-warrant: but, sir, if I go down, I will go down, like the heroes of the 'Cumberland,' with my flag still flying; and my last act shall be that of pouring a broadside into the ranks of treason. . . . I was charmed with the eloquence of the distinguished gentleman from Massachusetts (Mr. Thomas) a few days since. To his patriotic sentiments I heartily subscribe. In devotion to the Constitution, I claim to go as far as he. We look at it, however, from a different standpoint, and give it a different construction. When I heard his impassioned language, my pleasure was not unmixed with pain. My mind ran back to the desolation and ruin of my own section. I wondered how it could be that a gentleman hailing from a district in the Old Bay State, which had furnished so many jewels in the crown of our national glory, could find no balm in the Constitution to cure the ills of patriots and loyalists, or guaranties for their security and protection. Sir, must I go back to the persecuted Union men of Missouri, who have been robbed and plundered without mercy by their rebel enemies, and tell them that the Constitution is in the way of any effective legislation that would hold the enemy's property as security for their safety? Must I tell them that their wives will have again to do like the mother of Ishmael, — take up their little ones, and flee to the wilderness?"

"The men who have instigated this Rebellion," said Mr. Ely (Rep.) of New York, "not upon the impulse of a day, but as the culmination of passions which have been nursed for a generation, and which have not merely become as enduring as life, but which will be transmitted as heir-looms of hate from father to son, are the great land barons of the South. They have nursed their pride in stately mansions, and by the contemplation of broad acres. They will never forgive or forget the grief of the defeat which is impending over them. They never can or will become truly loyal; and, if we leave them in possession of the estates which have made them powerful, it is impossible that the South will be in our day any thing but a slumbering political volcano, liable at any moment to belch forth smoke and fire and devastating lava." Mr. Shanks (Rep.) of Indiana thought it "strange that an American Congress should be so unaccountably infatuated with the high crime of slavery as to falter and fall before it even in its treasons." Mr. Hutchins (Rep.) of Ohio could "see no reason why loyal white men should be obliged to go to the South, with its sultry climate, and endure all the dangers and hardships of that climate, from tenderness to the views of loyal slaveholders." Mr. Beaman (Rep.) of Michigan eloquently advocated these measures of confiscation and emancipation. "Can it be doubted that the rebels are in earnest? Does any man imagine that they will ever yield, and lay down their arms, until compelled to do so by force? Do they now employ any thing less than their entire resources, energy, and skill? Will the taking away of four millions of their population — three-fourths or more of their industrial classes — increase their hopes, courage, and capacity for evil? . . . It has been repeatedly intimated on this floor, that the passage of these bills, and especially of the one contemplating a contingent emancipation of slaves, would create dissensions at the North, and seriously impair the efficiency of the army. Indeed, gentlemen have gone the length to predict that it would result in mutiny, and cause the troops to lay down their arms, and disband. . . . Does any sane man believe that Northern freemen engaged in this war for the purpose of protecting and sustaining slavery? Why should they secure to the master his slave, rather than his cotton, his horse, or his ox? What cause of animosity have they against the poor bondman? What interest have they in maintaining and perpetuating the peculiar institution? What object have they in strengthening the resources of the enemy? Whence comes this deep and all-absorbing love of slavery in the hearts of Northern freemen, — a love that commands them to forget country, the graves of murdered brothers, and even the necessary means of self-preservation? Does it come from party ties and party influences? The love of country is stronger than the love of party. Republicans are not wedded to the institution, and Slavery slew Democracy in the Charleston Convention. Slavery, according to a senator from South Carolina, made these same Northern freemen mud-sills. Slavery made Kansas a field of blood. Slavery has destroyed freedom of speech, and freedom of the press. Slavery has whipped, driven from their homes, and even hung, inoffensive native-born American citizens. Slavery has smitten with blight and mildew fifteen States of the Union, and barbarized millions of our population. And, finally, Slavery has made war upon the United States, and has already slain fifty thousand of her loyal men. Mutiny, disband, and lay down their arms, because you remove poison from their cups, and turn pistols from their breasts! Mutiny, disband, and lay down their arms, lest you should, in self-defence, strangle the monster, the serpent in this our garden of Eden, — the author of all our woes!"—"Slavery, being in itself wrong," said Mr. Rice (Rep.) of Maine, "can, as a system, only be secure in wrong government; being contrary to natural right and justice, it knows no laws but those of aggression and force; being in the habitual exercise of despotic power over an inferior race, it learns to despise and disregard the rights of all races. It has 'sown the wind;' let it 'reap the whirlwind.' By the laws of peace, it was entitled to protection, and had it; by the laws of war, it is entitled to annihilation. In God's name, let it still have its right." Mr. Hanchett (Rep.) of Wisconsin declared, that he "who chooses to brave the moral sense of mankind, by affecting to *own* man as property, does so with a full appreciation of all moral, social, and political consequences. He who pays his money for human brains and human legs does so with the full knowledge that brains were made to think, and that legs were made to run. He takes his risk for time and for eternity, for peace and for war, for good or for evil, subject to all the incidents of his unnatural tenure." Mr. Hanchett closed his remarks with the declaration, that "all the people ask of the Administration is, that they yield neither to local prejudices or interest on the one hand, nor neglect the plain suggestions afforded by current events on the other; and that, to save the loyalty of a few slaveholders, the patriotic aspirations of millions of unconditional Union men be not divided and crushed.".

Mr. Price (Opp.) of Missouri was "utterly opposed to any measure which looks to the emancipation of slaves, without the free consent of their masters." Mr. Price thought, for "the origin of the war," we must "go quite behind the negro :" the true cause was "the lust of power, restless and unsatiable ambition. It is," he declared, "this unrepublican fondness for distinction, parade, and display, this itching for fame, and insatiable thirst for power, that has led to all our present troubles. South-Carolina politicians and wealthy planters desired to become lords temporal; and Charleston merchants desired to become princes under King Cotton, and control the commerce of the world. With the madman's purpose of accomplishing these objects, they inaugurated a revolution. I utter no threats nor imprecations, nor shall I shed tears of pity if the bold traitors who invoked this storm should be whelmed for ever beneath its fiery waves. It would only be poetic justice if that pestilent triangle, that has never grown any thing but rice, tar, and treason, should be devoured by the fires of its own kindling." Mr. Kellogg (Rep.) of Illinois would support these measures to cripple the energies of the rebels, and put an end to this desolating war. "We should not in our legislation," he said, "strike at the unthinking and the unwitting dupes of designing men; but we should strike at those whose heads have conceived, and whose hearts have been enlisted in, this work." Mr. Thomas (Opp.) of Massachusetts made an elaborate, able, and eloquent speech in opposition to these twin measures of confiscation and emancipation. "That the bills," he said, "before the House are in violation of the law of nations, and of the Constitution, I cannot — I say it with all deference to others — I cannot entertain a doubt. My path of duty is plain. The duty of obedience to that Constitution was never more imperative than now. I am not disposed to deny that I have for it a superstitious reverence. I have 'worshipped it from my forefathers.' In the school of rigid discipline by which we were prepared for it, in the struggles out of which it was born, the seven years of bitter conflict, and the seven darker years in which that conflict seemed to be fruitless of good, in the wisdom with which it was constructed and first administered and set in motion, in the beneficent Government it has secured for more than two generations, in the blessed influences it has exerted upon the cause of freedom and humanity the world over, I cannot fail to recognize the hand of a guiding and loving Providence. But not for the blessed memories of the past only do I cling to it. He must be blinded 'with excess of light,' or with the want of it, who does not see that to this nation, trembling on the verge of dissolution, it is the only possible bond of unity."

Mr. Train (Rep.) of Massachusetts thought the Virginia and Kentucky resolutions of 1798, originally brought forward to embarrass the administration of John Adams, have done their work; that " the germ of dissolution then planted has been industriously nursed by designing men and inborn traitors, until now the country is reaping the bitter fruit. Slavery has added its influence in bringing about the Rebellion, and a most potent and sinful one. It is an unmitigated curse, and a deadly evil; but this Rebellion would have occurred without it. When you add the workings of slavery to the doctrines

I have alluded to, every hour brings you with lightning speed to practical secession. Slavery debases every white person with which it comes in contact, socially and politically. It creates a difference of classes incompatible with a republican form of government; it makes the master impatient of control, and insubordinate as a citizen of the State, as it compels the master to hold a large amount of land to make slavery profitable; it creates a landed aristocracy, who, living upon the labor of others, learn to look down with contempt upon those who regard labor as honorable; and finally it creates a class of poor whites, who, with the rights of citizens, are as ignorant and degraded as the blacks, and who were easily inflamed to political madness, when the masters, rankling at the loss of political power, and to some of them the still greater loss of the opportunity to steal from the public treasury, applied the doctrine of State rights, and practically of open secession. If, then, the event of the Rebellion shall annihilate the doctrine of State rights, the Union may be restored, though slavery remains *stat nominis umbra.*" Mr. Whalley (Union) of Virginia briefly and earnestly advocated the pending bills. Virginia, he declared, was mobbed out of the Union; and the people of Western Virginia appealed to the people of the loyal States for aid, and " Massachusetts, responding to our call, loaned us ten thousand stand of arms." He emphatically declared, " If the policy is carried out which is contended for by some of the gentlemen who are opposed to confiscation, let me tell them, however honest they may be in their opinions to the contrary, the united South and their sympathizers in the North will once more take possession of this Government, and fill every seat in this House with traitors, and our liberty will be at an end. If we receive them back into full fellowship, with their hands all dripping with the blood of their countrymen, do you suppose that we of Western Virginia can live upon Virginia soil? Do you suppose that the patriots of East Tennessee can remain quietly in their homes? No, sir. I say to the gentleman from Massachusetts (Mr. Thomas), if it is unconstitutional to confiscate the property of these rebels, our Constitution is a failure, and our Government is at an end; and I had rather go with my family, and live among the wild savages of the West, than remain in Western Virginia." Mr. Ashley (Rep.) of Ohio asserted, that, "more than a year ago, I proclaimed, to the constituency which I have the honor to represent, my purpose to destroy the institution of slavery, if it became necessary to save the country, — as I believed then, and still believe it is, — in every State which had rebelled, or which should rebel, and make war upon the Government. I then demanded, as I now demand, 'that not a single slave claimed by a rebel slave-master shall be delivered up if he escape, or be left in the wake of our advancing and victorious armies.' I then declared, as I now declare, that 'justice, no less than our own self-preservation as a nation, required that we should confiscate and emancipate, and thus secure indemnity for the past, and security for the future.'" Mr. Killinger (Rep.) of Pennsylvania thought we were "in danger of doing too much, not too little, on this interminable negro question."

Mr. Gurley (Rep.) of Ohio earnestly pressed the duty of extending confiscation to the slaves of disloyal masters. "I see not," he said, "why property in slaves so called should be regarded as more sacred in title than houses, lands, gold, and silver. True, the man who is called a slave bears the image of God; there is upon him the moral impress of the Almighty; it is generally believed also that he has a soul, or spirit, that is immortal; and it is the common expectation, that he will sit down in heaven side by side with his master: but is it for this that *he* must, amid all the changes and chances of government, of war and peace, irrevocably remain in servitude, while every other species of property is taken from rebels? Is it, then, true that property in husbands, wives, and children, is so intensified in value, that even hard coin may be taken, but these never? By what rule, pray, of justice, human or divine, or of law, shall we seize the horses of rebels, and pass by their slaves, when one of the latter is practically worth in this war twenty of the former?" Mr. White (Rep.) of Indiana advocated the bills, and Mr. Nugen (Dem.) of Ohio opposed their enactment. Mr. Cox (Dem.) of Ohio delivered a lengthy and discursive speech on emancipation and its results. He denied that "slavery was the cause of the Rebellion:" it was "the occasion, not the cause." He believed secession "the worst crime since Calvary," but was "at as great a loss how to apportion the guilt between secession, and abolition which begat it, as I would be to apportion the guilt of the crucifixion between Judas and the Roman soldiers. . . . Must these Northern fanatics," he asked, "be sated with negroes, taxes, and blood, with division North and devastation South, and peril to constitutional liberty everywhere, before relief shall come? They will not halt until their darling schemes are consummated. History tells us that such zealots do not and cannot go backward." Mr. Wickliffe (Opp.) of Kentucky had been nearly fifty years devoted to the service of the country; and, old and crippled, he was sent there to do all he could to restore the Union as it was, to preserve the Constitution, and enforce the laws. He had served with John Quincy Adams in Congress, and he was "bound to ascribe his hatred of the South and its institutions to his overthrow in 1828 as President. Mr. Adams had been the founder, and for life the leader, of that party in the North which made constant war upon the institution of slavery within the States. It is on his wild, heated, and monstrous doctrine," he declared, "that the advocates of emancipation by the war of the present day base their claim of the power." No language could express his abhorrence of the act of organizing a brigade of slaves by Gen. Hunter. "I have," he declared, "introduced a bill to prohibit this outrage, this wrong upon humanity, this stigma upon the character of the nation, which no repentance, not of long rolling years, will efface." Mr. Walton (Rep.) of Vermont made an elaborate argument on the power to enact the pending bills, and in favor of the Senate bill. Mr. Law (Dem.) of Indiana emphatically declared that "the man who dreams of closing the present unhappy contest by reconstructing this Union upon any other basis than that prescribed by our fathers, in the compact formed by them, is a madman, — ay, worse, a traitor; and should be hung as high as Haman. Sir, pass these acts, confiscate under these bills the property of these men, emancipate their negroes, place arms in the hands of these human gorillas to murder their masters and violate their wives and daughters, and you will have a war such as was never witnessed in the worst days of the French Revolution, and horrors never exceeded in St. Domingo, for the balance of this century at least."

Mr. Maynard (Union) of Tennessee doubted "the power of Congress under the Constitution to pass either of these bills;" and he was "opposed to the exercise by Congress of any doubtful powers." Mr. Eliot, Chairman of the Select Committee, closed the debate in an earnest appeal to the House to "show, that so far as we are concerned, as the Legislature of the country, as the Congress of the United States, we are willing, so far as we are constitutionally able, to hearken to the cry of our people, to uphold and strengthen the arms of the Government, and condemn the property of rebel enemies, which is now employed for the overthrow of our Constitution and our laws." After the passage of the Confiscation Bill, the speaker stated that the next question was the House bill to free from servitude the slaves of rebels engaged in or abetting the existing Rebellion, and that the question was first on Mr. Blair's amendment to Mr. Sedgwick's amendment. Mr. Blair demanded the yeas and nays, and they were ordered, — yeas 52, nays 95. The question then recurred on Mr. Sedgwick's amendment; and Mr. Holman demanded the yeas and nays, and they were ordered, — yeas 32, nays 116. The question recurred on Mr. Walton's amendment to Mr. Morrill's amendment, and it was lost, — yeas 29, nays 121; and the question recurred on Mr. Morrill's substitute, and it was lost, — yeas 16, nays 126. Mr. Eliot's bill was then read a third time. Mr. Vallandigham demanded the yeas and nays on the passage of the bill, and they were ordered, — yeas 74, nays 78. So the bill was rejected on the 26th of May.

On the 27th, Mr. Porter moved a reconsideration of the vote, for the purpose of moving to recommit the bill, with instructions to report as a substitute the amendment he had proposed. The motion coming up on the 28th, Mr. Porter moved to postpone the consideration of the motion to the 4th of June. Mr. Holman moved to lay the motion to reconsider on the table, — yeas 69, nays 73. The motion to postpone to the 4th of June was agreed to. On the 4th of June, the Speaker stated the business in order to be Mr. Porter's motion to reconsider the vote rejecting the bill to free the slaves of rebels, and recommit the bill with instructions. Mr. Porter addressed the House in support of his motion to reconsider and recommit. Mr. Vallandigham moved to lay the motion to reconsider on the table, — yeas 65, nays 86; and Mr. Porter's motion to reconsider was then agreed to, — yeas 84, nays 64. Mr. Porter then moved to recommit the bill to the Special Committee, with instructions to report his substitute; and the motion was agreed to, — yeas 84, nays 66.

Mr. Eliot, Chairman of the Special Committee, on the 17th of June reported back the original bill, with Mr. Porter's substitute; and moved several amendments, all of which were ordered to be printed. On the 18th, Mr. Eliot moved a substitute for Mr. Porter's amendment, reported by the Select Committee, under the instructions of the House. Mr. Eliot's substitute provided that all right, title, interest, and claim whatever of every person belonging to six classes, — the sixth including all persons in armed rebellion sixty days after the President shall issue his proclamation, — in and to the service of any other persons, shall be forfeited, and such persons shall be for ever discharged from service, and be freemen; and that the President appoint commissioners to carry the act into effect. Mr. Eliot's amendment was agreed to, — yeas 82, nays 54; the substitute, as amended, was agreed to, — yeas 83, nays 52; and the bill, as amended, was passed, — yeas 82, nays 54.

On the 23d of June, the Senate proceeded to the consideration of the House bill, passed on the 26th of May, to confiscate the property of rebels. Mr. Clark moved to amend it by striking out all after the enacting clause, and inserting the bill reported by the Select Committee of the Senate, which combined confiscation and emancipation. Mr. Saulsbury (Dem.) of Delaware addressed the Senate on the 24th of June in opposition to the policy of confiscation and emancipation. On the 27th, the debate was resumed by Mr. Cowan, Mr. Trumbull, Mr. Howard, Mr. Browning, Mr. Dixon, and Mr. Sumner. Mr. Trumbull, in reply to Mr. Saulsbury, said, "When a negro rushes in to save the life of my brother or my son from the bayonet of a traitor against this Government, and knocks up the weapon that is aimed at his life, I will say 'God speed' to the negro, and I will encourage him to do it again. Sir, no traitor shall come and murder my child or my brother, or any soldier of my State or my country, who is fighting for this Union, with my consent. If there is a negro or anybody else in God's world that has got an arm to strike him down, I will say, 'Strike!' I care not who it is." — "Let me confess frankly," said Mr. Sumner, "that I look with more hope and confidence to liberation than to confiscation. To give freedom is nobler than to take property: and, on this occasion, it cannot fail to be more efficacious; for, in this way, the rear-guard of the Rebellion will be surely changed into the advance-guard of the Union. There is in confiscation, unless when directed against the criminal authors of the Rebellion, a harshness inconsistent with that mercy which it is always a sacred duty to cultivate, and which should be manifest in proportion to our triumphs, — 'mightiest in the mightiest.' But liberation is not harsh; and it is certain, if properly conducted, to carry with it the smiles of a benignant Providence." On the 28th, the debate was continued by Mr. Wilkinson, Mr. Cowan, Mr. Sumner, Mr. Clark, Mr. Doolittle, Mr. Pomeroy, Mr. Sherman, Mr. Wade, Mr. Fessenden, and other senators. Mr. Clark's amendment to the Confiscation Bill of the House was agreed to, — yeas 21, nays 17. Mr. Trumbull moved to amend by inserting the House bill to free the slaves of rebels. After debate, Mr. Trumbull withdrew his amendment. The vote was taken on concurring in Mr. Clark's amendment adopted in committee, — yeas 19, nays 17; and the bill as amended was then passed, — yeas 28, nays 13.

In the House, on the 3d of July, the Confiscation Bill, as amended by the Senate, was taken up for consideration. Mr. Crisfield (Dem.) moved to lay the amendment on the table, — yeas 48, nays 81. The question was then taken on the Senate amendment, and it was non-concurred in, — yeas 8, nays 124.

The Senate, on the 8th, proceeded to the consideration of the Confiscation Bill. Mr. Clark moved to insist, and ask a Committee of Conference. Mr. Sherman moved to recede, — yeas 14, nays 23. On Mr. Clark's motion to insist, and ask a Committee of Conference, the yeas were 28, and the nays 10; and Mr. Clark, Mr. Harris, and Mr. Wright, were appointed. The House, on the same day, on motion of Mr. Eliot, voted to insist on its disagreement to the Senate amendment, and appointed Mr. Eliot, Mr. Wilson (Rep.) of Iowa, and Mr. Corning (Dem.) of New York, a Committee of Conference on the part of the House. On the 11th of July, Mr. Eliot, from the Conference Committee, reported in substance the Senate amendment prepared by Mr. Clark. This report combined confiscation and emancipation in one bill. It provided that all slaves of persons who shall give aid or comfort to the Rebellion, who shall take refuge within the lines of the army; all slaves captured from such persons, or deserted by them, and coming under the control of the Government; and all slaves of such persons found on being within any place occupied by rebel forces, and afterwards occupied by the forces of the United States, — shall be deemed captives of war, and shall be for ever free, and not again held as slaves; that fugitive slaves shall not be surrendered to persons who have given aid and comfort to the Rebellion; that no person engaged in the military or naval service shall surrender fugitive slaves, on pain of being dismissed from the service; and that the President may employ persons of African descent for the suppression of the Rebellion, and organize and use them in such manner as he may judge best for the public welfare. Mr. Allen (Dem.) of Illinois moved to lay the report of the Conference Committee on the table, — yeas 42, nays 78; and the report was then agreed to, — yeas 82, nays 42. In the Senate, on the 12th, the Conference Committee's report was considered. Mr. M'Dougall moved to lay it on the table, — yeas 12, nays 28. Mr. Carlile demanded the yeas and nays on the acceptance of the report, — yeas 27, nays 12. So the report was accepted; and the bill received, on the 17th of July, the approval of the President of the United States.

CHAPTER VII.

HAYTI AND LIBERIA.

MR. SUMNER'S BILL TO AUTHORIZE THE APPOINTMENT OF DIPLOMATIC REPRESENTATIVES TO HAYTI AND LIBERIA. — MR. SUMNER'S SPEECH. — MR. DAVIS'S AMENDMENT. — MR. DAVIS'S SPEECH. — PASSAGE OF THE BILL. — THE BILL REPORTED IN THE HOUSE. — MR. GOOCH'S SPEECH. — MR. COX'S AMENDMENT. — MR. COX'S SPEECH. — MR. BIDDLE'S SPEECH. — MR. KELLEY'S SPEECH. — MR. M'KNIGHT'S SPEECH. — MR. ELIOT'S SPEECH. — MR. THOMAS'S SPEECH. — MR. FESSENDEN'S SPEECH. — MR. MAYNARD'S SPEECH. — MR. CRITTENDEN'S SPEECH. — PASSAGE OF THE BILL.

IN the Senate, on the 4th of February, 1862, Mr. Sumner (Rep.) of Massachusetts, from the Committee on Foreign Relations, to whom was referred so much of the President's message as relates to the opening of diplomatic relations with the republics of Hayti and Liberia, reported a bill to authorize the President of the United States to appoint diplomatic representatives to the republics of Hayti and Liberia; which was read, and passed to a second reading.

On the 22d of April, Mr. Sumner moved to take up the bill to authorize the President to appoint diplomatic representatives to the republics of Hayti and Liberia. The motion was agreed to, the bill read a second time, and made the special order for the next day. On that day, the Senate, as in Committee of the Whole, proceeded to its consideration. It proposed to authorize the President of the United States, by and with the advice and consent of the Senate, to appoint diplomatic representatives of the United States to the republics of Hayti and Liberia respectively. Mr. Sumner then addressed the Senate in support of the bill in a moderate and well-guarded speech. "The independence of Hayti and Liberia," he said, "has never yet been acknowledged by our Government. It would at any time be within the province of the President to do this, either by receiving a diplomatic representative from these republics, or by sending one to them. The action of Congress is not necessary, except so far as an appropriation may be needed to sustain a mission. But the President has seen fit, in his annual message, to invite such action. By this bill, Congress will associate itself with him in the acknowledgment, which, viewed only as an act of justice, comity, and good neighborhood, must commend itself to all candid minds. . . . A full generation has passed since the acknowledgment of Hayti was urged upon Congress. As an act of justice too long deferred, it aroused even then the active sympathy of multitudes; while, as an act for the benefit of our commerce, it was ably commended by eminent merchants of Boston and New York, without distinction of party. It received the authoritative support of John Quincy Adams, whose vindication of Hayti was associated with his best labors in the other House. The right of petition, which he steadfastly maintained, was long ago established. Slavery in the national capital is now abolished. It remains that this other triumph shall be achieved. Petitioners who years ago united in this prayer, and statesmen who presented the petitions, are dead; but they will all live again in the good work which they generously began."

On the 24th, the Senate resumed the consideration of the bill. Mr. Davis (Opp.) of Kentucky moved an amendment in the nature of a substitute, to strike out all after the enacting clause, and insert, "That the President of the United States be, and hereby is, authorized to appoint a consul to the republic of Liberia, and a consul-general to the republic of Hayti." Mr. Davis said, "I am weary, sick, disgusted, despondent, with the introduction of the subject of slaves and slavery into this Chamber; and, if I had not happened to be a member of the committee from which this bill was reported, I should not have opened my mouth upon the subject. If, after such a measure should take effect, the republic of Hayti and the republic of Liberia were to send their ministers plenipotentiary or their *chargés d'affaires* to our Government, they would have to be received by the President and by all the functionaries of the Government upon the same terms of equality with similar representatives from other powers. We recollect, that, a few years ago, the refined French court admitted and received the representative of Soulouque, who then denominated himself, or was called, the Emperor of Dominica, I think." Mr. Sumner: "Of Hayti."—"Well," continued Mr. Davis, "a big negro fellow, dressed out with his silver or gold lace clothes in the most fantastic and gaudy style, presented himself in the court of Louis Napoléon, and, I admit, was received. Now, sir, I want no such exhibition as that in our capital and in our Government. The American minister, Mr. Mason, was present on that occasion; and he was sleeved by some Englishman — I have forgotten his name — who was present, who pointed out to him the ambassador of Soulouque, and said, ' What do you think of him?' Mr. Mason turned round, and said, 'I think, clothes and all, he is worth a thousand dollars.'" Mr. Davis hoped that many colored people would go to Liberia, and cast their destinies in the land of their fathers. "I made," replied Mr. Sumner, "no allusion to the character of the population of those two republics. I made no appeal for them on account of their color. I did not allude to the unhappy circumstance in their history, that they had once been slaves. It is the senator from Kentucky who has introduced that topic into debate. And not only this, sir: he has followed it by alluding to some possible difficulties — I hardly know how to characterize them — which may occur here in social life, should the Congress of the United States undertake at this late day, simply in harmony with the law of nations, and following the policy of civilized communities, to pass the bill now under discussion. I shall not follow the senator on those sensitive topics. I content myself with a single remark. I have more than once had the opportunity of meeting citizens of these republics; and I say nothing more than truth when I add, that I have found them so refined, and so full of self-respect, that I am led to believe no one of them charged with a mission from his government will seek any society where he will not be entirely welcome. Sir, the senator from Kentucky may banish all anxiety on that account. No representative from Hayti or Liberia will trouble him." Mr. Davis's amendment was rejected, — yeas 8, nays 30. The yeas and nays were then ordered on the passage of the bill, — yeas 32, nays 7. So the bill passed the Senate.

In the House, June 2, Mr. Gooch (Rep.) of Massachusetts moved that the Committee on Foreign Affairs be discharged from the further consideration of the Senate bill authorizing the President of the United States to appoint diplomatic representatives to the republics of Hayti and Liberia. Mr. Gooch addressed the House in a clear, concise, and practical speech in support of the measure. He said, "Justice, sound policy, political wisdom, commercial interest, the example of other governments, and the wishes of the people of our own, all demand that we recognize the independence of Hayti and Liberia, and that, in our intercourse with them, we place them on the same footing as other independent nations." Mr. Cox (Dem.) of Ohio moved as a substitute the following amendment: "That there be appointed for each of the republics of Liberia and Hayti a consul-general, who shall be authorized to negotiate any treaties of commerce between said republics and this country." Mr. Cox said that this was "literally a Black-Republican measure. The gentleman from Massachusetts intends to let Hayti and Liberia send us ministers whomsoever they please to this country. If they send negro ministers to Washington City, the gentleman will say, they shall be welcomed as ministers, and have all the rights of Lord Lyons and Count Mercier." — "What objection," asked Mr. Fessenden (Rep.) of Maine, "can the gentleman have to such representatives?" — "Objection? Gracious heavens! what innocency!" exclaimed Mr. Cox. "Objection to receiving a black man on an equality with the white men of this country? Every objection which instinct, race, prejudice, and institutions make. What is it for, unless it be to outrage the prejudices of the whites of this country, and to show how audacious the abolitionists can behave? How fine it will look, after emancipating the slaves in this District, to welcome here at the White House an African, full-blooded, all gilded and belaced, dressed in court style, with wig and sword and tights and shoe-buckles and ribbons and spangles, and many other adornments which African vanity will suggest! How suggestive of fun to our good-humored, joke-cracking Executive! With what admiring awe will the contrabands approach this ebony demigod! while all decent and sensible white people will laugh the silly and ridiculous ceremony to scorn." Mr. Biddle (Dem.) of Pennsylvania followed Mr. Cox. "I cannot," he said, "recognize this measure as now prompted by that genuine philanthropy of which political abolitionism is the basest of counterfeits. Eminent members of the party in power laugh to scorn this colonization scheme."

On the 3d of June, the House resumed the consideration of the bill. Mr. Kelley (Rep.) of Pennsylvania said, "The gentleman from Ohio (Mr. Cox), acting under the new code, indulged himself in parading before the House the squalor and ignorance of the recently escaped slaves around us, as a fair portraiture of the condition of the negro race. He drew a melancholy picture. But how he enjoyed it! and with what evident satisfaction he added each sombre tint! The gusto with which he completed the work gave some indication of how jolly he would be, could he join a ring in derisive dance around some ulcerous Lazarus or blind Samson fallen by the wayside. And then his other picture of the negro official in shoe-buckles, knee-breeches, gold lace, and bag wig, — it was so funny! True, I did not hear the roars of laughter that should have followed it; but I am quite sure, that, if there was any such person as the elder Mr. Weller in the galleries, the effort to suppress his laughter must have brought him well-nigh to apoplexy." Mr. M'Knight (Rep.) of Pennsylvania followed in support of the measure. "It has been," he said, "to our glory that we planted the seeds of freedom, civilization, and Christianity, on the shores of heathen Africa, and to our shame that we have so long abandoned the culture and nature of the plant to others." Mr. Eliot (Rep.) of Massachusetts discussed the interests involved, and the duty of action. Mr. Thomas (Opp.) of Massachusetts spoke briefly but eloquently in favor of the bill. "I have no desire," he declared, "to enter into the question of the relative capacity of races; but, if the inferiority of the African race were established, the inference as to our duty would be very plain. If this colony has been built up by an inferior race of men, they have upon us a yet stronger claim for our countenance, recognition, and, if need be, protection. The instincts of the human mind and heart concur with the policy of men and governments to help and protect the weak. I understand, that to a child or to a woman I am to show a degree of forbearance, kindness, and of gentleness even, which I am not necessarily to extend to my equal." Mr. Fessenden of Maine would be willing to see any one, without regard to color, who might be sent as minister by a government with whom we have diplomatic relations. "The whole argument," he said, "of Mr. Cox, centred in this: Hayti and Liberia are not to be acknowledged, — no matter what reasons may be given to the contrary, — because, if otherwise, we shall see black ambassadors in Washington. In my opinion, the speech of the gentleman was unworthy of his head and heart." Mr. Maynard (Union) of Tennessee would pass the bill. "The policy of this, like all other nations, should be to recognize every nationality which has entitled itself to that degree of consideration. I suppose, if Liberia should send one of her citizens here, one of Afric's dusky sons, in some diplomatic character, — and even this by no means follows from the passage of this bill, — and he should occupy a seat in the diplomatic gallery, none of us would suffer more harm from the proximity than we now do from our contact with those of the same race who attend to the wants of our persons, brushing our coats and polishing our boots, in the lobbies of the House."

Mr. Crittenden (Opp.) of Kentucky said, "I will only say, sir, that I have an innate sort of confidence and pride that the race to which we belong is a superior race among the races of the earth, and I want to see that pride maintained. The Romans thought that no people on the face of the earth were equal to the citizens of Rome, and it made them the greatest people in the world. . . . The spectacle of such a diplomatic dignitary in our country, would, I apprehend, be offensive to the people for many reasons, and wound their habitual sense of superiority to the African race." Mr. Gooch closed the debate. "Why shall we," he asked, "in our intercourse with the world, make discriminations in relation to color not recognized by the other leading powers of the earth? Certainly the fact, that the great body of slaveholders in this country are to-day in rebellion against this Government, and seeking its overthrow, because they have not been able to control all its departments to promote the extension and perpetuation of slavery, does not make it obligatory upon us to do so." The first question was on the adoption of Mr. Cox's amendment. He called for the yeas and nays; and the yeas and nays were ordered. The question was taken; and it was decided in the negative, — yeas 40, nays 82. Mr. Gooch demanded the previous question on the passage of the bill. The previous question was seconded, and the main question ordered. Mr. Cox demanded the yeas and nays on the passage of the bill; and the yeas and nays were ordered. The question was taken; and it was decided in the affirmative, — yeas 86, nays 37. So the bill was passed, and received the approval of the President on the fifth day of June, 1862.

CHAPTER VIII.

EDUCATION OF COLORED YOUTH IN THE DISTRICT OF COLUMBIA.

MR. GRIMES'S BILL. — MR. GRIMES'S REPORT. — MR. WILSON'S AMENDMENT. — REMARKS OF MR. WILSON. — PASSAGE OF THE BILL. — BILL REPORTED IN THE HOUSE BY MR. ROLLINS. — PASSAGE OF THE BILL. — MR. LOVEJOY'S BILL. — REPORTED BY MR. FESSENDEN. — PASSAGE OF THE BILL. — BILL REPORTED IN THE SENATE BY MR. GRIMES. — PASSAGE OF THE BILL. — MR. WILSON'S BILL. — REPORTED FROM THE DISTRICT COMMITTEE. — REMARKS BY MR. CARLILE. — MR. GRIMES. — MR. DAVIS. — MR. MORRILL. — PASSAGE OF THE BILL IN THE SENATE. — PASSAGE IN THE HOUSE. — MR. WILSON'S BILL. — MR. GRIMES'S BILL. — PASSAGE IN THE SENATE. — MR. PATTERSON'S SUBSTITUTE. — PASSAGE OF THE BILL.

THE census of 1860 revealed the fact, that there were more than three thousand colored youth in the District of Columbia. These children were not permitted to enter the public schools, and no public provision whatever was made for their instruction. The property of colored parents was taxed for the support of schools from which their own children were excluded. The abolition of slavery, the repeal of the black code and ordinances, in the District, more distinctly revealed this neglect of colored children, and this injustice towards colored parents.

In the Senate, on the 29th of April, 1862, Mr. Grimes (Rep.) of Iowa introduced a bill providing for the education of colored children in the city of Washington. On the presentation of his bill, Mr. Grimes said, " In order that there may be no misapprehension as to what this bill seeks, I desire to say now, before it is referred, that, according to the census of 1860, there are three thousand one hundred and seventy-two colored children in this District. The amount of real estate then and now owned by colored persons within the District is in value $650,000. There is now levied a tax upon that property amounting to $36,000. The school-tax, as I understand, is ten per centum of that amount, or $3,600, which goes to the support of schools which are devoted exclusively to the education of white children. This bill simply provides that the tax which is levied on the property of colored persons shall be used exclusively in the education of colored children."

The bill was referred to the Committee on the District of Columbia; and, on the 30th, Mr. Grimes reported it with amendments. The Senate, on the 8th of May, on the motion of Mr. Grimes, proceeded to its consideration, and the amendments of the committee were agreed to. The bill, as amended, made it the duty of the municipal authorities of Washington and Georgetown to set apart ten per cent of the amount received from taxes levied on the real and personal property owned by persons of color, to be appropriated for the purpose of initiating a system of primary schools for the education of colored children. The board of trustees of public schools were to have sole control of the fund arising from the tax, as well as from contributions by persons disposed to aid in the education of the colored race, or from any other source, and to provide suitable rooms and teachers for such a number of schools as in their opinion would best accommodate the colored children.

Mr. Wilson (Rep.) of Massachusetts moved to amend the bill by adding as an additional section, —

"That all persons of color in the District of Columbia, or in the corporate limits of the cities of Washington and Georgetown, shall be subject and amenable to the same laws and ordinances to which free white persons are or may be subject or amenable; that they shall be tried for any offences against the laws in the same manner as free white persons are or may be tried for the same offences; and that, upon being legally convicted of any crime or offence against any law or ordinance, such persons of color shall be liable to the same penalty or punishment, and no other, as would be imposed or inflicted upon free white persons for the same crime or offence: and all acts, or parts of acts, inconsistent with the provisions of this act, are hereby repealed."

In support of his amendment, Mr. Wilson said, "We have some laws that everybody admits are very oppressive upon the colored population of this District; some of them old laws made by Maryland; others, ordinances of the cities of Washington and Georgetown. As we are now dealing with their educational interests, I think we may as well at the same time relieve them from these oppressive laws, and put them, so far as crime is concerned, and so far as offences against the laws are concerned, upon the same footing, and have them tried in the same manner, and subject them to the same punishments, as the rest of our people." The amendment was agreed to, the bill was reported to the Senate as amended, the amendment was concurred in, and the bill ordered to be engrossed. Mr. Saulsbury (Dem.) of Delaware demanded the yeas and nays on its passage, — yeas 27, nays 6. There being no quorum, the Senate adjourned.

On the 9th, the vote was taken, and resulted — yeas 29, nays 7. So the bill was passed in the Senate, and its title so amended as to make it read, " A bill providing for the education of colored children in the cities of Washington and Georgetown, in the District of Columbia, and for other purposes." In the House, on the 15th, Mr. Rollins (Rep.) of New Hampshire, from the Committee on the District of Columbia, reported back the bill without amendment, and demanded the previous question on its passage. It was ordered; the bill was passed, and approved by the President on the 21st of May, 1862.

In the House of Representatives, on the 23d of June, 1862, Mr. Lovejoy (Rep.) of Illinois introduced a bill relating to schools for the education of colored children in the cities of Washington and Georgetown, in the District of Columbia; and it was read twice, and referred to the District Committee. The bill provided that the duties imposed on the board of trustees of the public schools in the cities of Washington and Georgetown, by the act providing for the education of colored children in the cities of Washington and Georgetown, approved May 21, 1862, be transferred to Daniel Breed, Sayles J. Bowen, and Zenas C. Robbins, and their successors in office, who are created a board of trustees of the schools for colored children, and who shall possess all the powers and perform all the duties conferred upon and required of the trustees of public schools in the cities of Washington and Georgetown by that act. On the 3d of July, Mr. Fessenden (Rep.) of Maine, from the Committee on the District to whom was referred Mr. Lovejoy's bill, reported it back without amendment, and it passed the House. In the Senate, Mr. Grimes, on the 5th of July, reported back the bill from the District Committee; and, on his motion, it was enacted on the 11th of July, 1862.

In the Senate, on the 17th of February, 1863, Mr. Wilson (Rep.) of Massachusetts introduced a bill to incorporate "the institution for the education of colored youth," to be located in the District of Columbia. The objects of the institution were to educate and improve the moral and intellectual condition of such colored youth of the nation as may be placed under its care and influence. The bill was read twice, and referred to the District Committee. Mr. Grimes, on the 24th, from the Committee on the District of Columbia, to whom the bill was referred, reported it without amendment. On the 27th, the Senate, on motion of Mr. Grimes, proceeded to its consideration. "I should like to know," said Mr. Carlile (Dem.) of Virginia, "if these negroes cannot be educated without an act of incorporation." He did not "see any very good reason why the Government of the United States should enter upon the scheme of educating negroes." He understood "the reason assigned for the government of a State undertaking the education of the citizens of the State is that the citizens in this country are the governors;" but he presumed "we have not yet reached the point when it is proposed to elevate to the condition of voters the negroes of the land." Mr. Grimes in reply said, "It may be true, that, in that section of the country where the senator is most acquainted, the whole idea of education proceeds from the fact, that the person who is to be educated is merely to be educated because he is to exercise the elective franchise; but I thank God that I was raised in a section of the country where there are nobler and loftier sentiments entertained in regard to education. We entertain the opinion, that all human beings are accountable beings. We believe that every man should be taught, so that he may be able to read the law by which he is to be governed, and under which he may be punished. We believe that every accountable being should be able to read the word of God, by which he should guide his steps in this life, and shall be judged in the life to come. We believe that education is necessary in order to elevate the human race. We believe that it is necessary in order to keep our jails and our penitentiaries and our alms-houses free from inmates. In my section of the country, we do not educate any race upon any such low and grovelling ideas as those that seem to be entertained by the senator from Virginia." Mr. Davis (Opp.) of Kentucky thought the subject might be dropped. "I recollect," he said, "a fact in relation to the Island of St. Lucia, one of the West-India islands. When it became one of the British possessions, a great many Irish who spoke the Gaelic language migrated from the Island of Erin to St. Lucia. In the course of a few years, they possessed themselves of African slaves, — slaves from the continent; and, in adhering to their Gaelic language, the Africans whom they introduced, and the young ones that were raised, of course learned to speak the Gaelic too. After a while, some of their kinsfolk, who had been left behind in the mother country, visited the Island of St. Lucia, and they discovered all the negroes there talking the real Gaelic, the genuine

Irish; and they wrote back to their countrymen, for God's sake no more of them to come to St. Lucia; and, as they loved St. Patrick, not to come to St. Lucia, because all the Irish turned to be negroes there. I really think, sir, that, if the subject of negroes is handled much longer in the Senate, there is very great danger of some senators meeting such a fate as was feared by these visitors from Ireland would happen to their countrymen." Mr. Morrill (Rep.) of Maine thought the opposition to the bill, and the sentiments expressed, were extraordinary. "The senator from Virginia puts his opposition upon the ground of a protest against public education. Gracious God, sir, has it come to this, that in the American Congress, and at this late day, an honorable senator shall rise here, and enter his protest against a measure of public popular education? Coming from the region of country I do, I confess that it excites wonder and astonishment in my mind. Is there a civilized nation on the globe, that has not, within the last fifty years, turned its attention to the subject of the education of the people, and that has not embarked in it, and made it a matter of State concern, if you please, the highest State concern, not only as beneficial to the individuals, the social compact, but to the security of the State? I should like to know what sort of American statesmanship that is which enables a senator to rise here in his place, and arraign a measure designed to educate the people: for that, allow me to say, was one of the positions taken by the senator from Virginia; and he prided himself apparently on the fact, that, in the region of country in which he was raised, education was left to private enterprise. How well that great duty has been there performed, I care not to say: the history of the country shows. But, sir, I come from a region of country the people of which prize public education; who hold public education as a great duty, the first great duty of the State, to be religiously performed; and, if New England can boast of any thing, it is her system of education, her system of public instruction, which gives to every child, no matter whether he is high or low born, a fair chance in life, a fair chance to succeed in the world. That is her glory; and to-day, sir, amid the menaces, impotent as they are, that fall about New England, if there be any thing which will enable her to put them at defiance, it will be her moral power on the continent by reason of her system of public education. . . . The legislation of my State has adopted a system of education which enjoins it upon the people of every town and city to educate every child, without regard to color or complexion. The negro, if you please, in that regard, stands on an equal footing with every other child in the State. The law knows no complexion in its duty of public education, and the system of public education throughout New England knows no distinction whatever." Mr. Davis's motion to postpone the bill was lost, and the bill ordered to be engrossed. Mr. Carlile demanded the yeas and nays on its passage, and they were ordered; and, being taken, resulted — yeas 29, nays 9. In the House, on the 2d of March, the bill was taken from the Speaker's table. Mr. Wilson (Rep.) of Iowa called for the previous question: it was passed, and approved by the President on the 3d of March, 1863.

In the Senate, May 2, 1864, Mr. Wilson introduced

a bill granting one million acres of public land to the cities of Washington and Georgetown and the county of Washington, the proceeds to be used for the support of the public schools in proportion to the number of children. The bill also authorized the school commissioners to assess a poll-tax of one dollar on men of color for the education of colored children. The bill was referred to the Committee on Public Lands.

The Senate, on the 18th of February, 1864, on motion of Mr. Grimes, proceeded to the consideration of his bill to provide for the public instruction of youth in the primary schools throughout the county of Washington, in the District of Columbia, without the limits of the cities of Washington and Georgetown. Mr. Grimes suggested that the Senate consider the amendment reported from the District Committee as a substitute. This amendment established a public-school system in the county of Washington for the instruction of youth. The eighteenth section authorized the Levy Court at its discretion to levy a tax of one-eighth of one per cent on all taxable property owned by persons of color, for the purpose of initiating a system of education for colored children. The bill passed the Senate without a division.

In the House, on the 8th of June, Mr. Patterson (Rep.) of New Hampshire reported back, with an amendment in the nature of a substitute, the Senate bill to provide for the public instruction of youth in the county of Washington. A professor in Dartmouth College, familiar with the public-school systems of the Northern States, Mr. Patterson was admirably fitted to devise an improved system of public instruction for the national capital. The substitute reported by Mr. Patterson, with the unanimous approval of the District Committee, provided in the seventeenth and eighteenth sections, and in the proviso to the nineteenth section, for separate schools for colored children of the District. "To accomplish this," said Mr. Patterson, "we have provided that such a proportion of the entire school fund shall be set apart for this purpose as the number of colored children between the ages of six and seventeen bear to the whole number of children in the District. . . . We may have differences of opinion in regard to the proper policy to be pursued in respect to slavery; but we all concur in this, that we have been brought to a juncture in our national affairs in which four millions of a degraded race, lying far below the average civilization of the age, and depressed by an almost universal prejudice, are to be set free in our midst. The question now is, What is our first duty in regard to them? . . . I think there can be no difference of opinion on this, that it is our duty to give to this people the means of education, that they may be prepared for all the privileges which we may desire to give them hereafter." Mr. Patterson's substitute was adopted, and the bill passed the House as amended. The Senate readily concurred in the House amendment; and the bill received the approval of the President on the 25th of June, 1864.

By this beneficent act of legislation, it is made the duty of the school commissioners to establish public schools for colored children, to provide school-houses, to employ school-teachers, and " to appropriate a proportion of the school fund, to be determined by the numbers of white and colored children between the ages of six and seventeen years." Nearly four thousand colored children in the national capital have by the enactment of this law, in the public schools, the same rights and privileges as white children.

CHAPTER IX.

THE AFRICAN SLAVE-TRADE.

THE TREATY BETWEEN THE UNITED STATES AND GREAT BRITAIN FOR THE SUPPRESSION OF THE SLAVE-TRADE. — MR. SUMNER'S BILL. — REMARKS OF MR. SAULSBURY. — PASSAGE OF THE BILL. — MR. FOSTER'S BILL. — PASSAGE OF THE BILL.

THE American flag has been made to cover for many years the horrid and loathsome traffic in human flesh. The African-slave traders have pursued their foul and infamous work of sorrow and death under the protection of the flag of this Christian nation. This prostitution of the flag brought reproach and dishonor upon the Government and people of the United States. To suppress this traffic in men, to prevent this abuse of the flag of the country, a treaty was made with England for the more effectual suppression of the African slave-trade.

On the 12th of June, 1862, Mr. Sumner (Rep.) of Massachusetts, from the Committee on Foreign Relations, to whom was referred a message from the President of the United States in relation to the treaty between the United States and Great Britain for the suppression of the slave-trade, reported a bill to carry the treaty into effect. On motion of Mr. Sumner, the Senate, on the 26th, proceeded to the consideration of the bill. To carry into effect the provisions of the treaty between the United States and her Britannic

Majesty for the suppression of the African slave-trade, it was provided that the President should appoint, by and with the advice and consent of the Senate, a judge and also an arbitrator on the part of the United States to reside at New York; a judge and also an arbitrator to reside at Sierra Leone; and a judge and also an arbitrator to reside at the Cape of Good Hope. Mr. Saulsbury (Dem.) of Delaware wished to record his vote against the passage of the bill. "I do not," he said, "object to the suppression of the African slave-trade; but I do not believe that this Government has the constitutional right to establish any such court. I think the treaty ought not to have been adopted. There is no power under the Constitution for the establishment of such a court outside of the United States." Mr. Howard (Rep.) of Michigan demanded the yeas and nays on the passage of the bill, — yeas 34, nays 4. In the House, on the 7th of July, Mr. Gooch (Rep.) of Massachusetts reported back, from the Committee on Foreign Relations, the Senate bill to carry into effect the treaty between the United States and England for the suppression of the African slave-trade. "I desire only to state," remarked Mr. Gooch, "that the provisions of the treaty are necessary to carry the treaty recently made into effect." The bill was passed, and received the approval of the President on the 11th of July, 1862.

In the Senate, on the 8th of July, Mr. Foster (Rep.) of Connecticut introduced a bill to amend an act entitled "An act to amend the act entitled 'An act in addition to the acts prohibiting the slave-trade:'" it was read twice, and referred to the Judiciary Committee.

On the 9th, Mr. Foster reported back the bill, without amendment. It was taken up for consideration on the 12th; and Mr. Fessenden (Rep.) of Maine stated that he understood a division was to be called upon it, and moved that it be laid on the table. On the 15th, the Senate, on motion of Mr. Foster, proceeded to the consideration of the bill. It provided that the President might enter into arrangement, by contract or otherwise, with one or more foreign governments having possessions in the West Indies or other tropical regions, or with their duly constituted agent or agents, to receive from the United States, for a term not exceeding five years, at such place or places as shall be agreed upon, all negroes, mulattoes, or persons of color, delivered from on board vessels seized in the prosecution of the slave-trade by commanders of United-States armed vessels, and to provide them with suitable instruction, and with comfortable clothing and shelter, and to employ them, at wages under such regulations as shall be agreed upon, for a period not exceeding five years from the date of their being landed at the place or places agreed upon. Mr. King (Rep.) of New York regarded this as a sort of apprenticeship system to which he was opposed, and demanded the previous question on the passage of the bill, — yeas 30, nays 7. In the House, on the 16th, the bill was passed, and received the approval of the President on the 17th of July, 1862.

CHAPTER X.

ADDITIONAL ACT TO ABOLISH SLAVERY IN THE DISTRICT OF COLUMBIA.

MR. WILSON'S BILL. — REPORTED BACK WITH AMENDMENTS BY MR. GRIMES. — MR. GRIMES'S SPEECH. — MR. WILSON'S SPEECH. — COMMITTEE'S AMENDMENTS. — MR. SUMNER'S AMENDMENT. — PASSAGE OF THE BILL. — BILL IN THE HOUSE. — REMARKS OF MR. WICKLIFFE. — MOTION TO LAY ON THE TABLE BY MR. COX. — REMARKS BY MR. CRISFIELD. — PASSAGE OF THE BILL.

IN the Senate, on the 12th of June, 1862, Mr. Wilson (Rep.) of Massachusetts introduced a bill supplementary to the act for the release of certain persons held to service or labor in the District of Columbia, approved April 16, 1862; which was read twice, and referred to the Committee on the District of Columbia. Mr. Grimes (Rep.) of Iowa, Chairman of the District Committee, reported, on the 24th, the bill back with amendments. On the 7th of July, the Senate, on motion of Mr. Grimes, proceeded to its consideration. Mr. Grimes briefly explained its purpose and scope. "It will be remembered," he said, " that when the President of the United States notified the Senate of his approval of the act of the 16th of April last, emancipating slaves in this District, he stated that he had some objections to it, on the ground that the rights of *femes covert*, absent persons, minors, &c., were not saved. The first section of this bill is designed to cover cases of that kind;

and it provides that where persons were out of the country, officers of the army or navy, or idiots or minors, or persons who are laboring under any disability of that kind, they shall have an opportunity to come in and prove their claims to property of this description within a time limited. The second section of the bill, as the committee propose, is intended to cover cases of this kind. It has been discovered that there are some persons who have been held as slaves, whose owners are in arms against the country. There is nobody here to represent those owners; and it is impossible, therefore, for those colored persons to get any evidence of their manumission or their emancipation: and it is provided, that if any person, having claim to the service or labor of any person or persons in the District of Columbia by reason of African descent, shall neglect or refuse to file with the clerk of the Circuit Court the statement or schedule required by the ninth section of the act of April 16, 1862, it shall be lawful for the person or persons whose services are claimed to file such statement in writing or schedule, setting forth the particular facts mentioned in the ninth section of that act, and the clerk is to record the same; and the clerk is then to prepare, prescribe, and deliver the certificates, as described in the tenth section of that act, to such persons as shall file their statements. I understand that there are several cases — I am so informed by one of the commissioners — where this description of persons are claimed by persons now in rebellion and beyond our reach. The next section declares that all persons who are held to service under the laws of any State, and who, at any time since the 16th of April, have, by the consent of the persons who have held them, been forced to labor in this District, shall be free."

The President stating the question to be on the amendment of the committee to strike out the second section of the original bill, Mr. Wilson said, "The committee have inserted two very excellent sections; but they propose to strike out the second and fourth sections of the original bill. The second section was intended to cover the cases of persons who were held to service or labor in this District, who resided here with their masters, but who have been recently hired out in the neighboring States, especially the State of Maryland. There are cases of such persons whose names have not been returned by their masters, and who have no remedy unless we give it to them. I presented a petition, a short time ago, in relation to one case of this kind, — the petition of a person born in the District, held here to service, who had always lived here until recently, and was hired out over the line a few months ago. I think the commissioners ought to construe the law to cover those cases; for, in my judgment, the law should be construed in favor of personal rights: but there is some doubt about it, and hence the necessity for legislation on the subject. I have talked to some of the commissioners in regard to it, and find that there is doubt on the question. I think that section of the bill ought to stand, notwithstanding the dissent of the report of the committee."

"I will state," replied Mr. Grimes, "the reason why the committee recommended the striking-out of that section. As I understand it, the purport of that section was this: that if a person had been held to slavery in the District of Columbia prior to the emancipation act, and had been sent, by the man who claimed to be his master, out of the District prior to the passage of that act, then, under the law, he should become free. We did not believe we had that power. He was held as a slave under the law of the State of Maryland, to which he had been sent; and we did not suppose we could legislate for the State of Maryland." The second section of the bill was stricken out by the Senate.

The President stated the question to be on concurring in the new section proposed by the committee, giving to persons whose services are claimed the right to file the papers required by the act for the release of persons held to service in the District of Columbia, when persons claiming their services neglect or refuse to file such papers. The amendment was amended on the suggestion of Mr. Collamer (Rep.) of Vermont, and the amendment as amended was agreed to. The amendment proposed by the committee, to strike out the fourth section of the original bill providing for the appointment of a solicitor of the commission, was agreed to.

Mr. Sumner (Rep.) of Massachusetts offered as an additional section, that, in all the judicial proceedings in the District of Columbia, there shall be no exclusion of any witness on account of color. Mr. Powell (Dem.) of Kentucky demanded the yeas and nays on that amendment, — yeas 25, nays 11. Mr. Powell demanded the yeas and nays on the passage of the bill, — yeas 29, nays 6.

In the House, the bill was taken from the Speaker's table on the 9th of July; and Mr. Ashley (Rep.) of Ohio stated that the bill was supplementary to the act abolishing slavery in the District, approved the 16th of April. Mr. Calvert (Opp.) of Maryland desired "to strike out the fourth section. It was simply interfering with the rights of the slaveholders in the States." Mr. Wickliffe (Opp.) of Kentucky said, "As I understand the reading of the section, if a man in Montgomery County, or anywhere else in Maryland, sends his negro to market or into the city to do any business for him, he is set free." Mr. Cox (Dem.) of Ohio moved to lay the bill on the table, and Mr. Calvert demanded the yeas and nays: lost, — yeas 35, nays 67. Mr. Ashley moved the previous question. Mr. Crisfield (Dem.) of Maryland desired to offer an amendment to the fourth section. Mr. Ashley could not withdraw the demand for the previous question. "Then I hope," replied Mr. Crisfield, "there is patriotism enough in the House to vote down the demand." The House, by a large majority, seconded the previous question. Mr. Richardson (Dem.) of Illinois moved an adjournment, — yeas 28, nays 69. Mr. Pendleton (Dem.) of Ohio demanded the yeas and nays on the passage of the bill, — yeas 69, nays 36. So the bill passed the House, and was approved by the President on the 12th of July, 1862.

CHAPTER XI.

COLORED SOLDIERS.

MR. WILSON'S BILL. — MR. GRIMES'S AMENDMENT. — REMARKS OF MR. SAULSBURY. — MR. CARLILE. — MR. KING'S AMENDMENT. — MR. SHERMAN'S SPEECH. — MR. FESSENDEN'S SPEECH. — MR. RICE'S SPEECH. — MR. WILSON'S SPEECH. — MR. DAVIS'S AMENDMENT. — MR. COLLAMER'S SPEECH. — MR. TEN EYCK'S SPEECH. — MR. KING'S SPEECH. — MR. HENDERSON'S AMENDMENT. — MR. SHERMAN'S AMENDMENT. — MR. BROWNING'S AMENDMENT. — MR. LANE'S SPEECH. — MR. HARLAN'S SPEECH. — MR. WILSON'S BILL. — REMARKS OF MR. SHERMAN. — MR. LANE. — SPEECH OF MR. HOWARD. — MR. SHERMAN'S AMENDMENT. — MR. BROWNING'S AMENDMENT. — REMARKS OF MR. HENDERSON. — MR. WRIGHT. — MR. DOOLITTLE. — MR. POWELL. — PASSAGE OF THE BILL. — MR. STEVENS'S AMENDMENT. — REMARKS OF MR. CLAY. — MR. BOUTWELL. — MR. DAVIS'S AMENDMENT. — MR. MALLORY'S SPEECH. — MR. WEBSTER'S AMENDMENT. — MR. SCOFIELD'S SPEECH. — MR. WOOD'S SPEECH. — MR. WHALLEY'S AMENDMENT. — MR. STEVENS'S AMENDMENT ADOPTED. — CONFERENCE COMMITTEE. — REPORT ADOPTED.

IN the Senate, on the 8th of July, 1862, Mr. Wilson (Rep.) of Massachusetts reported, from the Committee on Military Affairs, a bill to amend the act calling forth the militia to execute the laws of the Union, suppress insurrection, and repel invasion, approved Feb. 28, 1795. On the 9th, on motion of Mr. Wilson, the Senate proceeded to consider the bill as in Committee of the Whole. Mr. Grimes (Rep.) of Iowa moved to amend it by adding three sections, providing that there shall be no exemption from military duty on account of color; that, when the militia shall be called into service, the President shall have full power and authority to organize them according to their race or color. Mr.

Saulsbury (Dem.) of Delaware denounced the attempt "made on every occasion to change the character of the war, and to elevate the miserable nigger, not only to political rights, but to put him in your army, and to put him in your navy." Mr. Carlile (Dem.) of Virginia declared that "the negro constituted no part of the militia of his State. I do not," he asserted, "think it is an effort to elevate the negro to an equality with the white man; but the effect of such legislation will be to degrade the white man to the level of the negro." Mr. King (Rep.) of New York moved to strike out the first two sections of Mr. Grimes's amendment, and insert these two sections: —

"That the President be, and he is hereby, authorized to receive into the service of the United States, for the purpose of constructing intrenchments, or performing camp service or any other labor, or any war service for which they may be found competent, persons of African descent; and such persons shall be enrolled and organized under such regulations, not inconsistent with the Constitution and laws, as the President may prescribe; and they shall be fed, and paid such compensation for their services as they may agree to receive when enrolled.

"That, when any man or boy of African descent shall render any such service as is provided for in the first section of this act, he, his mother, and his wife and children, shall for ever thereafter be free, any law, usage, or custom whatsoever, to the contrary notwithstanding."

Mr. King hoped that Mr. Grimes would accept the amendment. "I accept it," replied Mr. Grimes, "if it is in my power." Mr. Saulsbury pronounced this amendment "a wholesale scheme of emancipation." Mr. Sherman (Rep.) of Ohio said, "The question arises, whether the people of the United States, struggling for national existence, should not employ these blacks for the maintenance of the Government. The policy heretofore pursued by the officers of the United States has been to repel this class of people from our lines, to refuse their services. They would have made the best spies; and yet they have been driven from our lines."— "I tell the President," said Mr. Fessenden (Rep.) of Maine, "from my place here as a senator, and I tell the generals of our army, they must reverse their practices and their course of proceeding on this subject. . . . I advise it here from my place,—treat your enemies as enemies, as the worst of enemies, and avail yourselves like men of every power which God has placed in your hands to accomplish your purpose within the rules of civilized warfare." Mr. Rice (war Dem.) of Minnesota declared that " not many days can pass before the people of the United States North must decide upon one of two questions: we have either to acknowledge the Southern Confederacy as a free and independent nation, and that speedily; or we have as speedily to resolve to use all the means given us by the Almighty to prosecute this war to a successful termination. The necessity for action has arisen. To hesitate is worse than criminal." Mr. Wilson said, "The senator from Delaware, as he is accustomed to do, speaks boldly and decidedly against the proposition. He asks if American soldiers will fight if we organize colored men for military purposes. Did not American soldiers fight at Bunker Hill with negroes in the ranks, one of whom shot down Major Pitcairn as he mounted the works? Did not American soldiers fight at Red Bank with a black regiment from your own State, sir?

(Mr. Anthony in the chair.) Did they not fight on the battle-field of Rhode Island with that black regiment, one of the best and bravest that ever trod the soil of this continent? Did not American soldiers fight at Fort Griswold with black men? Did they not fight with black men in almost every battle-field of the Revolution? Did not the men of Kentucky and Tennessee, standing on the lines of New Orleans, under the eye of Andrew Jackson, fight with colored battalions whom he had summoned to the field, and whom he thanked publicly for their gallantry in hurling back a British foe? It is all talk, and idle talk, to say that the volunteers who are fighting the battles of this country are governed by any such narrow prejudice or bigotry. These prejudices are the results of the teachings of demagogues and politicians, who have for years undertaken to delude and deceive the American people, and to demean and degrade them."

Mr. Grimes had expressed his views a few weeks before, and desired a vote separately on each of these sections. Mr. Davis declared that he was utterly opposed, and should ever be opposed, to placing arms in the hands of negroes, and putting them into the army. Mr. Rice wished "to know if Gen. Washington did not put arms into the hands of negroes, and if Gen. Jackson did not, and if the senator has ever condemned either of those patriots for doing so." — "I deny," replied Mr. Davis, "that, in the Revolutionary War, there ever was any considerable organization of negroes. I deny, that, in the war of 1812, there was ever any organization of negro slaves. . . . In my own State, I have no doubt that there are from eighty to a hundred thousand slaves that belong to disloyal men. You propose to place arms in the hands of the men and boys, or such of them as are able to handle arms, and to manumit the whole mass, men, women, and children, and leave them among us. Do you expect us to give our sanction and our approval to these things? No, no! We would regard their authors as our worst enemies; and there is no foreign despotism that could come to our rescue, that we would not joyously embrace, before we would submit to any such condition of things as that. But, before we had invoked this foreign despotism, we would arm every man and boy that we have in the land, and we would meet you in a death-struggle, to overthrow together such an oppression and our oppressors." Mr. Rice remarked in reply to Mr. Davis, "The rebels hesitate at nothing. There are no means that God or the Devil has given them that they do not use. The honorable senator said that the negroes might be useful in loading and swabbing and firing cannon. If that be the case, may not some of them be useful in loading, swabbing, and firing the musket?"

The Senate, on the 10th of July, resumed the consideration of the bill. Mr. Collamer said, "I never could understand, and do not now understand, why the Government of the United States has not the right to the use of every man in it, black or white, for its defence; and every horse, every particle of property, every dollar in money, of every man in it. As to the using of colored men, that is entirely a question of expediency, whether you need them, whether you can use them to advantage; and that depends on so many contingencies, that I have always supposed the President, the generals, the men who are managing the war, actually engineering it along if you please, would lay their hands upon and use all means and appliances to that end which they found necessary. If gentlemen think it is any better to put it into a law that the President may do that, if that will help the matter, I have no sort of objection." Mr. Wilson thought that "it was necessary." — "Then," said Mr. Collamer, "I have no objection. . . . The second section of the amendment provides, that when any man or boy of African descent, who, by the laws of any State, owes service or labor to any person, who, during the present Rebellion, has borne arms against the United States, or adhered to their enemies by giving them aid or comfort, shall render to the United States any such service as is provided in the preceding section, he, his mother, and his wife and children, shall for ever thereafter be free, any law or usage to the contrary notwithstanding. I have a word to say about that. I am constrained to say, whether it is to the honor or dishonor of my country, that, in the land of slavery, no male slave has a child; none is known as father to a child; no slave has a wife, marriage being repudiated in the slave system. This is the condition of things; and, wonderful as it may be, we are told that that is a Christian institution!" Mr. Ten Eyck (Rep.) of New Jersey desired to strike out of the first section the words, "any military or naval," before "service." — "We may as well meet this question directly," said Mr. King, "and see whether we are prepared to use for the defence of our country the powers which God has given to it, — the men who are willing to be used to preserve it." — "My proposition is," said Mr. Ten Eyck, "to strike out the words, 'any military or naval,' before 'service.'"—"We have," said Mr. King, "in my judgment, nothing to fear from our enemies on account of the expression of our views on this point.... I have done talking in such a manner as to avoid giving offence to our enemies in this matter. I think it was the captain of the watch here at the Capitol who came and consulted about getting permission to omit, during the session of the Senate, to hoist the flag on the top of the Capitol; and, when he was asked what he wanted to omit that for, he said he feared it might be supposed that he desired to save labor and trouble, but he really suggested it because it hurt these people about here to look at it, — to see the flag on the top of the Capitol. I had not done much; but I wrote a letter very promptly to the Secretary of the Interior, stating the fact, and saying that I did not care whom he appointed, but I wanted that man removed. He was removed, and, within ten days, was with the enemy at Manassas."

The question on Mr. Davis's amendment to strike out the words, "or any military or naval service for which they may be found competent," was taken by yeas and nays, — yeas 11, nays 27. Mr. Henderson moved to amend the section by inserting the word "free," before "persons," in the sixth line, and also by adding after "descent," in the same line, the words, "and also such persons of African descent as may owe service or labor to persons engaged in the Rebellion." Mr. Henderson's amendment was lost, — yeas 13, nays 22. Mr. Saulsbury moved the indefinite postponement of the bill, — yeas 9, nays 27. Mr. Henderson moved to add at the end of the first section, "*Provided* that all loyal persons entitled to the service or labor of persons employed under the provisions of this act shall be compensated for the loss of such service." Mr. Hale would like to amend that by inserting the words, " by the laws of the State in which they reside." Mr. Henderson accepted the amendment. Mr. Powell demanded the yeas and nays, — yeas 20, nays 17. The first section, as amended, was agreed to. The President stated the question to be on the second section of the amendment of the senator from Iowa, " That when any man or boy of African descent shall render any such service as is provided for in the first section of this act, he, his mother, and his wife and children, shall for ever thereafter be free, any law, usage, or custom whatsoever, to the contrary notwithstanding." Mr. Sherman moved to amend it by adding, " who, during the present Rebellion, has levied war or borne arms against the United States, or adhered to their enemies by giving them aid and comfort." Mr. Sherman said, " When we take the slave of a loyal man, and make him work for us, I do not for that reason wish to deprive the master entirely of what he regards as his property, or what is regarded by local law as his property." — " When we take a slave," replied Mr. King, " to serve the country in this emergency, my own opinion is, that he should be made free, whether he belongs to a rebel or not." The secretary read the amendment to the amendment, to insert after the word " descent," in the second line, the words, " who by the laws of any State shall owe service or labor to any person, who, during the present Rebellion, has levied war or borne arms against the United States, or adhered to their enemies by giving them aid and comfort." The question, being taken by yeas and nays, resulted — yeas, 22, nays 16. So the amendment to the amendment was agreed to.

Mr. Browning (Rep.) of Illinois said, "I wish to move another amendment to that section in the seventh line, by striking out the words, "his mother, and his wife and children." Mr. Lane (Rep.) of Kansas asked Mr. Browning, "What would freedom be worth to you, if your mother, your wife, and your children, were slaves?" Mr. Browning replied, that " it would detract very greatly from the value of life with me, if it did not totally destroy it, to have my mother, my wife and children, in a state of hopeless bondage. I am no more the friend or advocate of slavery than the senator from Kansas, — not a bit more." On the 11th of July, the yeas and nays were taken on Mr. Browning's amendment, — yeas 17, nays 21. Mr. Harlan of Iowa addressed the Senate in a very elaborate and exhaustive speech in favor of the bill. "If I read," he said, "the signs of the times correctly, this has become a necessity. We cannot, if we persist in our folly, thwart the ultimate purposes of the Almighty. By his providential interposition, he has thrown open the door for the liberation of a nation of bondmen; he has removed the constitutional impediment; he has caused their assistance to be necessary for the perpetuity of the Union and the integrity of the nation. If we accept of this high destiny, all the nations of earth combined against us would be as flax in the flames; but if we are not equal to the demands of the age, and obstinately refuse to follow the plain intimations of Providence, this great work will be handed over to other nations, or will be wrought out by the rebels themselves, and our nation will become permanently divided." Mr. Harlan remarked, that Mr. Davis had predicted, when the bill for the abolition of slavery was pending, that the slaughters of St. Domingo would be re-enacted if the bill passed. . . . If senators will open their eyes, and look at these people, they will discover that they are no longer savages, but, in a comparative point of view, highly civilized. They provide for their own wants; they provide their own food and clothing and shelter, and for the education of their own children, for the support of their own churches and schools, and bury their own dead; and, during the seven years of my service at the capital of the nation, I have never seen a negro beggar, — not one. I have seen white beggars; I have seen white boys and girls begging for a penny of each passer-by at the crossings; I have seen stalwart men and women, of almost every nationality, begging in your streets and thoroughfares: but never yet have I seen a negro beggar in the streets of the capital of the nation." Mr. Davis followed in opposition to the bill; and, on motion of Mr. Wilson, it was further postponed.

On the 12th of July, Mr. Wilson, from the Committee on Military Affairs and the Militia, reported a new bill to amend the "Act calling forth the militia to execute the laws of the Union, suppress insurrections, and repel invasions," approved Feb. 28, 1795, and the acts amendatory thereof, and for other purposes; which was read twice by its title, and ordered to be printed. On the 14th of July, on motion of Mr. Wilson, the bill was taken up and considered as in Committee of the Whole. The bill proposed to authorize the President to receive into the service of the United States, for the purpose of constructing intrenchments, or performing camp service, or any other labor or any military or naval service for which they may be found competent, persons of African descent; and such persons are to be enrolled and organized under such regulations, not inconsistent with the Constitution and laws, as the President may prescribe, and are to be fed and clothed and paid such compensation for their services as they may agree to receive when enrolled. When any man or boy of African descent shall render any such service, he, his mother, and his wife and children, are for ever thereafter to be free, any law, usage, or custom to the contrary notwithstanding. All persons who have been or shall be hereafter enrolled in the service of the United States under the act are to receive the pay and rations now allowed by law to soldiers, according to their respective grades; except that persons of African descent who shall be employed are to receive ten dollars per month, and one ration. "I think, by an inadvertence," said Mr. Sherman ("for the senator from Massachusetts would not have done it otherwise), he has left out a very important clause in the thirteenth section, which was adopted by a deliberate vote of the Senate. I will therefore renew it. It is in section thirteen, line two, after the words 'African descent,' to insert the words, 'who by the laws of a State owes service or labor to any person, who, during the present Rebellion, has waged war against the United States, or has aided or assisted said Rebellion.'" Mr. Lane of Kansas said he must demand the yeas and nays on that amendment. Mr. Sherman wanted the Senate to understand, that by a deliberate vote, and by a considerable majority, the Senate determined that it would not apply the emancipation clause of the bill to any but the slaves of rebels. "By the section as it now stands, if any slave is employed to wheel a barrow of earth in making an intrenchment, or cutting down a tree, if he was the slave of the most loyal man in this country, he would thereby be made free." — "I am perfectly willing," replied Mr. Lane of Kansas, "to provide in the bill for remunerating the loyal master; but the idea in this amendment is to remand a man back to slavery, either to a loyal or a disloyal master, after he has fought in defence of his country!"

On the 15th, the Senate resumed the consideration of the bill; the pending question being Mr. Sherman's amendment to restrict the emancipation clause to the slaves of rebels. "Slave-masters," said Mr. Pomeroy, "have no loyalty to brag of. I do not propose to give them a bond in advance, and pledge the Government, that, if we use one of their slaves, we shall pay for him." Mr. Howard opposed Mr. Sherman's amendment. "I confess," he said, "that I am entirely opposed to the incorporation of the amendment of the senator from Ohio, in whatever form it may assume, into the bill. I cannot bear the idea; and it seems to me, that, if I were a slaveholder, I could not bear the idea of employing or suffering my slaves to be employed in defending me and my rights as a loyal man, taking arms in their hands, and going with me into the face of the battle, and risking their lives to defend my life and my family and my rights under my government, and afterwards reducing those poor creatures to slavery. I should regard it as a burning and eternal shame. I never could do it. I do not care how lowly, how humble, how degraded a negro may be, if he takes his musket, or any other implement of war, and risks his life to defend me, my countrymen, my family, my government, my property, my liberties, my rights, against any foe, foreign or domestic, it is my duty under God, it is my duty as a man, as a lover of justice, to see to it that he shall be free." — "I do not," said Mr. Harlan, "remember a single example since civilization commenced, when slaves have been mustered into the armed service of a country, and again attempted to be returned to slavery." The question being taken on Mr. Sherman's amendment, by yeas and nays, resulted — yeas 18, nays 17. Mr. Browning moved to strike out the words, "his mother, and his wife and children." Mr. Harris supported the amendment; believing it an impracticable thing, that could not be carried into effect, to free the wives and children of slaves used in the military service. The question was taken by yeas and nays, on Mr. Browning's amendment, — yeas 17, nays 20 : so the amendment was rejected. Mr. Browning moved to amend the thirteenth section by adding to it, "that the mother, wife, and children of such man or boy of African descent shall not be made free by the operation of this act, except where such mother, wife, or children owe service or labor to some person, who, during the present Rebellion, has adhered to their enemies by giving them aid and comfort." Mr. Henderson earnestly supported the amendment, as just to loyal slaveholders. The question, being taken by yeas and nays, resulted — yeas 21, nays 16. Mr. Wright desired "to see every thing on God's earth taken by our generals that will assist in the prosecution of the war. A general in the army, who will not employ every negro that comes within his lines to work, to labor, should be turned out instantly." — "The Revolution," said Mr. Doolittle, "and the seven-years' war with Great Britain, was the first parturition of America. During that long period of throes and pains and agony and blood, she gave her first-born birth, — liberty, ay, liberty; but it was liberty for the white man, and not liberty for the black. Now again, in God's own time, and in a way that man knows not of, America is in the agonies of her second childbirth, praying to be delivered. In some way no human being can foresee, this war, forced upon the country by the madness and fanaticism of the South, will, as all hearts believe, never end until slavery is put in the process of final extinction; until liberty for the black man, the second offspring of America, shall be born." — "I am as confident," said Mr. Powell, "as that I live and speak to the Senate of the United States to-day, that the policy of arming slaves, which has been adopted in one bill that has passed both Houses of Congress, and is proposed in the bill now under consideration, is the most disastrous measure for the integrity of this Union that has been or can be before this Congress." The bill was ordered to be engrossed for a third reading, and was read the third time. On its passage, Mr. Saulsbury called for the yeas and nays, and they were ordered; and, being taken, resulted — yeas 28, nays 9 — as follows: —

YEAS. — Messrs. Anthony, Browning, Chandler, Clark, Cowan, Doolittle, Fessenden, Foot, Foster, Hale, Harlan, Harris, Howard,

Howe, King, Lane of Indiana, Lane of Kansas, Morrill, Pomeroy, Rice, Sherman, Simmons, Sumner, Ten Eyck, Wade, Wilkinson, Wilson of Massachusetts, and Wright, — 28.

Nays. — Messrs. Bayard, Carlile, Davis, Kennedy, Powell, Saulsbury, Stark, Willey, and Wilson of Missouri, — 9.

So the bill was passed by the Senate.

In the House, on the 16th of July, the bill was taken up; and Mr. Stevens (Rep.) of Pennsylvania demanded the previous question on its passage, and it was ordered. Mr. Holman (Dem.) of Indiana moved to lay it on the table. Mr. Allen (Dem.) of Illinois demanded the yeas and nays, — yeas 30, nays 77. The bill was then passed, and received the approval of the President on the 17th of July, 1862.

On the 10th of February, 1864, in the House of Representatives, Mr. Stevens (Rep.) of Pennsylvania moved to amend the Enrolment Act by striking out the twenty-seventh section, and inserting, in substance, "that all able-bodied male persons of African descent between the ages of twenty and forty-five, whether citizens or not, shall be enrolled and made a part of the national forces; and, when enrolled and drafted into the service, his master shall be entitled to receive three hundred dollars, and the drafted man shall be free." Mr. Boyd (Union) of Missouri suggested that Mr. Stevens modify his amendment, so as to pay only loyal masters; and it was so modified. Mr. Clay (Union) of Kentucky opposed the amendment. Mr. Boutwell (Rep.) of Massachusetts moved to strike out "three hundred dollars," and insert "twenty-five dollars." "I desire," said Mr. Boutwell, "to say, in reply to the gentleman from Kentucky, that we have reached that emergency when men in the Border

States should understand, at least so far as I am concerned, that slaves as inhabitants of the country are to be used as other men are used to put down this Rebellion. No constitution or law of any State shall stand between me and what I believe to be my duty to my country." Mr. Morris (Rep.) of New York and Mr. Creswell (Union) of Maryland advocated Mr. Stevens's amendment. Mr. Smithers (Rep.) of Delaware said the people of that State had no scruples in relation to using colored soldiers. Mr. Davis (Rep.) of Maryland moved to strike out the proposed compensation to the masters of drafted slaves. The slaves " owe duty to the Government; and, if they do, we owe the masters nothing for taking them." Mr. Mallory (Dem.) of Kentucky said that "property is held in slaves. I do not mean that the person of the slave is property, and can be used as property; that he can be killed, and eaten like a hog; but that men own property in the labor and service of slaves in this country. The amendment of the gentleman from Maryland ignores this right, violates it in a plain, distinct, and palpable manner, and is contrary to the Constitution of the United States."

On the 11th, the House resumed the consideration of the Enrolment Bill; the pending question being Mr. Davis's amendment to Mr. Stevens's amendment. Mr. Stevens accepted the amendment. Mr. Davis then moved to amend by adding, that " the Secretary of War shall appoint a commission in each of the slave States represented in Congress, charged to award a just compensation to each loyal owner of any slave who may volunteer into the service, payable out of the commutation money." Mr. Anderson (Union) of Kentucky was "in favor of taking the slaves of rebels in Kentucky, and of rebel sympathizers." Mr. Davis's amendment to the amendment was agreed to. Mr. Webster (Union) of Maryland moved to so amend Mr. Stevens's amendment as "to put the drafted man on the same footing with the volunteer slave." — "We do not," said Mr. Kelley (Rep.) of Pennsylvania, "give the Northern father compensation for his minor son who is drafted; we do not give the Northern wife compensation for the husband whose labor was her support, if he be drafted; we do not give the Northern orphan child compensation for having withdrawn the father whose labor was its support; we do not give compensation to the poor wife and child of a poor man of Maryland or Kentucky when the draft designates her husband or its father: and I cannot see that the relation of this slave-owner to his slave is one whit more sacred than that of the father to his son, the wife to her husband, or the child to its parent." — "I deny," said Mr. Harris (Dem.) of Maryland, "that you have a right to enlist or enroll a slave." Mr. Kasson (Rep.) of Iowa would vote to give compensation in the case of slaves volunteering: he was against giving compensation in case of drafted slaves. Mr. Baldwin (Rep.) of Massachusetts moved to amend the amendment by striking out the words, "owner of any slave," and inserting, "the person to whom the colored volunteer may owe service;" and the amendment to the amendment was adopted. Mr. Broomall (Rep.) of Pennsylvania moved that the section shall not apply to any district if the representative expressly ask that the slaves be exempt from draft, letting it fall the more heavily upon the white man. He was opposed to it; but he wanted a test-vote on this proposition. "I have never found," he declared, "the most snaky constituent of mine, who, when he was drafted, refused to let the blackest negro in the district go as a substitute for him." Mr. Broomall's amendment was rejected. Mr. Webster moved to amend, so that the bounty now paid to the drafted man shall be paid to the person to whom any drafted man may owe any service or labor, — ayes 67, nays 44. Mr. Clay was opposed to sending a recruiting officer into Kentucky: "It will create a civil war among us." Mr. Scofield (Rep.) of Pennsylvania said, "There were two conditions of slavery, — non-instruction to the slave; non-discussion by the white man. These are acknowledged to be the two safeguards of slavery by the statutes of almost every slave State where ignorance is commanded to the slave, and silence to the white man. . . . Slavery is surrounded by a cordon of missionary schools for the black man. In those schools, the slaves of all ages are taught not only what can be learned from books and charts, but also that they are, and of right ought to be, free, — made so by the laws of God and the President's proclamation; and that it is a duty they owe to God and the President to maintain that freedom. When God shall please again to bless the land with peace, shall the negro lay aside his military belt, and resume the master's collar? If the country would allow it, the master would not. He would as soon introduce to his plantation a person charged with some fatal infection as his former slave, filled with antislavery ideas and military skill. He might court his industry, but not his *demoralized will*. But the other safeguard of slavery — the silence of the white man — is broken also.

Discussion has opened in all the Border States, and can never again be hushed."

Mr. Fernando Wood (Dem.) of New York desired "to call attention to the fact, that, while we are discussing a measure clearly and palpably in violation of the Constitution, the Confederate House of Representatives is discussing measures of peace, re-union, and conciliation." Mr. Cox proposed to send Mr. Wood to Richmond to negotiate a peace based upon the old Union. Mr. Harding moved to amend the proposed amendment by adding, "that the provisions of this section in regard to slaves shall not apply to the State of Kentucky." Mr. Higby (Rep.) of California thought "the Government might go into every district, and take men to fill up the Union armies, no matter what the color of their skin." Mr. King (Dem.) of Missouri moved to amend, so that no slave could be recruited or drafted in any State which has passed an ordinance of emancipation. Mr. Davis, in reply to Mr. Harris, said, "The gentleman spoke of robbery. Sir, the advocates of slavery should seek some other term of reproach. Its origin was in robbery; and, if time and law have sanctioned it, they have not obliterated its historic origin."

Mr. Whalley (Union) of West Virginia moved to amend by adding, that the troops of African descent shall be organized into companies and regiments of their own color, and shall be commanded by white officers. Mr. Boutwell moved to strike out the words, "shall be commanded by white officers." He said, "It is an imputation on the white people of the country to say, that, in a fair contest, they are not able to maintain, socially, intellectually, and morally, the ascendency. . . . If, with the ascendency which twenty-five million white people have in a struggle with four million of an oppressed and degraded race, we are not able to maintain the ascendency, then, I say, surrender. I believe we are able to maintain that ascendency; but whatever positions these people show themselves capable of holding, with honor to themselves and advantage to the country, never shall my vote restrain them from obtaining." Mr. Boutwell withdrew his amendment, and Mr. Whalley's amendment was rejected. Mr. Rollins (Union) of Missouri moved to amend so that slaves who have enlisted shall be placed on the same footing as those that shall hereafter enlist, — ayes 52, nays 51. Mr. Harrington moved to insert the word "white" before the word "volunteers;" and it was rejected. Mr. Stevens's amendment as amended was adopted. By its provisions, colored men, whether free or slave, were to be enrolled and considered part of the national forces. The masters of slaves were to receive the hundred-dollar bounty to each drafted man on freeing their slaves.

The Enrolment Bill was referred to a Conference Committee, consisting of Mr. Wilson of Massachusetts, Mr. Nesmith of Oregon, and Mr. Grimes of Iowa, on the part of the Senate; and Mr. Schenck of Ohio, Mr. Deming of Connecticut, and Mr. Kernan of New York, on the part of the House. In the Conference Committee, Mr. Wilson stated that he never could assent to the amendment, unless the drafted slaves were made free on being mustered into the service of the United States. Mr. Grimes sustained that position; and the

House committee assented to it. The House amendment was then modified so as to read, "That all able-bodied male colored persons between the ages of twenty and forty-five years, whether citizens or not, resident in the United States, shall be enrolled according to the provisions of this act, and of the act to which this is an amendment, and form part of the national forces; and, when a slave of a loyal master shall be drafted and mustered into the service of the United States, his master shall have a certificate thereof; and thereupon such slave shall be free; and the bounty of a hundred dollars, now payable by law for each drafted man, shall be paid to the person to whom such drafted person was owing service or labor at the time of his muster into the service of the United States. The Secretary of War shall appoint a commission in each of the slave States represented in Congress, charged to award, to each loyal person to whom a colored volunteer may owe service, a just compensation, not exceeding three hundred dollars, for each such colored volunteer, payable out of the fund derived from commutation; and every such colored volunteer, on being mustered into the service, shall be free."

The report of the Conference Committee was agreed to; and it was enacted that every slave, whether a drafted man or a volunteer, shall be free on being mustered into the military service of the United States, not by the act of the master, but by the authority of the Federal Government.

CHAPTER XII.

AID TO THE STATES TO EMANCIPATE THEIR SLAVES.

MR. WILSON'S JOINT RESOLUTION. — HOUSE COMMITTEE ON EMANCIPATION. — MR. WHITE'S BILL.— MR. WILSON'S RESOLUTION. — MR. HENDERSON'S BILL. — MR. NOELL'S BILL. — MR. WHITE'S REPORT. — REMARKS OF MR. CLEMENTS. — MR. WICKLIFFE. — MR. NOELL. — PASSAGE OF THE BILL. — HOUSE BILL REPORTED BY MR. TRUMBULL. — REMARKS OF MR. HENDERSON. — MR. WILSON'S AMENDMENT. — REMARKS OF MR. FESSENDEN. — MR. TRUMBULL. — MR. FOSTER. — MR. WILSON. — MR. SHERMAN. — MR. COWAN. — MR. BAYARD. — MR. CLARK. — MR. LANE OF KANSAS. — MR. MORRILL. — MR. WILSON'S AMENDMENT. — MR. GRIMES'S SPEECH. — MR. KENNEDY'S SPEECH. — MR. HARRIS'S REPORT. — MR. WILSON OF MISSOURI. — MR. WALL'S SPEECH. — MR. RICHARDSON'S AMENDMENT. — MR. COLLAMER'S AMENDMENT. — MR. SUMNER'S AMENDMENT. — REMARKS OF MR. POWELL. — MR. SUMNER'S AMENDMENT. — MR. SUMNER'S SPEECH. — PASSAGE OF THE BILL AS AMENDED. — MR. WHITE'S REPORT IN THE HOUSE. — BILL REFERRED TO COMMITTEE OF THE WHOLE.

IN the Senate, on the 7th of March, 1862, Mr. Wilson (Rep.) of Massachusetts asked leave to introduce a joint resolution to grant aid to the States of Maryland and Delaware to emancipate certain persons held to service or labor. It provided, that in case the States of Maryland and Delaware, within two years, shall enact that all persons held to service within those States shall be discharged from all claim to such service, and that neither slavery nor involuntary servitude shall thereafter exist in those States, the President may issue and deliver to those States the bonds of the United States, payable in twenty-five years, to an amount equal to two hundred and fifty dollars for each person so discharged and freed from service or labor. Mr. Saulsbury objected, and the resolution was not acted upon.

On the 10th, the Vice-President stated, that, "on Friday, the senator from Massachusetts (Mr. Wilson) sent to the chair a joint resolution, and it was objected to by the senator from Delaware (Mr. Saulsbury). It being a joint resolution, the objection of the senator from Delaware precluded its reception. It is now in order for the senator to renew it, if he chooses so to do." Mr. Wilson asked leave to introduce his joint resolution to grant aid to the States of Maryland and Delaware to emancipate their slaves. "I intend," said Mr. Saulsbury, "to object to the proposition in every stage, and fight it at every stage: I shall make all objections at all stages that I have a right to make." Mr. Wilson said he did not understand that it required unanimous consent, as he had given notice more than a week ago. The Vice-President stated that "the senator from Massachusetts did on Friday send to the chair the joint resolution, and the title was read. The chair rules that that was notice; and therefore the senator is entitled to ask leave to introduce his resolution to-day, under the notice already given." Leave was granted to Mr. Wilson to introduce his joint resolution; and it was read, and passed to a second reading.

In the House, on the 7th of April, 1862, Mr. White (Rep.) of Indiana introduced a resolution for the appointment of a select committee of nine members — the chairman and a majority of whom shall be members from the States of Delaware, Maryland, Virginia, Kentucky, Tennessee, and Missouri — to inquire and report whether any plan can be prepared and recommended for the gradual emancipation of all the African slaves and the extinction of slavery in those States by the people or local authorities. Mr. Roscoe Conkling (Rep.) of New York suggested the modification of the resolution, so as not to restrict the chair in the appointment of the committee; and Mr. White so modified his resolution. Mr. Mallory (Dem.) of Kentucky denounced the resolution as "an unconstitutional absurdity," and moved that it be laid on the table. Mr. Cox (Dem.) of Ohio demanded the yeas and nays on Mr. Mallory's motion, and they were taken, — yeas 51, nays 68. Mr. Vallandigham called for the yeas and nays on the passage of the resolution, — yeas 67, nays 52: so the resolution was passed. On the 14th of April, the Speaker announced as the select committee on the subject of gradual emancipation in the slaveholding States, — Messrs. Albert S. White of Indiana, Francis P. Blair of Missouri, George P. Fisher of Delaware, William E. Lehman of Pennsylvania, C. L. L. Leary of Maryland, K. V. Whaley of Virginia, James F. Wilson of Iowa, Samuel L. Casey of Kentucky, and Andrew J. Clements of Tennessee.

On the 16th of July, Mr. White, from the Select Committee on Emancipation, reported a bill granting the aid of the United States to certain States, upon the adoption by them of a system of emancipation, and to provide for the colonization of free negroes, accompanied by a report. The bill provided, that whenever the President shall be satisfied that any one of the States of Delaware, Maryland, Virginia, Kentucky, Tennessee, or Missouri, shall have emancipated the slaves therein, it shall be the duty of the President to deliver to such State an amount of bonds of the United States, payable at thirty years, equal to the aggregate value of all slaves within such State at the rate of three hundred dollars for each slave,—the whole amount for any one State to be delivered at once if the emancipation shall be immediate, or in ratable instalments if it shall be gradual; that no State shall make any compensation to the owner of any slave who shall be proved to have willingly engaged in or in any manner aided the present Rebellion. Mr. White, by unanimous consent, explained the action of the committee. "I will only add," he said, "that this measure has passed the committee with great unanimity; the slight dissent of any member being more to detail than to principle. It is addressed, not to the politician of an hour, but to historic men, conscious of the peril of their country, who know that great sacrifices must be made to save it, and look upon this as the most hopeful, as it will be the noblest, in its results." The bill was ordered to be printed, and referred to the Committee of the Whole on the State of the Union.

In the Senate, on the 8th of December, 1862, Mr. Wilson of Massachusetts introduced a resolution, instructing the Committee on Military Affairs to consider the expediency of providing by law for more effectually suppressing the Rebellion and securing domestic tranquillity in the State of Missouri. On the 19th, Mr. Henderson (Union) of Missouri introduced a bill granting aid to that State to emancipate the slaves therein; which was referred to the Judiciary Committee.

In the House, on the 15th, Mr. Noell (Union) of Missouri introduced a bill to secure the abolishment of slavery in the State of Missouri, and to provide compensation to loyal persons therein who own slaves; which was referred to the Select Committee on Emancipation. On the 22d, Mr. White, chairman of the committee, asked the consent of the House to report Mr. Noell's bill relative to the abolishment of slavery in Missouri, with a view to having it printed and recommitted. Mr. Vallandigham (Dem.) of Ohio objecting, Mr. White moved the suspension of the rules, — yeas 77, nays 36. Mr. Noell, on the 6th of January, 1863, reported back from the select committee, without amendment, his bill giving aid to Missouri, for the purpose of securing the abolishment of slavery therein. Mr. Vallandigham raised a point of order on the reception of the bill, which the Speaker overruled. The bill provided that the Government of the United States will, upon the passage by the State of Missouri of a good and valid act of emancipation of all the slaves therein, and to be irrepealable unless by the consent of the United States, apply the sum of ten million dollars in United-States bonds, redeemable in thirty years from their date.

Mr. Clements (Union) of Tennessee did intend to make a minority report, but was not aware the bill was to be reported : hence he desired to make an explanation. He was in favor of a general act to aid emancipation in the Border slave States ; but he thought the bill alone, by itself, "to be of a sectional character," and "for that reason I oppose it." — "I have seen it stated," said Mr. Wickliffe (Opp.) of Kentucky, "in the public prints, that, before the issuing of the President's proclamation, he received information from intelligent, unconditional Union men of Kentucky, which satisfied him that there was a great change in public sentiment among the people of Kentucky, and especially in the Union party, in favor of these miserable abolition schemes. I feel it my duty and my privilege to state on this floor, in the face of Heaven, in the presence of the Congress of the United States, and in the hearing of the nation, that there is not one in every three hundred men in Kentucky who is in favor of such a measure, or of the proclamation." The result of a measure for the emancipation of slaves in the Border States, by the aid of the national treasury, "would, in my judgment," said Mr. Clements, "deserve the thanks of all mankind; as it would, I believe, relieve our country, in time, of one of the greatest evils that disturb our national quietude." Mr. Noell advocated his bill as a just, wise, and beneficent measure. "I am aware," he said, "that some of the public men in my own State believe that that sum is not large enough. I differ from them in opinion on that point. . . . I believe that ten million dollars will be amply sufficient to pay for every slave of loyal owners at the rate of three hundred dollars each." Mr. Noell demanded the previous question. Mr. Price (Dem.) of Missouri asked Mr. Noell to withdraw it, to allow him to offer an amendment. Mr. Noell declared, if the amendment was to increase the amount named in the bill, he could not admit it. Mr. Price avowed that it did increase the amount. Mr. Holman (Dem.) of Indiana moved to lay the bill on the table, and demanded the yeas and nays. They were ordered, — yeas 42, nays 73. The question being on the passage of the bill, it was decided in the affirmative, — yeas 73, nays 46.

In the Senate, on the 14th of January, Mr. Trumbull reported back from the Judiciary Committee Mr. Henderson's bill, with a recommendation that it be indefinitely postponed; and the Senate concurred in the recommendation of the committee. Mr. Trumbull reported back from the committee Mr. Noell's House bill, with an amendment. On the 16th, on motion of Mr. Henderson, the Senate proceeded to the consideration of the House bill giving aid to Missouri for the abolishment of slavery; the question pending being upon the amendment reported by the Committee on the Judiciary to strike out all after the enacting clause of the bill, and insert, "That whenever satisfactory evidence shall be presented to the President of the United States that the State of Missouri has adopted a law, ordinance, or other provision, for the gradual or immediate emancipation of all the slaves therein, and the exclusion of slavery for ever thereafter from said State, it shall be his duty to prepare, and deliver to the Governor of said State, as hereinafter provided, to be used by said State to compensate for the inconveniences produced by such change of system, bonds of the United States to the amount of twenty million dollars, the same to bear interest at the rate of five per cent per annum, and payable thirty years after the date thereof." Mr. Henderson said this bill was substantially the one he introduced. "The decree had gone forth, that slavery must be destroyed. It is needless to argue that Missouri is beyond the limits of this decree. It is not beyond the influence of your past legislation, nor is it beyond the influence of events far more powerful than acts of legislation. . . . It is the best possible economy for the Government. If, in any manner, Missouri is held responsible for this state of things, she now presents her regrets. If it be charged that her admission into the Union gave origin to this unfortunate feud, she may at least claim the honor of fidelity to her pledge in the darkest hour of the nation's existence. If it be said that slavery is the cause of this Rebellion, she answers by placing slavery upon the altar of the country." On the 30th of January, the bill, on motion of Mr. Trumbull, was considered. "To carry out the pledge," said Mr. Sherman (Rep.) of Ohio, "we made one year ago, I am willing to vote ten million dollars in bonds of the United States to the State of Missouri. I will not vote for any more." — "We cannot," replied Mr. Henderson, "emancipate in the State of Missouri, under our Constitution, without paying the owners for their property. If we undertake to liberate at all, we are bound to pay." Mr. Wilson (Dem.) of Missouri gave notice that he should move to increase the amount. "I am ready," said Mr. Wilson of Massachusetts, "to give my vote to tax the toiling men of my State — to tax the farmers, the mechanics, the merchants, the fishermen on the coasts of New England — to blot slavery out of the State. Yes, sir: I am ready to tax my own barren New England so as to more effectually crush out this Rebellion, give domestic tranquillity, increase of population and of wealth, to that great Empire State of the West. I shall vote the money of Massachusetts with all my heart for emancipation in Missouri; but, sir, it must be emancipation now or within a few years. I care far less for the money than for the time. I am for making it a free State with free influences in my day and generation."

Mr. Wilson moved to amend the amendment proposed by the committee by inserting in lieu of it, "that whenever satisfactory evidence shall be presented to the President of the United States that either of the States of Missouri, Maryland, Delaware, or West Virginia, has adopted a law, ordinance, or other provision, for the emancipation of all the slaves therein, and for the exclusion of slavery for ever thereafter from such State, it shall be his duty to prepare, and deliver to the Governor of such State as shall so provide, — to the Governor of Missouri eighteen million dollars, to the Governor of Maryland eighteen million dollars, to the Governor of Delaware three hundred thousand dollars, and to the Governor of West Virginia one million five hundred thousand dollars, — bonds of the United States, bearing interest at the rate of five per cent per annum, and payable thirty years after the date thereof." Mr. Fessenden (Rep.) of Maine said, "I confess that I am somewhat surprised at the change that has been made by the Committee on the Judiciary in the bill passed by the House of Representatives. I rose, sir, to suggest that the bill before us is better than the proposed substitute, because it is satisfactory to the House of Representatives, satisfactory to the representative from the State of Missouri who introduced and advocated it; is less in amount, — proposing to appropriate only half as much, and yet, in my judgment, a sufficient amount."

Mr. Henderson made an earnest and eloquent appeal for prompt action. "Now is the moment," he asserted; "now is the accepted time. If ever you intend to do any thing to carry out your pledges that you are opposed to the institution of slavery, now is that time." Mr.

Trumbull explained the bill, and defended the action of the committee. "This bill," he said, "proposes that slavery shall cease once and for ever after thirteen years. That is the object of it. The object of it is to insure freedom, and not perpetuate slavery. I would be glad if the shackles could fall from every slave, not only in Missouri, but throughout the United States and the world, to-day; but, sir, I cannot accomplish it." Mr. Foster (Rep.) of Connecticut made an able and effective speech in favor of the substitute of the committee. He said, "In my opinion, Mr. President, no more grave question can be raised in this body. I think the decision of that question affects directly, more directly than any other question before us, the existence and perpetuity of the Government of the United States; I will add, than any other question which in the ordinary course of legislation can be brought before us. I will not say that the existence and perpetuity of the Union depend upon the manner in which that question may be decided; but I will say, that if it be decided to make this State a free State, and we actually make it a free State, we do more to perpetuate the existence of the Republic than we can do in any other one way." Mr. Wilson of Massachusetts, in response to Mr. Henderson, said, "I assure the senator from Missouri, to whose earnest tones I have listened to-day with unmixed pleasure, whose devotion to the country we all so fully applaud, that I am ready to vote any reasonable sum from the treasury of the nation to make Missouri free, — free now, when freedom will bring to her law, order, and tranquillity. I admit that it is important to take the first step; and if this were a proposition to aid a State situated like

Kentucky or Tennessee, then I should regard the first step as every thing gained : but for a great State like Missouri, with so few slaves, a State that has such mighty interests to become free at once, the proposition is one that we ought not to entertain ; and I hope it will be voted down by the Senate of the United States. Let us stamp upon her now war-desolated fields the words, ' Immediate emancipation,' and these blighted fields will bloom again, and law and order and peace will again bless the dwellings of her people." — " I want to say," remarked Mr. Pomeroy (Rep.) of Kansas, "that I think Missouri is destined to become a free State at any rate. You cannot keep slavery in Missouri thirteen years without a standing army."

On the 30th of January, the Senate, as in Committee of the Whole, resumed the consideration of the bill. "I believe," said Mr. Sherman, "that the condition of slavery as a fixed and permanent relation in Missouri tends to keep up civil war in the State; and that, the very moment she enters upon the path of gradual emancipation, all her sympathies and all her interests will be opposed to the present Rebellion, and in favor of the preservation of the Union. It is to accomplish this purpose, to create a spirit in the State of Missouri in favor of the perpetuity of the Union, that I am willing to vote the money of the people of Ohio to aid in this object. That can be accomplished better by gradual emancipation than by immediate emancipation." — " I should like to ask the senator from Ohio," said Mr. Cowan (Rep.) of Pennsylvania, " if a scheme of gradual emancipation be adopted, where would be the necessity for an appropriation at all ? I understand that the usual mode by which that is effected is by declaring the children, born after a certain time fixed, free." — "The right to the increase of slaves is now," replied Mr. Sherman, "under the local law, a property right, and that is estimated at a certain proportion of the value of the slaves. I should be willing to contribute from the treasury of the United States to the State of Missouri the value of that property right, according to their local law." — "The right," said Mr. Cowan, "remains in the State perfect over the condition of the children yet unborn." Mr. Wilson of Massachusetts, in reply to Mr. Sherman, said, " The senator from Ohio speaks with much feeling of the extreme views of some of us who desire, in contributing of the public money to make Missouri a free State, to give the priceless boon of personal freedom to her hundred thousand bondmen. The senator earnestly deprecates such radicalism as cares for the rights and interests of the slave. He announces that he is willing to tax the people of America to pay for children not yet born; no, not yet begotten. I am not. The senator talks of our extreme views, of our radicalism; while he accepts the abhorrent dogma, that slave-masters have a right to the unborn, unbegotten issue of their slaves, — a right he is willing to tax the people of Ohio to pay. I, sir, give no such vote. I will never consent to tax the people of Massachusetts to pay for unborn children twenty-two years hence." Mr. Henderson said, that, if a bill offering ten million dollars and immediate emancipation were passed, "I for one, though I as earnestly desire emancipation as any man in Missouri, will ask the Legislature of that State not to accept it. That is plain and honest.

In that event, I shall ask the Legislature of the State of Missouri, however, to adopt a gradual system of emancipation upon their own hook." — " I would not," said Mr. Bayard (Dem.) of Delaware, "throw a straw in the road of the people of Missouri, if it is the will of the people of that State to abolish slavery within its limits, either now or at a future day; but I am unable to find in the Constitution of the United States any authority for Congress interfering with that institution, or making an appropriation to aid any State for the purpose of emancipation."

Mr. Henderson said, "I now move in line twenty-one to strike out 'seventy-six,' and insert 'eighty-five,' so as to read, 'some day not later than the fourth day of July, 1885.'" — "That will allow," remarked Mr. Howard (Rep.) of Michigan, "to the State of Missouri the period of twenty-two years within which to bring about emancipation. It seems to me that that is an unnecessarily long period. 1876 will be a great epoch in the history of this nation, as I trust, if the people are true to themselves, true to their own interests, true to that tutelary Constitution under which we have lived and prospered for eighty long years past. I shall expect, if I shall have the good fortune to survive until that day, to see the Constitution in its vigor and purity restored, and the Union restored, and to see not one foot of slave soil within the territorial limits of the United States. I hope, sir, to live to see that day. I expect to live to see that day; and I want, when that great day shall arrive, to have the pleasure of joining in its festivities, and listening to the roar of its cannon, and to the joyous shouts of the people of the whole United States, that not only Missouri, but every other slaveholding State, is that day, at least, free, redeemed, emancipated from the pestilence." — "I am opposed," said Mr. Clark (Rep.) of New Hampshire, "to the amendment of the senator from Missouri. I am, with the senator from Michigan, willing to keep in good faith the resolution adopted by the Senate and House of Representatives at the last session. I am willing to aid any State in the gradual emancipation or in the immediate emancipation of its slaves; but I am not willing that we should bear, as the senator from Missouri intimates we should, the whole of this burden." Mr. Henderson said, "I hope that the amendment I propose will be adopted. There are some senators here, like the senator from Ohio (Mr. Sherman), who insist that emancipation must be gradual in my State. He cannot vote for any proposition of emancipation unless it is gradual. He does not want any immediate emancipation. The senator from Massachusetts (Mr. Wilson), with the very same integrity of purpose, with the same desire to accomplish the purpose, says he must have it immediate; and so says the senator from New Hampshire. If the bill is to fall between the contrariety of opinion that I find here, let it fall at once." Mr. Clark replied, that he was willing to give more to have it immediate, but was willing to give ten millions for gradual emancipation. He would propose an amendment giving fifteen million dollars for immediate emancipation, or ten million dollars for emancipation on the 4th of July, 1876." — "I should," said Mr. Lane (Rep.) of Kansas, "like to ask the senator from New Hampshire, if in time of peace the question was asked him, 'How much money will the people of New Hampshire give to extend the area of freedom over sixty-five thousand square miles of this country?' what his answer would be. I think I know the people of New Hampshire well enough to know that the answer would be, 'It is not to be estimated by dollars and cents.'"—"In requiring," said Mr. Wilson, "that a practical measure that shall secure the object intended shall be adopted, I have no fear of being accused of illiberality or of want of fidelity to the cause of the slave. I have a record, sir, of twenty-seven years; and no vote of mine during those years, for men or for measures or for principles, has been in support of slavery." Mr. Foster would stand by the amendment of the committee. "The only difference of opinion is that it appropriates more money than may be necessary: but the mistake of a few millions too much is not fatal; the mistake of a few millions below the point will be fatal." Mr. Morrill (Rep.) of Maine said, "If Missouri, that great State lying in the centre of the continent, would speak the word, 'We are on this side in this great contest; we are on the side of freedom, free men, and free labor,' it would be worth ten million dollars to have the word spoken, and to have it spoken now, and would place that State on the side of the Government of the country." The presiding officer: "The question recurs on the amendment of the senator from Missouri, to strike out 'seventy-six,' and insert 'eighty-five.'" Mr. Wilson said, "I want the privilege of voting to give ten million dollars for emancipation in 1876; so that the alternative presented to the people of Missouri will be this: Emancipation in 1865, twenty million dollars; emancipation in 1876, ten million dollars." — " I move," said Mr. Clark, "to fill the blank with ten million dollars; and on that amendment I will ask for the yeas and nays." The yeas and nays were ordered. Mr. Clark said, "The effect of the amendment will be precisely this, as I understand it: We pay twenty million dollars for immediate emancipation by 1865, and pay ten million dollars for gradual emancipation in 1876." The question, being taken by yeas and nays, resulted — yeas 16, nays 21. "I now move," said Mr. Wilson of Massachusetts, "to amend the amendment of the committee by striking out all after the word 'that,' and inserting the following: 'Whenever satisfactory evidence shall be presented to the President of the United States that the State of Missouri has adopted a law, ordinance, or other provision, for the emancipation of all the slaves therein, and for the exclusion of slavery for ever thereafter from the State, it shall be his duty to prepare and deliver to the Governor of Missouri twenty million dollars in bonds of the United States, bearing interest at the rate of five per cent per annum, and payable thirty years after the date thereof, to be used by that State to compensate for the inconveniences produced by such change of system.'" Mr. Grimes (Rep.) of Iowa moved to strike out "twenty million dollars," and insert "ten million dollars." — "I am willing," he remarked, "to go before the people of my State, and undertake to justify — I believe I shall be justified in making an appropriation of ten million dollars to create freedom, and only freedom, in the State of Missouri, from and after 1865. I am willing to take the responsibility of giving that vote, and stand the test before the freemen of Iowa; but informed as I am in regard to the condition of slavery in Missouri, knowing as little as I do of the number of slaves within the State, and of their value, I am unwilling at this time to vote more than ten million dollars."

Mr. Wilson of Massachusetts said, "One proposition is to put twenty million dollars in the pockets of the slaveholders, and give freedom to the slaves on the 4th of July, 1865: the other proposition is to give ten million dollars, and extend the time twelve years, — to 1876. One proposition fills the slaveholders' pockets with our money at once, gives freedom to the bondman, and brings content and peace there: the other proposition puts off emancipation for twelve years, and blasts the hopes of thousands of these people, and makes them discontented; and they will run away whenever they can." Mr. Lane of Kansas declared, "So far as the blacks are concerned, they will be practically as free under an act of gradual emancipation to take effect in 1876 as under an act to take effect in 1865. . . . I assure the senator from Massachusetts, with some knowledge of the subject of which I speak, that an emancipation bill to take full effect in 1876, so far as the black is concerned, is as potent in securing him freedom as an act to take effect in 1865." — "I confess I am surprised," replied Mr. Wilson of Massachusetts, "that the senator from Kansas, who has such practical views on these questions, and is so earnest in the cause, can think that these slaves, who are now kept under chain, to prevent whose running away, as he admits, armed men have to traverse the State, would be contented with an act promising them freedom thirteen years hence. Pass an act to make them all free in two years, and they will be contented at once. They will shout for joy, and offer up prayers to Almighty God for our action and the action of the emancipationists: but if you pass an act that they shall not be free for thirteen years, and that, in the mean time, they may be worked for nothing, sold, sent out of the State, and, if they run away, the Fugitive-slave Law may be brought to bear to bring them back, they will not be contented; they will be turbulent. The very hopes of freedom, thus baffled, will excite them to action, and they will run away; and there will be discontent and trouble in that State on the part of master and slave." Mr. Kennedy (Dem.) of Maryland was opposed to all these measures. "Let us alone. The laws of political economy, of inevitable destiny, are working out a remedy for slavery there. Do not trammel us with questions that may precipitate issues that we cannot control, and which may involve our beloved State in the most horrid scenes of fratricidal war."

On the amendment of the Committee on the Judiciary, by Mr. Harris, to strike out all after the enacting clause, and insert an amendment giving twenty million dollars for immediate emancipation, Mr. Wilson of Missouri moved to strike out "twenty million," and insert "twenty-five million" dollars, — yeas 2, nays 36. Mr. Davis spoke in opposition to the bill. Mr. Turpie (Dem.) of Indiana followed in opposition to the measure and the policy of the Administration. "Do senators," he asked, "still desire to continue to agitate this most odious doctrine of interference with the sovereignty of the States? Do they still desire to continue to agitate this dangerous and disgraceful element in the political history of the country? If they do, let them vote for the Missouri bill." Mr. Wall (Dem.) of New Jersey opposed the bill. He said, "The President of the United States, in his message, told the country that history would never forget him nor this Congress. Sir, I do not think it will. As Sir Charles Townshend once said to Lord Thurlow, who was an exceedingly profane man, when, in a burst of enthusiasm upon the floor of Parliament, he said, 'If I forget my sovereign, may my God forget me!' 'No, no,' said the witty Townshend: 'he will see you damned first!' And that, senators, I am afraid will be our condition with history, if we go on passing these enormous acts."

Mr. Ten Eyck (Rep.) of New Jersey addressed the Senate in favor of putting "the bill in such a shape that we may vote to aid the State of Missouri, and thus establish a precedent for the other States that may ask for assistance in the gradual abolition of slavery." Mr. Richardson (Dem.) of Illinois opposed the bill. "The Attorney-General," he said, "at the instance of the President, gives an opinion, announcing, for the first time from any national official position in this country, that Africans born here are citizens; disregarding the decision of the Supreme Court of the United States in the Dred Scott case, — the highest legal tribunal in the land. . . . The President wanted this opinion for some purpose. What was that purpose? Evidently for the advantage and benefit of the 'free American of African descent.' He has thought of nothing else, wrote of nothing else, talked of nothing else, dreamed of nothing else, since his election to the Presidency; and I fear he will think of nothing else until our Union is dissolved, our Constitution destroyed, and our nationality lost."

Mr. Wilson of Missouri moved to amend by inserting as a new section : 'That no part of the bonds herein specified shall be delivered until the act of the Legislature or the Constitutional Convention of the State of Missouri, providing for the emancipation of the slaves in said State, shall be submitted to a vote of the people, and approved by a majority of the legal voters of said State." Mr. Henderson opposed the amendment; and Mr. Powell and Mr. Saulsbury advocated it. The question, being taken by yeas and nays, resulted — yeas 13, nays 27.

"I am," said Mr. Harris, "an ardent friend of the measure proposed by this bill. I regard it as the most important measure that has been presented to the consideration of the Senate during its present session. Forty years ago, sir, the first great conflict between slavery and freedom took place in reference to the admission of the State of Missouri. In that conflict, slavery was successful. It secured a predominance of political power which was never effectually checked until the election of 1860. I desire exceedingly, that, in reference to this very State, we should begin to roll back the tide of slavery. There is peculiar fitness in it; but, sir, I see from the discussions here to-day that there is danger that this great and important measure may fail on account of some division of its friends in reference to the details. Apprehending that, and desiring to avoid it, I propose to make one further effort to prepare a bill which shall harmonize the friends of the measure of emancipation in Missouri; and, with a view to that, I move that the bill itself, with the proposition of the senator from Massachusetts, be recommitted to the Committee on the Judiciary." The motion was agreed to.

Mr. Harris, on the 2d of February, reported back from the Judiciary Committee the bill, with amendments. On the 6th, Mr. Henderson moved to take up the bill; and the motion was agreed to. On the 7th, the Senate resumed its consideration. Mr. Richardson moved that each one of the bonds issued by virtue of the provisions of this act shall have indorsed on the back thereof, in writing, as follows: "This bond was issued for the purpose of paying for slaves emancipated in the State of Missouri," — yeas 13, nays 27. Mr. Dixon (Rep.) of Connecticut moved to strike out "twenty million," and insert "eleven million" dollars, — yeas 14, nays 24. Mr. Collamer (Rep.) of Vermont moved to strike out "twenty million," and insert "fifteen million" dollars, — yeas 15, nays 21. Mr. Sumner (Rep.) of Massachusetts moved to strike out "1876," and insert "1864." — "I move," he said, "to strike out 'seventy-six,' and insert 'sixty-four,' so that the act of emancipation shall go into operation on the fourth day of July, 1864; and, sir, my reason for the amendment is this: this bill, as I understand it, is a bill of peace; it is to bring tranquillity to a disturbed State. . . . Sir, for the sake of the United States at this moment, for the sake of Missouri herself, for the sake of every slave-master in Missouri, and for the sake of every slave, I insist that this proposition shall go into execution at the nearest possible day. The testimony of reason, of common sense, and of history, is uniform in that direction; and I challenge any contradiction to it."

Mr. Willey (Union) of Virginia thought it would be much better for Missouri and for the slave, if, instead of "1876," it was "1900." Mr. Wilson of Missouri understood Mr. Sumner to desire to strike out "1876," "for the purpose of forcing immediate emancipation;" and therefore he could not vote for it. Mr. Henderson wished to stand by the bill as reported by the Committee on the Judiciary. Mr. Davis spoke at great length in opposition to the bill and amendment. In the course of his speech, he declared that "the negroes are reclaimed savages, and you want to put them in a position where they will relapse into savagism." — "Allow me to suggest," remarked Mr. Grimes, "that it cannot be possible that this race, after they have been under the humanizing effects of 'the domestic institution' as it is enjoyed by the State of Kentucky, can be regarded in the same light with the savages whose employment Lord Chatham denounced." The question, being taken by yeas and nays on Mr. Sumner's amendment, resulted — yeas 11, nays 26. Mr. Powell denounced the bill. "Is there," he asked, "any morality in it? What kind of morals is that, that will take from the people of a State, against their will, their property, not for the purpose of benefiting the State, but for the purpose of gratifying the fanatical zeal of a party temporarily in power?"

On the 12th, the Senate resumed the consideration of the bill, and Mr. Saulsbury spoke in opposition to the measure. Mr. Sumner moved to amend the amendment by striking out "three hundred," and inserting "two hundred" dollars, as the measure of value of slaves, — yeas 19, nays 17. Mr. Sumner then moved to strike out the words "gradual or," in section one, so that the money will be paid on evidence of "the immediate emancipation of all slaves therein." The question, being taken by yeas and nays, resulted — yeas 11, nays 27.

Mr. Sumner moved to amend the House bill by striking out "ten million," and inserting "twenty million" dollars. On motion of Mr. Fessenden, the yeas and nays were taken, — yeas 3, nays 37. The question recurring on the amendment reported by Mr. Harris to the House bill, Mr. Sumner closed the debate in a brief, concise, and eloquent speech. He said, "Procrastination is the thief, not only of time, but of virtue itself; but such is the nature of man, that he is disposed always to delay, so that he does nothing to-day which he can put off till to-morrow. Perhaps in no single matter has this disposition been more apparent than with regard to slavery. Every consideration of humanity, justice, religion, reason, common sense, and history, all demanded the instant cessation of an intolerable wrong, without procrastination or delay. But human nature would not yield; and we have been driven to argue the question, whether an outrage, asserting property in man, denying the conjugal relation, annulling the parental relation, shutting out human improvement, and robbing its victim of all the fruits of his industry, — the whole, in order to compel work without wages, — should be stopped instantly or gradually. It is only when we regard slavery in its essential elements, and look at its unutterable and unquestionable atrocity, that we can fully comprehend the mingled folly and wickedness of this question. If it were merely a question of economy or a question of policy, then the Senate might properly debate whether the change should be instant or gradual; but considerations of economy and policy are all absorbed in the higher claims of justice and humanity. There is no question whether justice and humanity shall be immediate or gradual. . . . If you would contribute to the strength and glory of the United States; if you would bless Missouri; if you would benefit the slave-master; if you would elevate the slave; and, still further, if you would afford an example which shall fortify and sanctify the Republic, making it at once citadel and temple, — do not put off the day of freedom. In this case, more than in any other, he gives twice who quickly gives."

The question was on Mr. Harris's substitute; and, being taken by yeas and nays, resulted — yeas 26, nays 10. So the amendment as amended was concurred in. The question was then taken on the passage of the bill as amended, — yeas 23, nays 18. So the bill was passed by the Senate.

In the House of Representatives, when the bill was taken from the Speaker's table, Mr. Norton (Dem.) of Missouri raised the point of order, that the bill must have its first consideration in the Committee of the Whole on the State of the Union. The Speaker ruled that the point of order was well taken. Mr. White (Rep.) of Indiana, Chairman of the Select Committee on Emancipation, moved its reference to that committee. Mr. Vallandigham demanded the yeas and nays on the motion of reference, — yeas 81, nays 51. On the 3d of March, Mr. White, from the Select Committee, moved to suspend the rules, so that the House may proceed to the consideration of the bill to aid the State of Missouri in emancipation, reported from the Select Committee on Emancipation. The question was taken; and there were — yeas 63, nays 57; and it was decided in the negative, two-thirds not voting for the suspension of the rules. So the bill to aid Missouri in the emancipation of the slaves therein was lost in the House of Representatives in the closing hours of the Thirty-seventh Congress.

CHAPTER XIII.

AMENDMENT OF THE CONSTITUTION.

MR. ASHLEY'S BILL. — MR. WILSON'S JOINT RESOLUTION. — HOUSE COMMITTEE ON THE JUDICIARY. — MR. HENDERSON'S JOINT RESOLUTION. — MR. SUMNER'S RESOLUTION. — MR. HENDERSON'S AMENDMENT REPORTED WITH AN AMENDMENT. — REMARKS OF MR. TRUMBULL. — MR. WILSON. — MR. DAVIS'S AMENDMENT. — REMARKS OF MR. SAULSBURY. — MR. CLARK. — MR. HOWE. — MR. JOHNSON. — MR. DAVIS'S AMENDMENTS. — MR. POWELL'S AMENDMENT. — REMARKS OF MR. HARLAN. — MR. HALE. — MR. M'DOUGALL. — MR. HENDRICKS. — MR. HENDERSON. — MR. SUMNER. — MR. SUMNER'S AMENDMENT. — REMARKS OF MR. TRUMBULL. — MR. HOWARD. — PASSAGE OF THE JOINT RESOLUTION IN THE SENATE. — MR. MORRIS'S SPEECH. — REMARKS OF MR. HERRICK. — MR. KELLOGG. — MR. PRUYN. — MR. WOOD. — MR. HIGBY. — MR. WHEELER'S AMENDMENT. — MR. KELLOGG OF MICHIGAN. — MR. ROSS. — MR. HOLMAN. — MR. THAYER. — MR. MALLORY. — MR. INGERSOLL. — MR. PENDLETON'S AMENDMENT. — JOINT RESOLUTION DEFEATED. — MR. ASHLEY'S MOTION TO RECONSIDER.

THE Speaker of the House of Representatives, on Monday the 14th of December, 1863, after announcing the standing committees, stated that the first business in order was the call of the States for bills and joint resolutions. When the State of Ohio was called, Mr. Ashley (Rep.), Chairman of the Committee on Territories, introduced a bill to provide for submitting to the States a proposition to amend the Constitution, prohibiting slavery. The proposed amendment declared that "slavery is hereby for ever prohibited in all the States of the Union, and in all Territories now owned, or which may hereafter be acquired, by the United States." Mr. William J. Allen (Dem.) of

Illinois demanded the reading of the bill, and it was read in full by the clerk. Mr. Ashley then moved its reference to the Committee on the Judiciary. Mr. Holman (Dem.) of Indiana objected to its second reading; but the Speaker overruled his point of order, and the bill was read twice, and referred to the Judiciary Committee.

When the State of Iowa was called, Mr. Wilson (Rep.), Chairman of the Committee on the Judiciary, introduced a joint resolution, submitting to the legislatures of the States this amendment to the Constitution: —

"SECT. 1. — Slavery, being incompatible with a free government, is for ever prohibited in the United States; and involuntary servitude shall be permitted only as a punishment for crime.

"SECT. 2. — Congress shall have power to enforce the foregoing section of this article by appropriate legislation."

Mr. Fernando Wood of New York, the acknowledged leader, in the House, of the peace Democrats, demanded the reading of the amendment; and it was read twice, and referred to the Judiciary Committee.

The Committee on the Judiciary, to whom the House committed the bill of Mr. Ashley and the joint resolution of Mr. Wilson, was made up, by Speaker Colfax, of five Republicans, three Democrats, and Ex-Governor Thomas of Maryland, who generally sustained the policy of the Administration. Mr. Wilson of Iowa, chairman of the committee, Ex-Governor Boutwell of Massachusetts, and Mr. Williams of Pennsylvania, were known to be earnest and uncompromising antislavery men; Mr. Woodbridge of Vermont and Mr. Morris of New York, though less known, were hardly less firm in adherence to the policy of emancipation; Ex-Governor King (Dem.) of Missouri had allied himself to the slave-preserving interests of his State; Mr. Bliss (Dem.) of Ohio was an avowed enemy of the emancipation policy of the Administration; and Mr. Kernan (Dem.) of New York, though an able lawyer and liberal legislator, was the personal associate and political adherent of Governor Seymour, and was generally regarded as too deeply interested in the aspirations and fortunes of his friend and leader always to follow the convictions of his judgment or the generous impulses of his heart. Ex-Governor Thomas of Maryland had recently committed himself to the policy of emancipation, and had allied himself to the party destined to make his native State a free commonwealth.

On the 11th of January, 1864, Mr. Henderson (Ind.) of Missouri introduced into the Senate a joint resolution, proposing an amendment to the Constitution, providing that slavery shall not exist in the United States. The proposed amendment was referred to the Committee on the Judiciary. That committee was composed of five Republicans, — Mr. Trumbull of Illinois, Mr. Foster of Connecticut, Mr. Ten Eyck of New Jersey, Mr. Harris of New York, and Mr. Howard of Michigan; and of two Democrats, — Mr. Bayard of Delaware and Mr. Powell of Kentucky.

Mr. Sumner of Massachusetts, on the 8th of February, introduced a joint resolution, providing that, "everywhere within the limits of the United States, and of each State or Territory thereof, all persons are equal before the law, so that no person can hold another as a slave." Mr. Sumner moved the reference of the resolution to the Select Committee on Slavery, of which he was chairman. Mr. Trumbull would refer it to the Committee on the Judiciary, that had under considertion the amendment introduced early in the session by Mr. Henderson of Missouri. Mr. Fessenden suggested that Mr. Trumbull move to amend the motion of reference so as to substitute the Committee on the Judiciary. Mr. Trumbull replied, that he had suggested that reference to the senator from Massachusetts, thinking he would give it that direction. Mr. Doolittle of Wisconsin had never before heard that an amendment to the Constitution was ever referred to any other than the Judiciary Committee, and he thought it clearly ought to go to that committee. Mr. Sumner thought the resolution under which the Select Committee on Slavery was raised broad enough to cover any proposition in regard to slavery; but if the senator from Illinois desired the resolution to go to the Judiciary Committee, of which that senator was the honored head, he should consent with the greatest pleasure. Mr. Saulsbury of Delaware moved the indefinite postponement of the resolution: eight senators voted yea, and thirty-one senators voted nay. The resolution was then referred to the Judiciary Committee.

On the 10th of February, Mr. Trumbull, from the Committee on the Judiciary, reported adversely on Mr. Sumner's resolution. At the same time, he made a report on the joint resolution originally introduced by Mr. Henderson, to strike out all after the resolving clause, and insert, —

"That the following article be proposed to the legislatures of the several States, as an amendment to the Constitution of the United States, which, when ratified by three-fourths of said legislatures, shall be valid, to all intents and purposes, as a part of the said Constitution; namely:—

"ART. 13, SECT. 1.— Neither slavery nor involuntary servitude, except as a punishment for crime, whereof the party shall have been duly convicted, shall exist within the United States, or any place subject to their jurisdiction.

"SECT. 2.— Congress shall have power to enforce this article by appropriate legislation."

On Monday, the 28th of March, the Senate, as in Committee of the Whole, proceeded to consider the joint resolution; the pending question being the amendment proposed by the Judiciary Committee to the original resolution introduced by Mr. Henderson. The chairman of the committee, Mr. Trumbull, opened the debate in a brief, clear, and comprehensive statement of the question. Speaking for the committee, he said, "I think, then, it is reasonable to suppose, that, if this proposed amendment passes Congress, it will, within a year, receive the ratification of the requisite number of States to make it a part of the Constitution. That accomplished, we are for ever freed of this troublesome question. We accomplish then what the statesmen of this country have been struggling to accomplish for years. We take this question entirely away from the politics of the country. We relieve Congress of sectional strifes; and, what is better than all, we restore to a whole race that freedom which is theirs by the gift of God, but which we for generations have wickedly denied them."

Mr. Wilson (Rep.) of Massachusetts followed Mr. Trumbull in advocacy of the proposed amendment. "The crowning act," he said, "in this series of acts for the restriction and extinction of slavery in America, is this proposed amendment to the Constitution, prohibiting the existence of slavery for evermore in the Republic of the United States. If this amendment shall be incorporated by the will of the nation into the Constitution of the United States, it will obliterate the last lingering vestiges of the slave system — its chattelizing, degrading, and bloody codes; its dark, malignant, barbarizing spirit; all it was and is; every thing connected with it or pertaining to it — from the face of the nation it has scarred with moral desolation, from the bosom of the country it has reddened with the blood and strewn with the graves of patriotism. The incorporation of this amendment into the organic law of the nation will make impossible for evermore the re-appearing of the discarded slave system, and the returning of the despotism of the slave-master's domination. Then, sir, when this amendment to the Constitution shall be consummated, the shackle will fall from the limbs of the hapless bondman, and the lash drop from the weary hand of the task-master. Then the sharp cry of the agonizing hearts of severed families will cease to vex the weary ear of the nation, and to pierce the ear of Him whose judgments are now avenging the wrongs of centuries. Then the slave mart, pen, and auction-block, with their clanking fetters for human limbs, will disappear from the land they have brutalized; and the schoolhouse will rise to enlighten the darkened intellect of a race imbruted by long years of enforced ignorance. Then the sacred rights of human nature, the hallowed family relations of husband and wife, parent and child, will be protected by the guardian spirit of that law which makes sacred alike the proud homes and lowly cabins of freedom. Then the scarred earth, blighted by the sweat and tears of bondage, will bloom again under the quickening culture of rewarded toil. Then the wronged victim of the slave system, the poor white man, the sand-hiller, the clay-eater, of the wasted fields of Carolina, impoverished, debased, dishonored by the system that makes toil a badge of disgrace, and the instruction of the brain and soul of man a crime, will lift his abashed forehead to the skies, and begin to run the race of improvement, progress, and elevation. Then the nation, 'regenerated and disinthralled by the genius of universal emancipation,' will run the career of development, power, and glory, quickened, animated, and guided by the spirit of the Christian democracy, that ' pulls not the highest down, but lifts the lowest up.' "

On the 30th, Mr. Davis of Kentucky addressed the Senate in opposition to the amendment, in a lengthy and discursive speech, in which he vehemently assailed the Administration. "The most effective single cause of the pending war," he avowed, "was the intermeddling of Massachusetts with the institution of slavery." He declared it to be an " objection of overruling weight, that no revision of the Constitution, in any form, ought to be undertaken under the auspices of the party in power." Mr. Davis closed his speech by the emphatic declaration, that "if the dominant party can continue their power and rule, either by the will or acquiescence of the people, or the exercise of the formidable powers which it has usurped, I am not able to see any termination of the present and still growing ills short of the ordeal of *general and bloody anarchy*." On the 3d of March, Mr. Davis had presented an amendment, in which he proposed that the States of Maine and Massachusetts should form and constitute one State of the United States, to be called East New England; and the States of New Hampshire, Rhode Island, Connecticut, and Vermont, should form and constitute one State of the United States, to be called West New England. This division of New England into two States — Maine and Massachusetts, separated by New Hampshire, constituting East New England; and New Hampshire and Vermont, Connecticut and Rhode Island, separated by Massachusetts, constituting West New England — seemed, to those familiar with the map of the country, to be rather an awkward geographical division. But, at the close of his speech, the senator from Kentucky, having doubtless extended his geographical researches, proposed a new arrangement, — that "the States of Maine, New Hampshire, and Vermont, are formed into and shall constitute one State of the United States, to be called North New England; and the States of Massachusetts, Connecticut, and Rhode Island, are formed into and constitute one State of the United States, to be called South New England." But this new geographical and political division of New England was not brought by its originator to the test of a vote of the Senate.

Mr. Saulsbury of Delaware followed on the 31st in opposition to the amendment, and in vindication of slavery on principle. "The Almighty," he said, "immediately after the Flood, condemned a whole race to servitude. He said, 'Cursed be Canaan.' Slavery continued among all people until the advent of the Christian era. It was recognized in the new dispensation which was to supersede the old. It has the sanction of God's own apostles; for, when Paul sent back Onesimus to Philemon, he sent his *doulos*, a slave born as such." Mr. Clark of New Hampshire followed Mr. Saulsbury, in a speech of much clearness and force, in favor of the amendment. "I am told," he said, "that this is not the time for such an amendment of the Constitution. Pray when, sir, will it come? Will it be when the President has issued more and more calls for two or three hundred thousand men of the country's bravest and best? Will it be when more fathers and husbands and sons have fallen, and their graves are thicker by the banks of the rivers and streamlets and hillsides? Will it be when there are more scenes like this I hold in my hand,— an artist's picture, a photograph of an actuality,— a quiet spot by the side of a river, with the moon shining upon the water, and a lonely sentinel keeping guard; and here, in the open space, the head-boards marking the burial-places of many a soldier-boy, and an open grave to receive another inmate; and, underneath, the words, 'All quiet on the Potomac'? Will it be when such scenes of quiet are more numerous, not only along the Potomac, but by the Rapidan, the Chickahominy, the Stone, the Tennessee, the Cumberland, the Big Black, and the Red? Sir, *now*, in my judgment, is the time, and the fitting time. Never until now could this amendment have been carried; and now I hope and believe it can."

On the 4th of April, Mr. Howe of Wisconsin made a quaint and earnest speech for the amendment. "What," he asked, "are the apologies for this institution? I have heard them. We hear them daily. That which we hear the oftenest, that which is insisted upon the loudest, is, that slaves are only made of negroes, or of the descendants of negroes, and that they, as a race, are inferior to the whites. Whether the fact is so or not, I shall not spend a moment in arguing; but I affirm this, that if, in the whole catalogue of excuses that are offered for crimes and offences, one single excuse could be found more odious than the crime itself, it is this one excuse for slavery. Admit that, as a race, they are inferior to the race of the whites: I ask senators, I ask men, if that is a fact which authorizes you or me to enslave them. Sir, the excuse not only shames what sense of manhood there is in us who are grown up, but it shames all the manliness of the boys of the country." Mr. Johnson, on the 5th of April, addressed the Senate in support of the amendment. The representative of a slave State just casting aside its burden, a lawyer of acknowledged eminence, and a statesman of large experience, his speech commanded the marked attention of the Senate. In the outset of his remarks, he most emphatically avowed, "I am satisfied now, and I was satisfied throughout all the contests in which that question has been presented, that, sooner or later, the present condition of things was inevitable, or something nearly like them. If," said he, "there be justice in God's providence, if we are at liberty to suppose that he will not abandon man and his rights to their own fate, and suffer their destiny to be worked out by their own means and with their own lights, I never doubted that the day must come when human slavery would be exterminated by a convulsive effort on the part of the bondmen, unless that other and better reason and influence which might bring it about should be successful, — the mild though powerful influences of that higher and elevated morality which the Christian religion teaches."

At the close of Mr. Johnson's speech, Mr. Davis moved to strike out all after the word "namely" in the amendment reported by the committee, and insert, "No negro, or person whose mother or grandmother is or was a negro, shall be a citizen of the United States, and be eligible to any civil or military office, or to any place of trust or profit, under the United States." The question, being taken by yeas and nays, resulted — yeas 5, nays 32. Mr. Davis then proposed to amend the amendment reported by the committee by adding these words to the first section of the proposed article : "But no slave shall be entitled to his or her freedom under this amendment, if resident, at the time it takes effect, in any State the laws of which forbid free negroes to reside therein, until removed from such State by the Government of the United States." Upon this amendment he asked the yeas and nays ; but only four senators sustained his call, and his amendment was rejected without a division. Mr. Davis further proposed to amend the amendment by adding at the end of the second section, that Congress shall distribute the emancipated slaves among the free States. This amendment was rejected without a division. Mr. Powell now moved to amend the amendment of the committee by adding at the end of the first section, "No slaves shall be emancipated by this article, unless the owner thereof shall be first paid the value of the slave or slaves so emancipated," — yeas 2, nays 34. On the 6th of April, Mr. Harlan of Iowa addressed the Senate in an exhaustive speech in favor of the amendment of the Constitution. He emphatically denied any just title to the services of the adult offspring of the slave mother, and pronounced it "a mere usurpation, without any known mode of justification under any existing code of laws human or divine. . . . The justice of this claim," he declared, "cannot be found either in reason, natural justice, or the principles of the common law, or in any positive municipal or statute regulation of any State, or in the Hebrew code written by the finger of God protruded from the flame of fire on the summit of Sinai." Mr. Harlan was followed by Mr. Saulsbury in a labored defence of slavery, and in denunciation of the proposed amendment of the Constitution, as a "fraud" upon the nation. He pronounced "such an amendment to be the clearest cause of secession that could possibly be furnished or that ever has been furnished to any State." Mr. Hale made an earnest, eloquent, and effective appeal in favor of placing the nation in harmony with the laws of God. He closed his speech by saying, "Sir, when the great founder of the Dutch Republic (William the Silent, I think he was called), after losing his armies, his treasure, his finances, and every thing but his own indomitable courage and his Christian faith, counselled his followers again to rally, and again to strike for freedom, they asked him, 'Have you secured any alliances? are there any of the potentates and powers of the earth that you could associate with, that will aid you in the struggle in which you propose to engage?' his answer was, 'Yes: I have allied myself to the King of kings, and in his strength I invite you to go to battle.' Sir, that is the position, and the only position, this nation can occupy. If we cannot do that; if we cannot put away from us the great sin and the great crime which has separated us, not only from the sympathies of the Christian world, but from the blessings of the God of the Christian world, — then indeed is our cause hopeless and our struggle desperate." Mr. M'Dougall of California, in a brief, clear, and emphatic speech, denounced the proposed amendment of the Constitution, and the entire antislavery policy of the Government. He would vote against the amendment of the Constitution if he stood alone in the Senate. The adoption of the amendment "would add twenty-five or fifty per cent to the vital forces of the Southern Confederacy." He had opposed the antislavery policy. "It achieves," he declared, "nothing that tends toward victory: it only arouses the fiercer animosity of an already violent foe." Mr. Powell was opposed to any amendment; but, if we are to enter upon that work, let us exhibit to the world that our ideas are not restricted to one, — the subject of African slavery; and he proposed several amendments, which were voted down, without reference to their merits, by the friends of the amendment to the Constitution for the extinction of slavery. Mr. Davis proposed an amendment concerning the election of President, which was rejected without a division. The amendment of the Judiciary Committee was then adopted, and the joint resolution reported to the Senate as amended.

On the 7th, Mr. Hendricks of Indiana spoke in opposition to the amendment of the Constitution. He had never, he said, discussed the moral question of slavery before the people. "I do not," he said, "intend to discuss it here, because with the moral questions of slavery the Federal Government has nothing to do. Are the negroes," he asked, "to remain among us? I can say to the senator, that they never will associate with the white people of this country upon terms of equality." Mr. Henderson of Missouri, the mover of the original proposition, followed Mr. Hendricks in a lengthy, thorough, and effective speech in advocacy of the extinction of slavery by a constitutional amendment. "Our ancestors," he said, "acknowledged the truth, when they proclaimed the inalienable right of liberty unto all men. That declaration gave *them* liberty. It fired the world, and enlisted the sympathies of civilization. So soon as they obtained it for themselves, however, the false counsels of expediency came to refuse it to others."

Mr. Sumner, on the 8th, spoke in favor of the extinction of slavery by constitutional amendments and by other modes of legislation. "There is nothing," he declared, "in the Constitution, on which slavery can rest, or find even the least support. Even on the face of that instrument, it is an *outlaw;* but, if we look further at its provisions, we find at least four distinct sources of power, which, if executed, must render slavery impossible, while the preamble makes them all vital for freedom: first, the power to provide for the common defence and general welfare; secondly, the power to raise armies and maintain navies; thirdly, the power to guarantee to every State a republican form of government; and, fourthly, the power to secure *liberty* to every person restrained without due process of law. But all these provisions are something more than powers: *they are duties also.* And yet we are constantly and painfully reminded in this Chamber that pending measures against slavery are unconstitutional. Sir, this is an immense mistake. *Nothing against slavery can be unconstitutional.* It is only hesitation which is unconstitutional." Mr. Sumner closed by moving to amend the bill by striking out the words of the proposed article, and inserting the following : "All persons are equal before the law, so that no person can hold another as a slave; and Congress may make all laws necessary and proper to carry this article into effect everywhere within the United States and the jurisdiction thereof."

Mr. Powell did not believe, with Mr. Clark, that " slavery was the cause of all our woes. The bad faith of the abolitionists had done more to bring this war about than all the efforts of the fire-eaters of the South." At the close of Mr. Powell's speech, the Vice-President stated the question to be on the amendment moved by Mr. Sumner. "In placing," said Mr. Sumner, " a new and important text into the Constitution, it seems to me we cannot be too careful in the language we adopt." The amendment proposed by the committee, he thought, started with the attempt to reproduce the Jefferson Ordinance; and he doubted the expediency of reproducing that ordinance : for he objected " to the Jefferson Ordinance, even if it were presented in its original text. He should prefer the form sent to the Chair, which he offered as a suggestion; but, if senators did not incline to it, he had no desire to press it." — "At an early stage of the session," said Mr. Trumbull, "the senator from Missouri introduced a proposition to amend the Constitution of the United States so as for ever to prohibit slavery. That resolution was referred to the Committee on the Judiciary. At a later day, a month or two afterwards, the senator from Massachusetts also introduced a proposition to prohibit slavery. The committee had both those propositions before them. . . . I do not know that I should have adopted these precise words; but a majority of the committee thought they were the best words: they accomplish the object; and I cannot see why the senator from Massachusetts should be so pertinacious about particular words." — "I wish, as much as the senator from Massachusetts," said Mr. Howard of Michigan, "in making this amendment, to use significant language, — language that cannot be mistaken or misunderstood: but I prefer to dismiss all reference to French constitutions or French codes, and go back to the good old Anglo-Saxon language employed by our fathers in the Ordinance of 1787; an expression which has been adjudicated upon repeatedly, which is perfectly well understood both by the public and by judicial tribunals; a phrase, I may say further, which is peculiarly near and dear to the people of the North-western Territory, from whose soil slavery was excluded by it." Mr. Sumner withdrew his proposition. Mr. Saulsbury offered an amendment embodied in twenty sections; but, on a division, only two votes were given for it. Mr. M'Dougall thought, before the final vote was taken, it was due to himself to make a few remarks. "I look upon this policy," he said, "as being a policy for sacrificing the whole of the colored people now occupying parts of this Republic. This policy will ingulf them. They can never commingle with us."

The yeas and nays were then taken on the passage of the joint resolution, submitting to the legislatures of the several States a proposition to amend the Constitution of the United States; and 38 senators voted yea, and 6 senators voted nay, as follows: —

YEAS. — Messrs. Anthony, Brown, Chandler, Clark, Collamer, Conness, Cowan, Dixon, Doolittle, Fessenden, Foot, Foster, Grimes, Hale, Harding, Harlan, Harris, Henderson, Howard, Howe, Johnson, Lane of Indiana, Lane of Kansas, Morgan, Morrill, Nesmith, Pomeroy, Ramsey, Sherman, Sprague, Sumner, Ten Eyck, Trumbull, Van Winkle, Wade, Wilkinson, Willey, and Wilson, — 38.

NAYS. — Messrs. Davis, Hendricks, M'Dougall, Powell, Riddle, and Saulsbury, — 6.

In the House of Representatives, on the 31st of May, the joint resolution, submitting to the legislatures of the several States a proposition to amend the Constitution of the United States, was taken up. Mr. Holman (Dem.) of Indiana objected to its second reading; and the Speaker stated the question to be, "Shall the joint resolution be rejected?" Mr. Wilson (Rep.) of Iowa demanded the previous question, and Mr. Schenck (Rep.) of Ohio demanded the yeas and nays, — yeas 55, nays 76.

Mr. Wilson, Chairman of the Judiciary Committee, having, at an early day before the proposed amendment was discussed in either House, made an elaborate speech in favor of the extinction of slavery by the adoption of a constitutional amendment, yielded the floor to Mr.

Morris of New York, a member of the Judiciary Committee. "I aver," declared Mr. Morris, in opening the debate, "that no nation can violate any moral law, without incurring a penalty. No member of society, no matter how weak or humble, can be oppressed, without injury to the whole. It is an inexorable law. There is a system of compensation in the economy of God, and applicable to nations and individuals, as inevitable as that fire will burn. We may not admit it; but time will realize the fact. We may not recognize the hand; but the chastening will come as certainly as that God is just. Legislators as well as divines should remember these truths."

Mr. Herrick (Dem.) of New York followed Mr. Morris in opposition to the amendment. He declared that " the adoption of this measure could have no other effect than to seal for ever the dissolution of the Union: it meant nothing else than eternal disunion, continuous war." Mr. Kellogg (Rep.) of New York followed in support of the amendment, and for the suppression of the Rebellion. "No expense," he said, "no sacrifice, no allurement, must deter or divert us; but rising with the emergency, and equal to every fate, we must meet and master every obstacle that stands in the way of the complete supremacy of the Constitution and the laws."

The consideration of the question was resumed on the 14th of June; and Mr. Pruyn (Dem.) of New York addressed the House in opposition to the amendment. Mr. Fernando Wood (Dem.) of New York said that " the bloody and brutal policy of the Administration party had well-nigh destroyed all hope of reconstruction. This proposed alteration of the Constitution was beyond the power of the Government. It involves the extermination of the white men of the Southern States, and the forfeiture of all the land and other property belonging to them. Negroes and military colonists will take the place of the race thus blotted out of existence. Is this intended as the last scene of the bloody drama of carnage and civil war now being prosecuted? The world looks on with horror, and it will leave to future ages a fearful warning to avoid similar acts of perfidious atrocity." Mr. Higby (Rep.) of California said, " The Constitution should be adapted to the condition of the country where the noble men of the loyal States are giving up their lives and where they have given them up by thousands. Their bones are bleaching upon hundreds of battle-fields. They are drenching with their blood the soil over which they are moving, with Victory perching on their banners, and killing out the roots of slavery so that it cannot exist." " It is an attempt," said Mr. Kalbfleisch (Dem.) of New York, " to replenish their almost exhausted stock of political capital by creating a new issue based upon the slavery question before the people, in the hope of renewing that agitation upon the turbulent waves of which they were swept into the power which they have so deplorably abused." Mr. Wheeler (Dem.) of Wisconsin presented an amendment to add to the resolution, — " that this article shall not apply to the States of Kentucky, Missouri, Delaware, and Maryland, until after the expiration of ten years from the time the same shall be ratified." " Slavery," said Mr. Shannon (Rep.) of California, " is paganism refined, brutality vitiated, dishonesty corrupted ; and, sir, we are asked to retain this curse, to protect it, after it has corrupted our sons, dishonored our daughters, subverted our institutions, and shed rivers of the best blood of our countrymen." Mr. Marcy (Dem.) of New Hampshire assured the supporters of the Administration that their "career was fast drawing to a close." Mr. Coffroth (Dem.) of Pennsylvania opposed the bill, and bitterly assailed the policy of the Administration. "Slavery," he exclaimed, "is denounced as the cause of the Rebellion. I deny this, though it may be the occasion, as money is the occasion of larceny, robbery, or burglary." — "I was here," said Mr. Kellogg (Rep.) of Michigan, "when the Rebellion broke out; and I do not believe the adoption of the Crittenden Compromise would have postponed the war a single week. Southern senators laughed at the idea of being satisfied in such a way. They were determined to dissolve the Union, and establish a separate government in conformity with their ideas; and they firmly believed that we would allow them to do so. They had a supreme contempt for the people of the North, and never dreamed of the difficulties in the way, or the opposition they were to encounter. They had made up their minds to do as they pleased, and set the Government of the United States at defiance." Mr. Ross (Dem.) of Illinois advocated peace. He suggested that "we first agree upon an armistice, and then send commissioners, to meet, on the 4th of July, at Mount Vernon, around the grave of Washington." He declared that "suggestions in favor of an amicable adjustment" would not meet the approbation of the adherents of the Administration. Mr. Holman (Dem.) of Indiana said, "This bill, having passed the Senate, only awaits the approval of the House. Of all the measures of this disastrous Administration, each in its turn producing new calamities, this attempt to tamper with the Constitution threatens the most permanent injury."

The debate was continued, on the 15th of June, by Mr. Farnsworth (Rep.) of Illinois. "When," said he, "we stood in the breach, and declared that slavery should go no further; that it should not spread over the land; that they should not 'call the roll of their slaves under the shadow of Bunker Hill,' nor 'flog them in the corn-fields of Illinois,' — then the slaveholders brought on the Rebellion." Mr. Thayer (Rep.) of Pennsylvania declared that "humanity and civilization revolt against a sentiment so inhuman in itself, and so debasing to the mind that holds it, as the sentiment which we listened to yesterday, — that slavery is the best possible condition of the negro race." — "I re-affirm it," said Mr. Fernando Wood. "I am willing," replied Mr. Thayer, "that he should re-affirm it. . . . I can only say, that, for myself, I would not hold or avow a sentiment so barbarous, so cruel, and so inhuman in its character, as that, for all the wealth and honor that are embraced within the four quarters of the world."

Mr. Mallory (Dem.) of Kentucky denounced the proposed amendment of the Constitution as a palpable violation of the reserved rights of the States." — "Madness and despair rule," said Mr. Kelley (Rep.) of Pennsylvania; "and I shall consume none of the brief time allotted to me by following the gentleman from Kentucky. . . . But, sir, the privilege is not often given to men to perform an act, the influence of which will be felt beneficently by the poor, the oppressed, the ignorant, and the degraded of all lands, and which will endure until terminated by the wreck of matter and the crush of worlds. I rise that I may thus publicly thank God, and the good people by whose suffrages I am here to-day, for the golden opportunity afforded me of doing such an act."

Mr. Edgerton (Dem.) of Indiana avowed that it was "better for our country, better for man, that negro slavery exist a thousand years, than that American white men lose their constitutional liberty in the extinction of the constitutional sovereignty of the Federal States of this Union." — "Never," said Mr. Arnold (Rep.) of Illinois, "since the day when John Adams pleaded for the Declaration of Independence, has so important a question been submitted to an American Congress as that upon which you are now about to vote. The signing of the immortal Declaration is a familiar picture in every log-cabin and residence all over the land. Pass this resolution, and the grand spectacle of this vote, which knocks off the fetters of a whole race, will make this scene immortal." Mr. Ingersoll (Rep.) of Illinois, the successor of Owen Lovejoy, followed Mr. Arnold in an earnest and eloquent appeal for the amendment. "I know full well," he said, "if the lamented Lovejoy, my honored and noble predecessor, could come to-day from the unseen world, and take his place among us, his manly and eloquent voice would be heard in this hall, as in days past, with all the earnestness of his great soul, pronouncing in favor of the adoption of this resolution in favor of universal liberty and the rights of mankind."

Mr. Randall (Dem.) of Pennsylvania maintained that "the only mode in which the Union can be restored, and put on the march of a newer and more glorious progress, is by having due regard to the mutual advantages and interests of the States." Mr. Rollins of Missouri opposed the amendment in an earnest speech. Mr. Pendleton (Dem.) of Ohio moved, as a substitute for the joint resolution, a provision submitting it to the conventions of the several States, so that the ratification, if at all, shall be by conventions of three-fourths of the States. Mr. Pendleton made an elaborate speech in opposition to the amendment of the Constitution. "We must," he said, "retrace our steps; we must return to State rights." At the close of Mr. Pendleton's speech, the House proceeded to vote. The amendments proposed by Mr. Wheeler and Mr. Pendleton were rejected. Mr. Holman demanded the yeas and nays on the passage of the joint resolution, and they were ordered.

The question was taken; and it was decided in the negative, — yeas 93, nays 65, not voting 23, — as follows: —

YEAS. — Messrs. Alley, Allison, Ames, Anderson, Arnold, Baily, John D. Baldwin, Baxter, Beaman, Blaine, Blair, Blow, Boutwell, Boyd, Brandegee, Broomall, Ambrose W. Clark, Freeman Clarke, Cobb, Cole, Creswell, Dawes, Deming, Dixon, Donnelly, Driggs, Eckley, Eliot, Farnsworth, Fenton, Frank, Garfield, Gooch, Griswold, Hale, Higby, Hooper, Hotchkiss, Asahel W. Hubbard, John H. Hubbard, Hulburd, Ingersoll, Jenckes, Julian, Kasson, Kelley, Francis W. Kellogg, Orlando Kellogg, Littlejohn, Loan, Longyear, Marvin, M'Clurg, M'Indoe, Samuel F. Miller, Moorhead, Morrill, Daniel Morris, Amos Myers, Leonard Myers, Norton, Odell, Charles O'Neill,

Orth, Patterson, Perham, Pike, Price, Alexander H. Rice, John H. Rice, Schenck, Scofield, Shannon, Sloan, Smith, Smithers, Spalding, Starr, Stevens, Thayer, Thomas, Tracy, Upson, Van Valkenburgh, Elihu B. Washburne, Webster, Whaley, Wheeler, Williams, Wilder, Wilson, Windom, and Woodbridge, — 93.

NAYS. — Messrs. James C. Allen, William J. Allen, Ancona, Ashley, Augustus C. Baldwin, Bliss, Brooks, James S. Brown, Chanler, Coffroth, Cox, Cravens, Dawson, Denison, Eden, Edgerton, Eldridge, English, Finck, Ganson, Grider, Harding, Harrington, Herrick, Holman, Hutchins, Philip Johnson, William Johnson, Kalbfleisch, Kernan, King, Law, Lazear, Le Blond, Long, Mallory, Marcy, M'Allister, M'Dowell, M'Kinney, William H. Miller, James R. Morris, Morrison, Noble, John O'Neill, Pendleton, Pruyn, Radford, Samuel J. Randall, Robinson, Rogers, James S. Rollins, Ross, Scott, John B. Steele, William G. Steele, Stiles, Strouse, Stuart, Sweat, Wadsworth, Ward, Chilton A. White, Joseph W. White, and Fernando Wood, — 65.

NOT VOTING. — Messrs. William G. Brown, Clay, Henry Winter Davis, Thomas T. Davis, Dumont, Grinnell, Hall, Benjamin G. Harris, Charles M. Harris, Knapp, M'Bride, Middleton, Nelson, Perry, Pomeroy, William H. Randall, Edward H. Rollins, Stebbins, Voorhees, William B. Washburn, Winfield, Benjamin Wood, and Yeaman, — 23.

So the joint resolution was not passed; two-thirds not having voted in favor thereof. Mr. Odell (Dem.) of New York, Mr. Griswold (Dem.) of New York, Mr. Baily (Dem.) of Pennsylvania, and Mr. Wheeler (Dem.) of Wisconsin, voted for the joint resolution. Mr. Ashley (Rep.) changed his vote from the affirmative to the negative, for the purpose of submitting, at the proper time, a motion to reconsider. Mr. Ashley entered his motion to reconsider the vote; and that motion is now the pending question in the House.

CHAPTER XIV.

REPEAL OF FUGITIVE-SLAVE LAWS.

MR. HOWE'S BILL. — MR. WILMOT'S BILL. — MR. WILSON'S BILL. — MR. STEVENS'S BILL. — MR. ASHLEY'S BILL. — MR. JULIAN'S BILL. — SPECIAL COMMITTEE ON SLAVERY. — MR. SUMNER'S BILL AND REPORT. — MR. FOSTER'S SPEECH. — MR. SHERMAN'S AMENDMENT. — MR. JOHNSON'S SPEECH. — MR. SUMNER'S SPEECH. — MR. SAULSBURY'S AMENDMENT. — MR. BROWN'S SPEECH. — MR. HOWARD'S AMENDMENT. — REMARKS OF MR. CONNESS. — MR. MORRIS'S BILL. — REMARKS OF MR. MALLORY. — MR. MORRIS. — MR. WILSON. — MR. PENDLETON. — MR. KING. — MR. COX. — MR. HUBBARD. — MR. FARNSWORTH. — PASSAGE OF MR. MORRIS'S BILL IN THE HOUSE. — MR. MORRIS'S BILL REPORTED BY MR. SUMNER. — MR. SAULSBURY'S AMENDMENT. — MR. JOHNSON'S AMENDMENT. — PASSAGE OF THE BILL.

IN the Senate, on the 26th of December, 1861, Mr. Howe (Rep.) of Wisconsin introduced a bill to repeal the Fugitive-slave Act of 1850. In presenting the bill, Mr. Howe declared that " the act has had its day. As a party act, it has done its work. It has probably done as much mischief as any other one act that was ever passed by the National Legislature. I am not sure but it has done as much mischief as all the acts ever passed by the National Legislature since the adoption of the Federal Constitution." The bill was read twice, referred to the Committee on the Judiciary, and reported back adversely by Mr. Ten Eyck (Rep.) of New Jersey, on the 11th of February, 1863.

On the 23d of May, 1862, Mr. Wilmot (Rep.) of Pennsylvania introduced a bill requiring an oath of allegiance in certain cases and for other purposes. The bill provided, that before any person owing service shall be delivered up, and before any process shall be hereafter issued for the arrest of any fugitive from service, the person so claiming such service shall solemnly swear that he will support and defend the Constitution and Government of the United States against all enemies, domestic or foreign; and that he has not, by word or deed, given aid, comfort, or encouragement to the Rebellion; that, in all cases of arrest of persons claimed as fugitives from service, it shall be the duty of the officer before whom such fugitive shall be taken to summon before him such witnesses as the fugitive shall, on oath, declare to be material to disprove any of the allegations of the claimant, or to establish his freedom; and, in the examination and trial of such cases, no witness shall be excluded on account of color. Mr. Wilmot's bill was read twice, referred to the Committee on the District of Columbia, and reported back on the 27th of May by Mr. Wade (Rep.) of Ohio without amendment.

On the 24th of May, 1862, Mr. Wilson (Rep.) of Massachusetts introduced a bill to amend the Fugitive-slave Act of 1850. The bill secured to persons claimed as fugitives from service or labor in one State a right to a trial by jury in the District Court of the United States for the district in which they may be; the proceedings to be the same as on an indictment, subject to a writ of error from the Circuit Court and from the Supreme Court, as provided in the Judiciary Act of 1789. It gave to such persons held for trial the right to bail before and pending the trial. It required that the person claiming the service of any fugitive should prove that he was loyal to the Government, and had not in any manner aided the Rebellion; and it repealed sections six, seven, eight, nine, and ten, and part of section five, of the act of Sept. 18, 1850. Mr. Wilson, on the 10th of June, moved to take up the bill for consideration. Mr. Powell (Dem.) of Kentucky demanded the yeas and nays; and they were ordered, — yeas 25, nays 10. So the motion was agreed to; and the Senate proceeded to its consideration. Mr. Trumbull (Rep.) of Illinois, remarking that the bill was a long one, and the hour was late, moved an adjournment; which was carried.

In the House of Representatives, after the announcement of the standing committees of the Thirty-eighth Congress, on the 14th of December, 1863, the Speaker stated that the first business in order was the call of the States for bills and joint resolutions. Mr. Stevens (Rep.) of Pennsylvania introduced a bill to repeal the Fugitive-slave Act, approved Feb. 12, 1793, and the act amendatory thereto, approved Sept. 18, 1850; Mr. Ashley (Rep.) of Ohio introduced a bill to repeal the Fugitive-slave Act of 1850, and all acts and parts of acts for the rendition of fugitive slaves; Mr. Julian (Rep.) of Indiana introduced a bill to repeal the third and fourth sections of the act respecting fugitives from justice, and persons escaping from the service of their masters, approved Feb. 12, 1793, and the act to amend and supplementary to the aforesaid act, approved Sept. 18, 1850; and these bills were referred to the Judiciary Committee. On the same day, Mr. Julian submitted a resolution, instructing the Judiciary Committee to report a bill to repeal the third and fourth sections of an act respecting fugitives from justice and persons escaping from the service of their masters, approved Feb. 12, 1793; and the act to amend and supplementary to the aforesaid act, approved Sept. 18, 1850. Mr. Holman (Dem.) of Indiana moved to lay the resolution on the table, and demanded the yeas and nays, — yeas 82, nays 73.

In the Senate, on the 13th of January, 1864, Mr. Sumner moved that a select committee of seven be appointed to take into consideration all propositions concerning slavery and the treatment of freedmen. The resolution was agreed to; and the Vice-President appointed Mr. Sumner (Rep.) of Massachusetts, Mr. Howard (Rep.) of Michigan, Mr. Carlile (Dem.) of Virginia, Mr. Pomeroy (Rep.) of Kansas, Mr. Buckalew (Dem.) of Pennsylvania, Mr. Brown (Rep.) of Missouri, and Mr. Conness (Union) of California. Mr. Sumner, Mr. Howard, Mr. Pomeroy, and Mr. Brown, are recognized as thorough, earnest, radical antislavery men; Mr. Carlile is a proslavery man from conviction; Mr. Buckalew is a fair representative of the sentiments, opinions, and policy of the leaders of the Northern Democracy; Mr. Conness, though trained in the faith of the Democratic party, is an earnest and uncompromising opponent of slavery and its champions in every form.

On the 8th of February, Mr. Sumner asked and obtained leave to introduce a bill to repeal all laws for the rendition of fugitive slaves; which was read twice by its title, and referred to the Select Committee on Slavery and Freedmen. Mr. Sumner, on the 29th of February, from the Select Committee on

Slavery, reported a bill, accompanied by a report, for the repeal of all acts, and parts of acts, requiring the rendition of fugitive slaves. The bill was read twice, and the report ordered to be printed. Mr. Sumner stated that the minority of the committee desired to present their views in the form of a minority report. Mr. Conness moved to print ten thousand extra copies of the report. Mr. Buckalew, on the 1st of March, asked leave of the Senate to present a report from the minority of the Committee on the Repeal of the Fugitive-slave Acts; and the report was received; and, on motion of Mr. Powell, it was ordered to be printed. He also moved to print ten thousand extra copies of the report; and the motion was referred to the Committee on Printing. Mr. Sumner's report in support of the bill was lengthy, elaborate, and exhaustive. The legal, political, and moral aspects of the question were fully presented. Mr. Buckalew's report discussed the questions involved in the light of the legislation and judicial decisions of the Government, and the avowals of the public men of the past.

On the 7th of March, Mr. Sumner asked the Senate to take up the bill, with a view to make it the special order for a future day. His motion was agreed to; and he moved to make it the special order for the 9th of March, and it was carried. On Wednesday, the 9th, Mr. Sumner called for the special order. Mr. Davis of Kentucky expressed a desire to debate the bill; and on motion of Mr. Sumner, at the suggestion of Mr. Hendricks, it was postponed to Wednesday, the 16th, and made the special order for one o'clock. On the 19th, Mr. Sumner moved that the Senate proceed to the consideration of the bill. Mr. Trumbull demanded the yeas and nays, — yeas 26, nays 10; Mr. Cowan, Mr. Willey, and Mr. Van Winkle, voting with the Democratic senators in the negative. The bill was reported to the Senate, ordered to be engrossed, and read a third time. Mr. Foster of Connecticut was "not prepared to see the bill pass just now." Mr. Sumner had "not the least desire to address the Senate. It seems to be perfectly plain. It is like a diagram; it is like the multiplication-table; it is like the ten commandments." Mr. Foster did not apprehend that the bill was to be put on its passage at the present time: he confessed he expected to say something upon it. Mr. Pomeroy thought "we might as well pass the bill now." Mr. Buckalew called for the yeas and nays, and they were ordered. Mr. Hendricks said, "It may be that our fathers erred in the agreement among themselves that a fugitive slave should be returned; it may be that it was a mistake on their part: but while their agreement stands, and while my oath is upon my conscience to respect that agreement, I cannot vote for a bill like this." Mr. Sherman had "some doubt about the expediency of now repealing the law of 1793." Mr. Sumner said the committee felt "that we had better make a clean thing of it, purify the country, lift the country up before foreign nations, and let us now wash our hands of all support of slavery." Mr. Sherman said that "the law of 1793 was framed by the men who framed the Constitution. It has been declared to be valid and constitutional by every tribunal that has acted upon it." Mr. Sumner replied that "it was declared to be unconstitutional by the Supreme Court of the United States in the Prigg case; and the senator knows very well that it is among the records in the life of Judge Story, who gave the opinion in the Prigg case, that the fatal objection to the act of 1793, that it did not give a trial by jury in a case of human freedom, was never argued before the court, and that he personally considered it an open question." Mr. Sherman said, "Under these circumstances, I prefer not to repeal the law of 1793, about the constitutionality of which I have little doubt." Mr. Sherman then moved to reconsider the vote ordering the bill to be engrossed, for the purpose of offering an amendment; and the vote was reconsidered. He then moved to add at the end of the bill the words, "except the act approved Feb. 12, 1793, entitled 'An act respecting fugitives from justice, and persons escaping from the service of their masters.'" Mr. Henderson moved to amend the amendment of the senator from Ohio by repealing the act of 1850; and then the act of 1793 will certainly remain in force, because the act of 1850 is merely amendatory of the act of 1793. Mr. Sherman thought "we had better repeal all the laws on the subject, except the act of 1793." Mr. Johnson said that "the Constitution as it is now, according to my interpretation of it, not only authorizes the passage of the act of 1793, and the passage of the act of 1850, but made it the duty of Congress to pass some law of that description. The honorable member from Massachusetts is mistaken, I think, in supposing that Mr. Justice Story ever even doubted the constitutionality of the act of 1793." Mr. Sumner would "simply refer the senator to the Life of Judge Story, by his son, and the elaborate chapter on the Prigg decision." Mr. Johnson had seen it. "There is," he said, " one question which is perfectly plain under the adjudications of the Supreme Court, and particularly in the judgment pronounced by Mr. Justice Story, that the Constitution itself is a fugitive-slave act." — " To my mind," said Mr. Sumner, "nothing is clearer than that, according to unquestionable rules of interpretation, the clause of the Constitution, whatever may have been the intent of its authors, cannot be considered applicable to slaves. Such is slavery, that, from the nature of the case, it cannot be sanctioned or legalized except by 'positive' words. *It cannot stand on inference.*" The question, being taken by yeas and nays on Mr. Sherman's amendment, resulted — yeas 24, nays 17 — as follows : —

YEAS. — Messrs. Buckalew, Carlile, Collamer, Cowan, Davis, Dixon, Doolittle, Foster, Harris, Henderson, Hendricks, Howe, Johnson, Lane of Indiana, M'Dougall, Nesmith, Powell, Riddle, Saulsbury, Sherman, Ten Eyck, Trumbull, Van Winkle, and Willey, — 24.

NAYS. — Messrs. Anthony, Brown, Clark, Conness, Fessenden, Grimes, Hale, Howard, Lane of Kansas, Morgan, Morrill, Pomeroy, Ramsey, Sprague, Sumner, Wilkinson, and Wilson, — 17.

Mr. Saulsbury moved an amendment of two sections concerning arrests without due process of law : 9 senators voted yea, and 27 senators voted nay. " I do not wish," said Mr. Conness, "to cast a vote for this measure in its present shape. I had intended, before the debate closed, if it was debated, to say something on the subject. I do not design that now ; and, as the Senate have seen fit to amend the bill, I cannot vote for it. At present, therefore, I move that it lie on the table." Mr. Sumner hoped the senator " would withdraw that motion." — " For what reason ? " asked Mr. Conness. " For the reason," replied Mr. Sumner, "that we get something by this bill." Mr. Wilson asked for the yeas and nays on the motion to lay the bill on the table, and they were ordered. The vote, being taken, resulted — yeas 9, nays 31. Mr. Powell moved the reference of the bill to the Judiciary Committee. The motion was rejected. Mr. Johnson said, "I understand, as the bill now is, it repeals all the fugitive-slave acts, except that of 1793." — "Yes," answered senators. "Then I shall vote for it; because, as I never would have voted for the Fugitive-slave Act of 1850, I shall certainly vote for its repeal." Mr. Foster expressed a wish to make a few remarks upon the bill, and the Senate adjourned. On the 20th, the Senate proceeded to the consideration of the bill; and Mr. Foster made an elaborate speech in favor of the bill as amended on motion of Mr. Sherman. "I shall give," he said, "my vote on its passage with very great pleasure. Its effect will be to repeal the law of 1850, popularly known as the Fugitive-slave Law; in my opinion a most iniquitous measure, and certainly most obnoxious to the people of the free States from the day of its passage to the present hour. That bill was passed in a period of great excitement in the country. A malicious and malignant spirit had been excited. Sectional and partisan feeling raged over the land. An arrogant and defiant party, in their pride of power, passed that bill through both Houses of Congress. It has the forms of law, and has stood unrepealed to this day. From the first day I had the honor of a seat in this body until now, I should have voted cheerfully for its repeal at any time."

Mr. Brown of Missouri declared that "the amendment of the senator from Ohio (Mr. Sherman), which has been adopted by the Senate, makes this bill, as it now stands, tantamount to a revival of the Fugitive-slave Act of 1793. It is a virtual re-instating and re-authorization, so far as the vote of the Senate can go, of that act."

Mr. Van Winkle of West Virginia, on the 21st, addressed the Senate in opposition to "the series of projected measures now pending in one or both Houses of Congress," and in vindication of the policy of organizing the State of West Virginia, and abolishing slavery therein. Mr. Howard expressed a desire to offer an amendment. Mr. Wilson moved a reconsideration of the vote ordering the bill to be engrossed, to allow that motion to be made; and the vote was reconsidered. Mr. Howard moved to insert at the end of the bill the following amendment: "But no person found in any Territory of the United States or in the District of Columbia shall be deemed to have been held to labor or service or to be a slave, nor shall he or she be removed under said act of 1793; and the fourth section of said act is hereby repealed." Mr. Doolittle moved an executive session. Mr. Sumner suggested that it should be an hour later. Mr. Brown thought we could not finish the bill this evening. Mr. Fessenden did not like to interfere with this bill, but he must "give notice to gentlemen, that, unless they choose to dispose of it this afternoon or by to-morrow at one o'clock, I must then move to go on with the Army-appropriation Bill." Mr. Sumner hoped we should go on with the bill at least for another hour. Mr. Conness hoped we should not go on with the consideration of this bill. "I do not understand the anxiety of my honorable friend from Massachusetts in pressing this bill in its present condition." Mr. Pomeroy hoped the senator from Massachusetts would let the question go over: there were half a dozen amendments to be proposed. Mr. Sumner said, if the friends of the measure request that it shall not be pressed to-day, he would not throw himself in their way. Mr. Conness moved that it be postponed to, and made the order of the day for, Wednesday, the 27th of April, at one o'clock; and the motion was agreed to; and Mr. Sumner's bill was postponed, and not again called up for consideration.

The several bills to repeal the Fugitive-slave Act, introduced on the 14th of December, 1863, by Mr. Stevens, Mr. Ashley, and Mr. Julian, and the bill afterwards introduced by Mr. Spaulding, were referred to the Judiciary Committee. On the 6th of June, Mr. Morris (Rep.) of New York reported, for the several bills referred to the Judiciary Committee on that subject, a substitute, entitled "A bill to repeal the Fugitive-slave Act of 1850, and all acts, and parts of acts, for the rendition of fugitive slaves." The bill was read twice, ordered to be printed, and recommitted. Mr. Holman (Dem.) of Indiana moved to reconsider the vote by which the bill was recommitted to the Committee on the Judiciary, and also moved to lay the motion to reconsider on the table. The House divided, — ayes 26, noes 57; no quorum voting. Mr. Wilson of Iowa called for the yeas and nays, and they were ordered. The question was taken, and it was decided in the negative, — yeas 44, nays 66. The vote by which the bill was recommitted was then reconsidered. Mr. Morris withdrew the motion to recommit; and the bill was ordered to be engrossed, and read a third time. Mr. Morris moved the previous question on the passage of the bill, and the main question was ordered. Mr. Holman called for the yeas and nays on its passage, and they were ordered. Mr. Mallory (Dem.) of Kentucky desired to ask Mr. Morris a question, if he would withdraw the previous question. Mr. Morris declined to withdraw it. Mr. Mallory wished to state to the House the reason why he asked Mr. Morris to withdraw the previous question. Mr. Morris said, if the gentleman does not want over two minutes, I will yield to him. "Think of it!" exclaimed Mr. Cox (Dem.) of Ohio: "they condescend to give us two minutes to discuss the repeal of the Constitution."—"Kentucky is the only State," said Mr. Mallory, "still adhering to the Union, which has not abolished or taken the initiatory steps to abolish slavery. . . . I demand, as an act of justice to my State, that the Fugitive-slave Act be permitted to remain on the statute-book. . . . If the Fugitive-slave Law is repealed, and your provost marshals and recruiting officers draft and recruit the slaves of Kentucky, if this policy is continued, what need, think you, will there be to abolish slavery by constitutional amendment? Sir, I warn you against the course this Congress is pursuing. Already you have crushed out every feeling of love of the Union in the people of the revolted States; and you are besotted if you think that acts of oppression and wrong can be perpetrated in the Border slave States, without producing estrangement and even enmity there. Kentucky has remained true to her faith pledged to the Government, and I warn you not to persevere in inflicting on her insult and outrage." Mr. Morris said he must decline to withdraw the call for the previous question. Mr. Mallory did not expect that he would yield: "Justice is a thing that I have long ceased to hope for from that side of the House."

A series of motions designed to stave off or delay the passage of the bill were then made, in which Holman (Dem.) of Indiana, Pendleton (Dem.) of Ohio, Ancona (Dem.) of Pennsylvania, Strouse (Dem.) of Pennsylvania, Dawson (Dem.) of Pennsylvania, and Eldridge (Dem.) of Wisconsin, took part; but these motions were voted down by large majorities. Mr. Davis of Maryland suggested the postponement of the bill. Mr. Cox, by unanimous consent, appealed to Mr. Morris to postpone it for the present. "To what time," asked Mr. Morris, "does that side of the House propose to postpone the question, and have a vote taken upon it?" Mr. Cox would refer it back to the Judiciary Committee. "If the other side of the House," replied Mr. Morris, "will consent to the designation of a particular day when action shall be had, I shall be inclined to postpone the consideration of the question." Mr. Wilson of Iowa said "it was the intention of the Judiciary Committee to allow every member of the House full time to examine it. I presume it will be satisfactory to the committee if a particular time is agreed upon for taking this vote." Mr. Morris renewed the inquiry, "How long a time do gentlemen ask for discussing this question?" Mr. Holman wanted such time as may be deemed reasonable. Mr. Mallory did not think it would be proper to fix any time within which this discussion must take place. Mr. Pendleton would not agree to any understanding with reference to a vote on this bill. Mr. Morris was willing to postpone the bill to Monday, the 13th of June, and, after reasonable discussion, take the vote that day. Mr. Pendleton declared that there can be no unanimous consent in regard to taking the vote, but he did not object to making it a special order; and the further consideration of the bill was postponed to Monday, the 13th of June. On that day, the bill came up by special order; and Mr. Morris, who reported it, withdrew the previous question, and gave notice that he should renew the motion after the bill should have been debated. Mr. King (Dem.) of Missouri made an elaborate speech in opposition to the passage of the bill. "The law," he said, "now sought to be repealed, was passed in the discharge of a solemn duty to the slaveholding States, — a duty enjoined by the Constitution, and which cannot, in my opinion, be repealed by Congress without a total disregard of an imperative obligation." Mr. Hubbard (Rep.) of Connecticut advocated the bill in a brief, earnest, and emphatic speech. "I make," he said, "no distinction whatever between the act of 1793 and the act of 1850. To-day they are equally obnoxious; and, in my opinion, equally infamous. I revere the memory of the founders of the Republic; but I am not so infatuated as to believe that the fathers would ever have passed the act of 1793 had slavery then been in rebellion against them. It is fit that American statesmen in this age of the world; at this period of the great American war; at a time when the Republic is smarting and bleeding, if not reeling, under the blows that slavery has given it; and at a time when a hundred thousand black men are fighting for the flag, and not one against it,—it is fit that American statesmen, here assembled to deliberate and act upon this momentous question, should have an opportunity to record their votes for posterity to read." Mr. Cox next addressed the House in opposition to the passage of the bill in a sharp, pungent, partisan speech, during which he had a running debate with Baldwin of Massachusetts, Blaine of Maine, Cole of California, and Sloan of Wisconsin. He closed his speech by an arraignment of the supporters of the Administration. "Your Executive," he said, "is a usurper of the powers wisely distributed to the other departments of the Government. Here you sit to-day, striving to strike down the only mode whereby one peculiar clause of the Constitution can be carried out, and propose no mode as a substitute either by State or Federal action. Your ideas are not those of the higher, but of the *lower* law. They do not come from the sources of law and light and love *above*. They sunder all the ties of allegiance, and all the sanctions of faith. You are destructionists: you would tear down all that is valuable and sacred in the past, and build up nothing in their place. You are revolutionists." Mr. Sloan (Rep.) of Wisconsin defended his State for its action in regard to the Fugitive-slave Act of 1850. Mr. Morris made a brief speech in advocacy of his bill. "These statutes," he said, "are repugnant to the sense of every good man who has not been educated to believe that the slave code is more imperative than the Constitution itself. I say, sweep out a law which no man respects who is not a votary of human slavery. It is an abomination." Mr. Farnsworth (Rep.) of Illinois closed the debate in a very brief speech. In reply to the attack made by Mr. Cox upon the Administration for the surrender, to the authorities of Cuba, of Arguelles, Mr. Farnsworth said, "Oh! Mr. Speaker, I understand where the trouble is with that side of the House. The effect of the action of sending back this rascal to Cuba was the emancipation of *eighty human beings:* that is where the shoe pinches. All the trouble is, that, upon Arguelles landing in Cuba, the chains fell from the limbs of eighty men: that is what troubles my friends upon the other side of the House. If he had stolen money or horses, some petty crime, it would have been all well enough, and you would have heard no dissent; but he is so infamous, his crime so high-handed and God-defying, that he is worthy of a plank in the Democratic platform, and a wail from the Democratic party." Mr. Morris demanded the previous question upon the passage of the bill; and the main question was ordered to be put. Mr. Hubbard of Connecticut demanded the yeas and nays; and they were ordered. The question was taken; and it was decided in the affirmative, — yeas 82, nays 57. Mr. Morris moved to reconsider the vote by which the bill was passed, and to lay that motion on the table; and it was agreed to. So the bill prepared by Mr. Morris, and reported by him from the Judiciary Committee, passed the House on the 13th of June.

In the Senate, on the 21st of June, Mr. Sumner moved that the Senate proceed to the consideration of the House bill for the repeal of all laws for the rendition of fugitive slaves. Mr. Hendricks of Indiana opposed the motion. Mr. Howard of Michigan said, "I think it is high time that the Senate of the

United States should take this subject under their consideration, and should pass upon the great questions which have so long agitated the people of the United States connected with the rendition of fugitive slaves." Mr. Saulsbury opposed taking up the bill, as "no practical good can result from it." Mr. Doolittle moved "to go into executive session." Mr. Sumner hoped not. "I know," he said, "of nobody who proposes to discuss it, unless it is the senator from Wisconsin, if he proposes to make a plea for slave-hunting." Mr. Davis of Kentucky said, "I tell the senator from Massachusetts, that I have, as I said some days ago, the sequel of the story of slavery in his State to tell; and I expect to tell it upon this bill. I have no doubt it will be very edifying to the honorable senator." Mr. Doolittle said in reply, that "when the senator from Delaware expressly declares to the Senate that this question must be discussed, and shall be discussed; that it cannot pass in an hour nor in a day; and when the senator from Kentucky, with whom he ought certainly to be somewhat acquainted, and to have some practical sense of his powers of endurance, — when he comes to discuss this question of repealing the Fugitive-slave Law, I think the honorable senator from Massachusetts does great injustice in turning upon me, and asking if I want to make a 'plea for slave-hunting;' and that there will be no speaking, unless it is by the honorable senator from Wisconsin." — "The speech of the senator from Wisconsin," replied Mr. Sumner, "belongs to the class of what may be called dilatory motions, or a speech to sustain a dilatory motion. He announces to us that there is to be an opposition to this bill, and mentions several senators who menace speeches." Mr. Hale was against both motions, — "against taking up the Fugitive-slave Bill, and against going into executive session. There are several very important bills, relating to the navy, on the calendar; and I have received urgent and pressing letters from the Secretary of the Navy to call the attention of the Senate to them." Mr. Powell was opposed to all the motions, and for taking up his bill to secure freedom of elections. He did "not see what good armies or navies are going to do us, if we have no freedom of elections." Mr. Hale was not willing to go into executive session, as he was not ready to proceed to the consideration of the unfinished business under consideration in executive session when we adjourned. Mr. Wilson said, "We have but very little business in executive session to attend to, and I hope we shall take up the measure indicated by my colleague." The motion to go into executive session was lost. Mr. Conness called for the yeas and nays on Mr. Sumner's motion to take up the House bill to repeal the fugitive-slave acts; and they were ordered, — yeas 25, nays 17. The bill was taken up for consideration, and the Senate took a recess until evening.

On the 22d, Mr. Sumner moved to proceed to the consideration of the bill of the House to repeal the fugitive-slave acts. Mr. Hale opposed the motion, as he desired to take up some naval bills; and demanded the yeas and nays: and Mr. Sumner's motion was lost, — yeas 14, nays 22. At the evening session, Mr. Sumner moved to take up the House bill to repeal the fugitive-slave acts. Mr. Chandler said, "I will spend the night with great pleasure with the senator from

Massachusetts on his bill; but to-morrow I shall demand the day for the Committee on Commerce." Mr. Saulsbury would adjourn: he wanted a day without the "nigger." The motion to adjourn was lost, — yeas 8, nays 28. On Mr. Sumner's motion to take up the bill, the yeas were 26, and the nays 12. Mr. Lane of Indiana moved that the Senate proceed to the consideration of executive business, — yeas 16, nays 19. Mr. Saulsbury moved to postpone the bill indefinitely; and the question, being taken by yeas and nays, resulted — yeas 11, nays 25. Mr. Sherman was willing to give to Mr. Davis from Kentucky, who was absent, a right to be heard, as he desired to speak on the bill; but if senators " propose to resort to parliamentary tactics for delay, merely to defeat a vote upon the bill, which the majority have a right to pass, I am perfectly willing to go into a contest of physical endurance."—"I am governed entirely," said Mr. Johnson, " by the wishes of the senator from Kentucky, who desires an opportunity to be heard." Mr. Willey was one of those who had voted against taking up this bill. "I did so," he said, " simply because I was told by the friends of the senator from Kentucky that he desired to be heard. If a majority of the Senate say that this matter is to be pressed to-night, I will yield at once." Mr. Sumner would meet senators half-way. "I propose that we shall go on to-night, and perfect the bill, but suspend taking the vote on its final passage, in order to give the senator from Kentucky an opportunity of being heard." Mr. Powell accepted Mr. Sumner's proposition, and withdrew his motion to postpone the further consideration of the bill till the first Monday of December next; and it was reported to the Senate without amendment.

On the 23d of June, the bill was again taken up; and Mr. Davis of Kentucky addressed the Senate in opposition to its passage. Mr. Saulsbury moved to strike out all after the enacting clause, and to insert the words of the Constitution concerning fugitives, "and that Congress shall pass all necessary laws for the rendition of all persons who shall escape." He demanded the yeas and nays; and they were ordered, — yeas 9, nays 29. Mr. Johnson moved to strike out after the word "that," in the third line, the following words: "Sections three and four of an act entitled 'An act respecting fugitives from justice, and persons escaping from the service of their masters, passed Feb. 12, 1793.'" Mr. Wilson asked for the yeas and nays; and they were ordered. Mr. M'Dougall said, "I am governed by the Constitution of the United States, and the laws passed under the Constitution; and I shall govern myself accordingly in my votes." The question, being taken by yeas and nays, resulted — yeas 17, nays 22. Mr. Saulsbury demanded the yeas and nays on the passage of the bill; and they were ordered, — yeas 27, nays 12, as follows: —

YEAS. — Messrs. Anthony, Brown, Chandler, Clark, Conness, Dixon, Fessenden, Foot, Grimes, Hale, Harlan, Harris, Hicks, Howard, Howe, Lane of Indiana, Lane of Kansas, Morgan, Morrill, Pomeroy, Ramsey, Sprague, Sumner, Ten Eyck, Trumbull, Wade, and Wilson, — 27.

NAYS. — Messrs. Buckalew, Carlile, Cowan, Davis, Johnson, M'Dougall, Powell, Richardson, Riddle, Saulsbury, Van Winkle, and Willey, — 12.

So Mr. Morris's bill repealing the fugitive-slave acts passed the Senate on the 23d, and received the approval of the President on the 28th, of June, 1864.

CHAPTER XV.

PAY OF COLORED SOLDIERS.

MR. WILSON'S BILL. — MR. GRIMES'S AMENDMENT. — MR. WILSON'S JOINT RESOLUTION. — MR. CONNESS'S AMENDMENT. — REMARKS OF MR. FESSENDEN. — MR. WILSON. — MR. FOSTER. — MR. SUMNER. — MR. JOHNSON. — MR. GRIMES. — MR. HOWE. — MR. WILSON. — MR. GRIMES. — MR. COWAN'S AMENDMENT. — MR. SUMNER'S AMENDMENT. — MR. WILSON'S AMENDMENT. — MR. DOOLITTLE'S AMENDMENT. — MR. SUMNER'S AMENDMENT TO MR. COWAN'S AMENDMENT. — MR. WILSON'S AMENDMENT. — REMARKS OF MR. CLARK. — MR. DAVIS'S AMENDMENT. — MR. COLLAMER'S AMENDMENT. — REMARKS OF MR. FOOT. — MR. SUMNER'S AMENDMENT. — REMARKS OF MR. WILKINSON. — MR. WILSON. — MR. HOWARD. — MR. JOHNSON. — MR. FESSENDEN. — MR. WILSON'S BILL. — MR. DAVIS'S AMENDMENT. — PASSAGE OF THE BILL. — MR. WILSON'S AMENDMENT TO THE ARMY APPROPRIATION BILL. — MR. STEVENS'S AMENDMENT. — REMARKS OF MR. HOLMAN. — MR. PRICE. — MR. HOLMAN'S AMENDMENT. — CONFERENCE COMMITTEES. — REPORT ACCEPTED.

IN the Senate, on the 8th of January, 1864, Mr. Wilson (Rep.) of Massachusetts introduced a bill to promote enlistments. It was read twice, referred to the Committee on Military Affairs, and reported back on the 18th with amendments. On the 21st, the Senate, on motion of Mr. Wilson, proceeded to its consideration. The second section provided that all persons of African descent, who have been or may be mustered into the military service of the United States, shall receive the same uniform, clothing, arms, equipments, camp-equipage, rations, medical and hospital attendance, pay and emoluments, as other soldiers of the regular or volunteer forces of the like arm of the service; and that every such person hereafter mustered into service shall receive two months' pay in advance. Mr. Grimes asked if bounties were given to colored soldiers by the bill. Mr. Wilson replied, that bounties were not given, but that two months' pay in advance was given. Mr. Pomeroy (Rep.) of Kansas desired to know if there was any law allowing the master of a slave compensation for the services of the slave. Mr. Wilson replied, that there was no law authorizing the War Department to allow compensation for slaves, other than the general authority to use the commutation-money to obtain substitutes.

On the 27th of January, on motion of Mr. Wilson, the Senate took up the bill to promote enlistments; and Mr. Grimes moved to amend the second section by striking out the words, "two months' pay in advance," and inserting, "such sums in bounty as the President shall order, in different States, and parts of States, not exceeding a hundred dollars;" and the amendment was agreed to.

On the 3d of February, Mr. Wilson, from the Committee on Military Affairs, reported a joint resolution to equalize the pay of colored soldiers. It provided that all persons of color, who have been or may be mustered into the military service of the United States, shall receive the same uniform, clothing, arms, equipments, camp-equipage, rations, medical and hospital attendance, pay and emoluments other than bounty, as other soldiers of the regular or volunteer forces of the United States of like arm of service, during the whole term in which they shall be or shall have been in such service; and every person of color who shall hereafter be mustered into the service is to receive such sums in bounty as the President shall order, in the different States and parts of the United States, not exceeding a hundred dollars. The Senate, on the 4th, proceeded to the consideration of the joint resolution. Mr. Fessenden (Rep.) of Maine wished " to inquire what propriety there is in our going back, and paying them this increase for services already rendered." Mr. Wilson thought, " as an act of justice, the bill should be retrospective. Gross injustice has been done towards these men, and it ought to be corrected." Mr. Ten Eyck (Rep.) of New Jersey thought " the withholding of the full pay to men who were led to believe they would receive the same pay as other soldiers has occasioned great dissatisfaction, not only in the minds of those troops, but of all their friends at home." Mr. Lane (Rep.) of Kansas hoped " the joint resolution would be retrospective." Mr. Fessenden was in favor, and had ever been in favor, of putting colored soldiers on a level with white ones; but he was opposed to paying men for services already rendered, unless the men were promised full pay by orders emanating from the War Department. Mr. Conness (Union) from California moved to strike out the words, " during the whole time in which they shall be or shall have been in such service," and insert, " from and after the passage of this act." Mr. Lane hoped the amendment would not be adopted: " The senator from California should not attempt to perpetrate such an outrage upon a gallant regiment of his State." Mr. Conness was in favor of equality of compensation in the future; but " neither the condition of the treasury, nor the public credit, can afford ' these acts of justice,' as they are termed." Mr. Pomeroy (Rep.) of Kansas thought we should give colored soldiers the precise pay, and place them in precisely the same position, as white soldiers. Mr. Doolittle (Rep.) of Wisconsin said, "If the Government has in good faith made a promise to soldiers who have enlisted in any particular regiment, whether in Massachusetts or anywhere else, that promise ought to be kept." He thought there were differences in the condition of colored troops in the States. In the Northern States, they were in the same condition as the white soldiers; but, in the Southern States, the Government was doing much to support their wives and children, and some account should be made of this expenditure. "I wish," said Mr. Sumner, "to see our colored troops treated like white troops in every respect. But I would not press this first principle by any retro-active proposition, unless where the faith of the Government is committed; and there I would not hesitate. The treasury can bear any additional burden better than the country can bear to do an injustice." On the 10th, the Senate resumed the consideration of the joint resolution equalizing the pay of soldiers. Mr. Foster (Rep.) thought, "If it is just to do this, it is certainly expedient; for justice is always the highest expediency." He thought justice required that we carry out the pledges of the Government or of public officers; " but justice especially requires it when we consider that we are dealing with men, a great portion of whom, as I have suggested, were never taught to read, and never could, therefore, know what the written law of the country was." Mr. Sumner quoted the order of the Secretary of War to Governor Andrew of Massachusetts, and maintained that it was issued under the law of 1861, not the act of 1862. Mr. Fessenden could not concur in Mr. Sumner's construction of the act of 1862. Mr. Lane (Rep.) of Indiana thought, "If we place colored troops hereafter on an equality with the white troops, it is surely as much as they can ask, either from the justice or the generosity of this Senate; for no man in his sober senses will say that their services are worth as much, or that they are as good soldiers." Mr. Wilson said, "A colonel of a colored regiment stated to me, the other night, that his regiment made a march of forty-three miles in the late expedition to North Carolina, without one straggler; that he had seen but one case of drunkenness in his regiment for six months. All the testimony of our officers who took these troops with prejudices against them goes to show that they are industrious; that they are obedient; that they are deferential in their manners; that they make the best kind of scouts; that they know the country well; that they are performing their duty with a zeal and an earnestness unsurpassed. There is a reason for this. Take a colored man who has been degraded by popular prejudice, or by law, or in any other way, put the uniform of the United States upon him, and let him follow the flag of the country, and he feels proud and elevated. They are fighting for the elevation of their race, as well as for our country and our cause, and for the emancipation of their race; and well may they perform that duty." Mr. Sumner said, "I hope the senator from Indiana will pardon me if I refer to him for one minute. He is so uniformly generous and just, that I was the more surprised when I listened to his remarks just now. I was surprised at his lack of generosity and his lack of justice — he will pardon me — toward these colored soldiers. I was surprised — he will pardon me — at his injustice to the State of Massachusetts. He spoke disparagingly of the colored soldiers. He thought they had been paid enough. He thought that the gallant blood shed on the parapets of Fort Wagner had been paid enough; and he failed to see that those men who died for us on that bloody night, and were buried in the same grave with their colonel who led them, now stood alive in this presence to plead for the equality of their race."

The Senate, on the 13th, resumed the consideration of the joint resolution; and Mr. Conness withdrew his amendment to strike out the retrospective clause. Mr. Sumner offered an amendment, that in regard to all past services, if it shall appear to the satisfaction of the Secretary of War that the persons were led to suppose they were mustered into the service under the act of July 22, 1861, they shall receive full pay. Mr. Anthony thought the amendment did not cover the case. "I think there were a number of these men — I know it was so in my State — who were led to suppose that they would have the same pay as the white soldiers as soon as Congress assembled; that the manifest injustice of paying white soldiers one price, and colored soldiers another price, would be at once corrected." — "In my view," said Mr. Johnson, "there is no obligation, either legal or moral, upon the Government to pay these men more than the law entitles them to." Mr. Grimes thought "this matter is being compromised by attempting to cover some individual cases in a general law. I think, however, that the Chairman of the Committee on Military Affairs had better not involve this bill with any reference to the Massachusetts regiments or to the Rhode-Island men who have been enlisted, or to the South-Carolina regiments." Mr. Howe rose "to assent to the advice given by the senator from Iowa: it is eminently sensible."—"It is evident," said Mr. Wilson, "after what has been said here this morning, that this joint resolution is delayed by the attempt to do justice to some ten or fifteen or twenty regiments to whom this promise was made. I think the amendment proposed by my colleague would not apply to more than fifteen or twenty regiments at most, and it would be at the discretion of the Secretary of War. I should be perfectly willing to trust it in his hands. But, as I see that I cannot get the resolution through promptly in its present shape, I propose to amend it by striking out that portion which makes it retrospective, — by striking out all after the word 'service' in the ninth line, down to the word 'and' in the tenth line, and inserting 'from the first day of January, 1864;' so that it will read, 'As other soldiers of the regular or volunteer forces of the United States of like arm of the service, from and after the first day of January, 1864." Mr. Johnson thought, "If the Governor of Massachusetts has made a promise which the law did not authorize; if he has created, as between the Massachusetts soldiers and the Governor of Massachusetts, an obligation which ought to be redeemed, let Massachusetts redeem it." — "They have passed," said Mr. Fessenden, "a law to redeem it; but these regiments refuse to receive it of Massachusetts." Mr. Wilson explained the action of the State, and the position of the colored regiments in declining to receive the money of Massachusetts. "They enlisted under the expectation of receiving the same pay as other troops, and they hold the Government to its pledges." Mr. Johnson, in reply, said, "They are gentlemen of most extraordinary sensibility." — "They will not receive," said Mr. Collamer, "the three dollars from the State, or the ten dollars from the United States." — "I will say," replied Mr. Johnson, "if they are made up of that material, they will not be as good soldiers as we hope the others will be." — "They have made their record on that point," replied Mr. Wilson. "I sympathize," said Mr. Grimes, "a great deal with those gallant and patriotic noble young men who have gone out in command of the Massachusetts fifty-fourth and fifty-fifth regiments, and who are in command of the first and second South-Carolina regiments. I know a great many of them. I know them to be gallant and patriotic young men. But I cannot help thinking that they have involved us unnecessarily in trouble in connection with this subject; for I know perfectly well that it was through their persuasions that these colored troops in South Carolina declined to receive the money that Massachusetts voted to pay them." Mr. Cowan (Rep.) would vote to equalize the pay, but was opposed to retrospective legislation in this case. Mr. Collamer thought Mr. Sumner's amendment did "not reach the case at all. It puts the question of paying these men back to the time of their enlistment, upon whether they were led to believe or did believe that they were to receive thirteen dollars a month. I do not think it makes any difference what they were led to believe or did believe. It is not to be put upon any contingency of that kind. There is the written enlistment; and it speaks for itself." The amendment was lost.

Mr. Wilson then moved to strike out the words, "during the whole time in which they shall be or shall have been in such service," and to insert in lieu thereof, "from and after the first day of January, 1864." The amendment was agreed to. Mr. Doolittle moved to amend by reserving out of the pay of colored soldiers from the States in rebellion four dollars per month to reimburse the Government for expenses incurred in feeding and clothing women and children of color in those States. Mr. Conness opposed the amendment. Mr. Sherman thought it not only just, but in accordance with the practice of the Government. Mr. Grimes objected to this amendment. "Is it just," he inquired, "to take four dollars from the pay of a man who has no wife, and put it into a common fund?" Mr. Wilson believed that the women and children, being accustomed to outdoor work, instead of being a burden to the Government, are a benefit to it. Mr. Lane of Kansas believed that "the families of the colored soldiers are self-sustaining machines almost from the moment they enter our lines. I hope," he said, "that this amendment will not receive a single vote in this Chamber; for it is a discrimination between the soldiers of the army of the United States, and an invitation to Jeff. Davis to persist in his brutal treatment of our gallant troops." Mr. Doolittle's amendment was rejected. Mr. Cowan moved to strike out all after the enacting clause, and insert, "That, from and after the passage of this resolution, the soldiers of the United States of

America, of the same grade and service, shall be entitled to the same pay, rations, and pension. Mr. Sumner moved to amend the original bill by adding as a proviso: "*Provided*, that in all cases of past service, where it shall appear to the satisfaction of the Secretary of War, by the actual papers of enlistment, that such persons were enlisted as volunteers under the act of July, 1861, the pay promised by that act shall be allowed from the commencement of such service." The question, being taken by yeas and nays, resulted — yeas 16, nays 21. Mr. Cowan earnestly advocated his amendment. He was in favor of "treating the negro precisely the same as any other man. He was a citizen of the United States. When I say that the negro is a citizen, I do not mean to say that he is equal to the white man." Mr. Saulsbury rose to enter his "protest against the constitutional views of the senator from Pennsylvania." He objected to the words "colored soldiers" and "colored persons." They used the word "negro" in his State. "Now, lo and behold, in the advancement of civilization and Christianity and refinement of which we hear so much, the negro has got to be a 'colored person;' and, when you come to provide for calling him into the public service, there must be perfect equality!"

On motion of Mr. Wilson, the Senate resumed, on the 16th, the consideration of the joint resolution. Mr. Wilson moved to amend Mr. Cowan's amendment by striking out all after the word "that," and inserting, "From and after the passage of this resolution, the soldiers of the United States of America, of the same grade and service, shall be entitled to the same pay, rations, and pension." Mr. Davis then gave notice that he would move to amend Mr. Cowan's substitute. He addressed the Senate for two days in denunciation of the policy of the Government, and in reviewing the history and criticising the action of Massachusetts.

On the 23d, the Senate resumed the consideration of the joint resolution; the pending question being on Mr. Wilson's amendment to Mr. Cowan's substitute for the original resolution. Mr. Wilson modified his amendment: the vote was taken upon it, and it was lost. Mr. Davis moved three resolutions as an amendment in the nature of a substitute to Mr. Cowan's amendment. The amendment proposed that all negroes and mulattoes — by whatever term designated — in the military service of the United States, be, and the same are hereby, declared to be discharged from such service, and shall be disarmed as soon as practicable. Mr. Conness demanded the yeas and nays, and they were ordered. Mr. Clark opposed this proposition to disband thousands of soldiers. "I want," said Mr. Clark, "the black man to have arms in his hands. I glory in the opportunity of putting arms in his hands, that, when he puts down the Rebellion, he may put down for ever the institution which has enslaved him. I hail in it the safety of the black man. I glory in his elevation: and I say here to the senator from Kentucky, — and I say it unhesitatingly, — that, when you have put arms in the hands of the black man, you cannot enslave him; and therefore I would give him arms. I would make his arms his protection. I would teach him to respect himself as a man, and to feel that he is respected, and his rights preserved. . . . When the negro was brought into the service of the country, he vindicated himself;

he showed that he could make a good soldier; he showed that he could make a good fighter; he showed that he could make a good marcher; he showed that he was obedient to discipline; he showed, that, in some cases, he could endure more than the white man, and was equally loyal and ready to fight. Then, if the black man makes a good soldier; if he goes readily to the fight; if he stands up firmly and bravely, and gives his blood and his life to the country, — I ask, Why should he not be paid? Can anybody tell me?" The vote was taken on Mr. Davis's amendment, — yeas 7, nays 30.

Mr. Collamer proposed to amend the original joint resolution by adding to it, "All persons enlisted into the service as volunteers under the call dated Oct. 17, 1863, who were at the time of enlistment actually, and for six months previous had been, resident inhabitants of the State in which they volunteered, shall receive from the United States the same amount of bounty, without regard to color; *provided, however*, that the foregoing provision shall not extend to any State which the President by proclamation has declared in a state of insurrection." Mr. Foot earnestly and eloquently advocated this amendment. The War Department, after the call of October for three hundred thousand men, offered a bounty, to all accepted volunteers, of $300. "This is simply," he said, "a proposition to redeem that promise, — a promise published and proclaimed everywhere throughout the country; in every nook and corner of the country, at the threshold of every hamlet in the country, — a promise everywhere and by everybody understood as applying to and embracing all accepted volunteers, without exception of class or color,—a promise everywhere and by everybody so *interpreted* and so *relied upon*, and so *acted upon*." Mr. Sumner moved to amend Mr. Collamer's amendment by adding, "that all persons whose papers of enlistment shall show that they were enlisted under the act of Congress of July, 1861, shall receive, from the time of their enlistment, the pay promised by that statute,"—yeas 19, nays 18. Mr. Wilson moved to amend Mr. Collamer's amendment by adding the word "free" after the word "all," for the reason that all slaves are now provided for by law. Mr. Wilkinson earnestly opposed this amendment, and severely criticised the provisions of the Enrolment Act for drafting and enlisting slaves. "I am willing," said Mr. Wilson in reply, "that he shall denounce that measure. That act says to every slave in the loyal States, 'Enroll your name among the defenders of the Republic; and, the hour you are mustered into our armies, you are a free man for evermore.' The Government of the United States by that act, for the first time in our history, has declared tens of thousands of slaves in the loyal States free, upon their own will to become free. It is incomparably the greatest emancipation measure that was ever passed by the Congress of the United States; and I would rather have my name to that bill, which asserts the power of this nation to emancipate every slave in the country who will enroll his name among the defenders of the Union, than to any measure for which my name stands recorded in favor of the freedom of mankind. Sir, I glory in the vote, and I glory in that measure." Mr. Howard eloquently defended his vote against that portion of the Enrolment Act relating to mustering slaves into the service. "You call him to aid you in your wars," he said: "your necessities remit him to the condition in which Nature herself placed him. The hand of robbery becomes palsied. Freedom, his birthright, accrues to him as a responsible being; and he again enjoys what was not yours to give, and which human force and crime have withheld. The Almighty, not you, restores to him the gift of liberty. He owes you nothing for it; not even gratitude." — "The senator from Michigan," said Mr. Johnson, "seems to think that nothing has been gained by the slave. Nothing! What was his condition before? That of a slave, — slavery for himself and his posterity for ever. What do we tell him? Come into the service of the United States, and you shall be free, you and yours; the shackles that have bound your limbs shall fall from them; you shall stand erect in the presence of your Maker, as free as any white man who treads the soil. Is that nothing?"

Mr. Fessenden addressed the Senate, on the 29th, in explanation of his sentiments and opinions. He had, from the beginning, been in favor of placing colored soldiers on the same footing as white soldiers. "Pass," he said, "the bill, and settle the principle as it ought to be settled; place the colored troops on the same level with the white troops in all cases; let them receive the same pay and rations, and every thing else." Mr. Grimes moved to recommit the joint resolution to the Military Committee; and the motion was agreed to.

On the 2d of March, Mr. Wilson reported a new bill, in lieu of the original joint resolution to equalize the pay of soldiers. The first section placed colored soldiers on an equality with white soldiers from the 1st of January, 1864; the second section gave the same bounties to colored volunteers in the loyal States, under the call of October, 1863; the third section gave to all persons of color, who have been enlisted and mustered into the service of the United States, the pay allowed by law to other volunteers in the service, from the date of their muster, if it has been pledged or promised to them by any officer or person, who, in making such pledge or promise, acted by authority of the War Department; and the Secretary of War is to determine any question of fact arising under this provision. Mr. Davis moved to amend the bill by adding a section to give to loyal owners of slaves such compensation as should be determined by commissioners appointed by the Circuit Court. On the 9th, Mr. Davis spoke at great length upon matters pertaining to slavery: his amendment was rejected on the 10th, — yeas 6, nays 31. Mr. Davis then demanded the yeas and nays on the passage of the bill, — yeas 31, nays 6. So the joint resolution passed the Senate.

On the 22d of April, Mr. Wilson moved to amend the Army-appropriation Bill by adding as an amendment the bill, which passed the Senate on the 10th of March, to equalize the pay of soldiers in the army. In support of his amendment, he said, "The failure of Congress to increase the pay of colored soldiers is not only checking enlistments, but disastrously affecting the men in the field. Sir, can we, dare we, hope for the blessing of Heaven upon our cause, while we perpetrate these wrongs, or suffer them to remain unredressed? Can we demand that the rebels shall give to our colored soldiers the rights of civilized warfare, while we refuse to them equality of rights? Can we redress the brutal and bloody butchery at Fort Pillow, while we continue this injustice? Sir, the whole country is horrified at the barbarities perpetrated by the rebels upon our colored soldiers. The civilized world will be shocked as it reads of the bloody butchery at Fort Pillow. Sir, I feel that the nation is doing a wrong to the colored soldiers hardly less wicked than the wrongs perpetrated upon them by slaveholding traitors." Mr. Fessenden thought the measure ought to be passed, and passed at once. If the Senate would waive the objection to put it on the Appropriation Bill, he would not object to it. The amendment was agreed to, — yeas 32, nays 6.

In the House, on the 30th of April, Mr. Stevens (Rep.) of Pennsylvania asked leave to report from the Committee of Ways and Means the Senate amendments to the Army-appropriation Bill. Mr. Holman (Dem.) of Indiana opposed the amendment equalizing the pay of soldiers. "I protest against it," he said, "as but a part of your general policy, which seeks by the force of power to extinguish every vestige of the old Republic of our fathers, wild, reckless, impracticable. I protest against it in the name of a distracted and bleeding country, which, struggling with defiant treason, and demanding prudence and patriotism in the conduct of its affairs, and the noblest incentives to constancy and courage, receives at your hands only the paralyzing counsels of fanaticism and passion." Mr. Price (Rep.) of Iowa said, "Gen. Jackson, in his day, knew something of the value of negro soldiers as well as white soldiers; and he placed them upon an equality as to pay and rations." — "I despise the principle," said Mr. Stevens, "that would make a difference between them in the hour of battle and of death. The idea that we are to keep up that distinction is abhorrent to the feelings of the age, is abhorrent to the feelings of humanity, is shocking to every decent instinct of our nature; and I take it that no man who is not wedded to the institution of slavery, or does not foster it for the sake of power, will go with the gentleman from Indiana." Mr. Holman moved to strike out the word "pay," — yeas 52, nays 84. Mr. Schenck (Rep.) of Ohio moved to amend the Senate amendment: lost, — ayes 58, noes 65. The Senate amendment equalizing the pay of soldiers was agreed to, — yeas 80, nays 49. Mr. Schenck moved to amend that portion of the Senate amendment giving to colored volunteers the same bounties allowed to white volunteers under the call of October, 1863; so that the bounty should not exceed a hundred dollars, — yeas 78, nays 51. Mr. Stevens moved to strike out the section of the Senate amendment authorizing the Secretary of War, on proof, to allow full pay to volunteers who were promised it, and to insert that all free persons of color shall receive the same pay as other soldiers, — yeas 73, nays 54.

The Senate, on the 3d of May, disagreed to the House amendments, asked a Committee of Conference; and the Chair appointed Mr. Fessenden, Mr. Wilson, and Mr. Henderson, conferrees. The House insisted on its amendments; and the Speaker appointed Mr. Stevens, Mr. Schenck, and Mr. Morrison, conferrees on the part of the House. The Conference Committee were unable to agree. A second Conference Committee was appointed, and the Conference Committee's report was rejected by the House on the 26th of May; and the House appointed Mr. Stevens, Mr. Pendleton, and Mr. Davis of New York, conferrees, and asked another conference. The Senate, on the 27th, agreed to another Conference Committee; and Mr. Howe, Mr. Morrill, and Mr. Buckalew, were appointed conferrees. On the 10th of June, the committees reported that the House recede from its amendment reducing the bounty of volunteers enlisted under the call of October, 1863, from three hundred dollars to one hundred dollars; and that "all persons of color who were free on the nineteenth day of April, 1861, and who have been enlisted and mustered into the military service of the United States, shall from the time of their enlistment be entitled to receive the pay, bounty, and clothing allowed to such persons by the laws existing at the time of their enlistment. And the Attorney-General of the United States is hereby authorized to determine any question of law arising under this provision; and if the Attorney-General aforesaid shall determine that any of such enlisted persons are entitled to receive any pay, bounty, or clothing, in addition to what they have already received, the Secretary of War shall make all necessary regulations to enable the pay department to make payment in accordance with such determination." Mr. Pendleton refused to sign the report. Mr. Sumner desired to know in what condition the report left the colored troops enlisted in South Carolina. Mr. Howe, Chairman of the Conference Committee replied, that it made no provision for them, unless they were free at the breaking-out of the war. Mr. Sumner, as a senator from Massachusetts, might be content, as the regiments from his State were cared for;

but he was interested in the adjustment, on principles of justice, of colored troops from other States. Mr. Wilson said there was no doubt that the South-Carolina regiments ought to have full pay, and it was wrong to quibble about it: to limit the provision to men who were free in 1861 leaves out the men who were slaves then, and who ought to have justice done them. Mr. Pomeroy thought injustice was done to regiments from his State. Mr. Conness opposed the report as an "unjust discrimination." Mr. Howe explained and defended the report. Mr. Sumner said, "The last chapter of 'Rasselas' is entitled, 'A conclusion in which nothing is concluded;' and I think that title may be properly given to the report of this committee." — "The report of the committee," said Mr. Johnson, "really does settle nothing; and it is not intended to settle any thing, except contingently." Mr. Fessenden appealed to senators to concur in the adoption of the report. "I shall," said Mr. Wilson, "run the risk of it, for the reason that the bill, as it now stands, settles the question of equality from the 1st of January last; and, in the next place, it settles the question of bounty to colored men who are liable to be drafted in the loyal States, and it puts their matter in the control of the Attorney-General, whose opinion, I think, cannot be any thing else than that these men have the right which they claim." Mr. Henderson was unwilling to pay colored troops more than they agreed to receive when they enlisted.

On the 11th, Mr. Wilson moved to take up for consideration the report of the Conference Committee. Mr. Sumner did not think the report creditable to Congress; and he concurred in its acceptance with reluctance.

"It is," he said, "in the full confidence that in this way we shall at last, through the opinion of the Attorney-General, obtain that justice which Congress has denied, that I consent to give my vote for this report." The report was accepted by the Senate. In the House, the report was accepted on the 13th, — yeas 71, nays 58. By the provisions of this legislation, colored troops were in all respects placed on the same footing as white troops from the 1st of January, 1864. Colored volunteers in the loyal States, under the call of the 17th of October, 1863, were allowed the same bounty as white volunteers; all colored soldiers free on the 19th of April, 1861, were to receive full pay; and the Attorney-General was authorized to decide whether colored men not free on the 19th of April were entitled to the same pay as white soldiers. The Attorney-General has finally decided that colored soldiers are in all respects entitled to the same compensation as white soldiers.

CHAPTER XVI.

TO MAKE FREE THE WIVES AND CHILDREN OF COLORED SOLDIERS.

MR. WILSON'S BILL TO PROMOTE ENLISTMENTS. — MR. POWELL'S MOTION TO STRIKE OUT THE SECTION TO MAKE FREE THE MOTHERS, WIVES, AND CHILDREN OF COLORED SOLDIERS. — MR. HENDERSON'S AMENDMENT. — REMARKS OF MR. GRIMES. — MR. WILKINSON. — REMARKS OF MR. JOHNSON. — MR. SHERMAN'S SPEECH. — MR. CARLILE'S SPEECH. — REMARKS OF MR. DOOLITTLE. — MR. BROWN'S AMENDMENT. — MR. WILSON'S AMENDMENT. — MR. WILKINSON'S AMENDMENT. — REMARKS OF MR. SHERMAN. — MR. GRIMES. — MR. CONNESS'S MOTION TO REFER THE BILL. — REMARKS OF MR. CLARK. — MR. HOWARD. — MR. FESSENDEN. — MR. DAVIS'S AMENDMENT. — MR. WILKINSON'S SPEECH. — MR. WILSON'S JOINT RESOLUTION.

THE third section of the bill to promote enlistments, introduced into the Senate on the 8th of January, 1864, by Mr. Wilson of Massachusetts, declared that when any man or boy of African descent, owing service or labor in any State, under its laws, shall be mustered into the military or naval service of the United States, he, and his mother, wife, and children, shall be for ever free. On the 27th of January, the Senate proceeded to the consideration of the bill to promote enlistments. Mr. Powell (Dem.) of Kentucky moved to strike out the third section giving freedom to the mother, wife, and children of the colored soldier. Mr. Powell pronounced the section "clearly and palpably unconstitutional. There is certainly no power in this Congress to pass any such law. It is depriving loyal men of loyal

States of their property, by the legislative enactment of this Congress." Mr. Henderson moved to strike out the words, "his mother, and his wife and children," and insert, "and his mother, his wife and children, shall also be free, provided that, by the laws of any State, they owe service or labor to any person or persons who have given aid or comfort to the existing Rebellion against the Government, since the 17th of July, 1862." Mr. Grimes said, "That is substantially the law now. The reason why I shall vote for this section is, that I am exceedingly anxious to pass a law by which it shall be declared, that if a man who has perilled his life for me and for the institutions of my country at Port Hudson — I care not what kind of a claim may be set up to his service, or who may set it up — is claimed by any one, that claim shall not be regarded. I am unwilling that after he has thus perilled his life, and been wounded in my defence, he shall be taken off to slavery by any person, or under any sort of institution. I think that such a proposition as this will meet the approval and commendation of the country; and I rejoice that the senator from Massachusetts, and the Committee on Military Affairs, have given us an opportunity to record our votes in favor of it." Mr. Wilkinson said, " That is the law as it now stands; and if the senator from Missouri wishes to carry out the purpose, or to retain this provision of the existing law, all he has to do is to oppose this section entirely. I think that law is the most disgraceful legislation of the Congress which passed it. It is a disgrace to the nation to pass such a law; and I am very much rejoiced that the Committee on Military Affairs have introduced this bill wiping it out." Mr. Henderson did not offer the amendment, to protect slavery. "I have not been engaged," he said, "very recently in the protection of that institution; and, so far as I can go constitutionally to abolish the institution throughout the country, I most unhesitatingly would do so. My impression is, that, when you put this Rebellion down, slavery for ever dies, because of the fact that they have organized this Rebellion on the existence of the institution; and, if the Rebellion goes by the board, the institution itself goes. I can further state to those gentlemen, that I believe no State will again take its place in the Union, without first, by the action of its own people, abolishing slavery."

The Senate on the 28th resumed, on motion of Mr. Wilson, the consideration of the bill. Mr. Wilkinson demanded the yeas and nays on Mr. Henderson's motion to strike out "his mother, and his wife and children;" and they were ordered. Mr. Johnson should vote in favor of the amendment. "I doubt very much," he said, "if any member of the Senate is more anxious to have the country composed entirely of free men and free women than I am. Sir, the bill provides that a slave enlisted anywhere, no matter where he may be, whether he be within Maryland or out of Maryland, whether he be within any other of the loyal States, or out of the loyal States altogether, is at once to work the emancipation of his wife and children. He may be in South Carolina; and many a slave in South Carolina, I am sorry to say it, can well claim to have a wife, or perhaps wives and children, within the limits of Maryland. It is one of the vices and the horrible vices of the institution, one that has shocked me from infancy to the present hour, that the whole marital relation is disregarded. They are made to be, practically and by education, forgetful or ignorant of that relation. When I say they are educated, I mean to say they are kept in absolute ignorance; and, out of that, immorality of every description arises; and among other immoralities is that the connubial relation does not exist."

On the 2d of February, Mr. Sherman addressed the Senate upon the general questions of employing colored men as soldiers, and of emancipation. "On the subject of emancipation," he declared, "I am ready now to go as far as any one. Like all others, I hesitated at first, because I could not see the effect of the general project of emancipation. I think the time has now arrived when we must meet this question of emancipation boldly and fearlessly. There is no other way. Slavery is destroyed, not by your act, sir, or mine, but by the act of this Rebellion. I think, therefore, the better way would be to wipe out all that is left of the whole trouble, — the dead and buried and wounded of this system of slavery. It is obnoxious to every manly and generous sentiment. From the beginning, we should have armed the slaves; but before doing so, in my judgment, we ought to secure them by law, by a great guaranty, in which you and I, and all branches of the Government, would unite in pledging the faith of the United States, that, for ever thereafter, they should hold their freedom against their old masters." Mr. Carlile followed Mr. Sherman, on the 8th, in opposition to the bill. He emphatically declared, that, "if it shall become necessary in this struggle for the confederates to arm their slaves, they will arm and emancipate them too; and I will say further, if their confederacy never crumbles into dust until it does so from the arming and emancipating their slaves, it will last until —

'Heaven's last thunder shakes the world below.'

The slaves know that their owners have the legal right to emancipate them. Many of them know that you have not."

On the 9th, the Senate resumed the consideration of the bill; the pending question being Mr. Henderson's amendment to strike out "his mother, wife, and children." Mr. Doolittle (Rep.) of Wisconsin opposed the bill, but favored an amendment of the Constitution. "Slavery," he said, "is dying, dying, all around us. It is dying as a suicide dies. It is dying in the House, and at the hands of its own professed friends. The sword which it would have driven into the vitals of this Republic is parried, and thrust back into its own. And, sir, let it die; let it die. Without any sympathy of mine, slavery with all its abominations may die, and go into everlasting perdition." Mr. Richardson (Dem.) of Illinois asserted, that, "while senators are struggling for the rights of the negro, they forget the white race, — the race that has made this country so great and so glorious; that has upheld your flag in triumph on every ocean, and has carried your commerce to all the civilized ports of the earth." On the 8th of March, Mr. Brown (Rep.) of Missouri moved to amend the bill by striking out the third section, making the "mother, wife, and children" of the colored soldier free, and inserting an amendment re-affirming the President's proclamation of emancipation, and abolishing slavery throughout the United

States. He affirmed, in an elaborate speech of rare beauty and force, "that slavery yet liveth, the discussion which has attended every measure introduced here trenching upon it sufficiently attests. Neither dead, nor willing to die, but struggling for being, by joint and ligature and tissue and nerve, that some centre of future growth may lurk under proviso or exception, its vitality 's upheld in this hour by appeal to the same constitutionalisms and local countenance that will be swift to maintain it hereafter if this epoch shall pass without its utter extinction. The soldier who has worn our uniform and served under our flag must not hereafter labor as a slave. Nor would it be tolerable that his wife, his mother, or his child, should be the property of another. The instinctive feeling of every man of generous impulse would revolt at such a spectacle. The guaranty of freedom for himself, his mother, his wife, and his child, is the inevitable incident of the employment of a slave as a soldier. If you have not the power, or do not mean, to emancipate him, and those with whom he is connected by domestic ties, then, in the name of God and humanity, do not employ him as a soldier!"

On the 18th of March, Mr. Brown withdrew his amendment; and Mr. Wilson moved to strike out the entire bill, and insert, "That when any person of African descent, whose service or labor is claimed in any State under the laws thereof, shall be mustered into the military or naval service of the United States, his wife and children, if any he have, shall for ever thereafter be free, any law, usage, or custom whatsoever, to the contrary notwithstanding; that it shall be the duty of the commission appointed in each of the slave States represented in Congress under the provisions of the twenty-fourth section of the 'Act to amend an act entitled "An act for enrolling and calling out the national forces, and for other purposes," approved March 3, 1863,' approved Feb. 24, 1864, to award to each loyal person, to whom the wife and children aforesaid may owe service, a just compensation, to be paid out of any moneys which may be appropriated by Congress for that purpose." "I propose," he said, "in this amendment, to make the soldier's wife and children free, no matter to whom they belong. We have provided in the Enrolment Act, that a slave enlisted into the military service of the United States is free when he is mustered into the service. We have exercised that great power to strengthen the Government in putting down the Rebellion. We have enlisted about eighty thousand colored men, and we are continuing to enlist colored men, in all parts of the country. But, sir, the enlistment of colored men causes a vast deal of suffering; for a great wrong is done to their families, and especially is that so in the State of Missouri. Those wives and children who are left behind, may be sold, may be abused; and how can a soldier fight the battles of our country when he receives the intelligence that the wife he left at home, and the little ones he left around his hearth, were sold into perpetual slavery, — sold where he would never see them more? Sir, if there be a crime on earth that should be promptly punished, it is the crime of selling into slavery, in a distant section of the country, the wives and children of the soldiers who are fighting the battles of our bleeding country. Now wife and children plead to the husband and father not to enlist, — to remain at home for their protection. Pass this bill, and the wife and children will beseech that husband and father to fight for the country, for his liberty, and for their freedom." Mr. Wilkinson moved to strike out the second section of the amendment, which proposed to pay the estimated value of wives and children of colored soldiers. Mr. Pomeroy would amend that section. "I should like," he said, "to have that section amended in the eighth line by striking out the words, 'to award to each loyal person to whom the wife and children aforesaid may owe service a just compensation,' and inserting, 'to settle the account between each such person made free and his or her owner, and award to each party such just compensation as may be found due.'"

Mr. Sherman moved to postpone the bill until Thursday next, with a view that we may act upon the main proposition, the amendment to the Constitution to abolish slavery in the United States. Mr. Sumner said the main question was to hit slavery wherever and whenever it could be found. "I think it is a measure to fill up our armies," said Mr. Wilson; "and it ought not to be postponed an hour. Then, as a matter of justice, how can you go to a man, and ask him to enlist to fight the battles of his country, when he knows, that, the moment his back is turned, his wife and children will be sold to strangers?" Mr. Wilkinson believed the vote to be a most important one, and the proposition of Mr. Sherman would allow it to be more fully considered. Mr. Lane of Kansas differed with Mr. Wilkinson "as to the question of time. This is a bill, that, in my opinion, should be voted upon at the very earliest day, or else we should stop enlisting black men." Mr. Grimes said, "Here is a bill, which, it seems to me, it is very important that we should pass at an early day in some shape or other, either in the shape in which the senator from Massasachusetts (Mr. Wilson) presents it to us, and which I do not really approve, or as proposed to be amended by the senator from Minnesota (Mr. Wilkinson), or as proposed to be amended by the senator from Missouri (Mr. Brown); and I do not know of any bill that is before us, or that is likely to be before us to-day, which deserves the careful and the immediate attention of Congress more than this bill does." — "I suggested," said Mr. Sherman, "in its discussion, a long time ago, practical difficulties which the senator from Massachusetts has not met. Who is the wife of a slave? Who is the child of a slave? What is the use of passing this bill, without employing some definite and distinctive language that will embrace the persons whom it is designed to embrace?" Mr. Brown said, "You have the fact before you, that these colored soldiers are going into the army of the United States: You have the further fact before you, that slave-owners are hounding on a persecution in the Border States, and selling the wives and children of those soldiers, making merchandise of their flesh and blood, and doing it as a punishment for their entry into our army as volunteers for our defence. Shall we tolerate that scene? Shall we legislate here, sending men day after day to sacrifice their lives for our protection, and yet sit quietly by, with no legislation to prevent, and see others sending the wives and children of those men day after day into further and harsher bondage because they have done so?" — "I do not," said

Mr. Grimes, "apprehend that there is going to be any great trouble in ascertaining who are the wives and children of these men. As has been well said by the senator from Missouri, we all know that the laws of the slave States do not recognize the relation of husband and wife, or parent and child; but we recognize the fact that such relations do *de facto* exist, and that is enough for our purpose: it ought to be enough; and we shall be justified by the people of the country who sent us here in regarding it as enough for all the purposes of this bill."

"There are," said Mr. Sherman, "grave questions of constitutional power involved in this proposition. The general object proposed to be accomplished, I desire as much as any one; but I want to do it in an effective way: and I think it is much wiser for us to defer all these propositions in regard to slavery, until we can, by a general plan based upon a constitutional amendment proposed by Congress, and submitted to the people, aided by auxiliary legislation, wipe out the whole system in the mode provided by the Constitution." — "The senator from Ohio," said Mr. Wilson, "takes the position, that, because there is a proposition pending to amend the Constitution of the United States to abolish slavery, we are to do nothing else against slavery. Sir, I say it is sound policy to strike this system of slavery whenever and wherever you can get a blow at it. It is to perish, if it perish at all, by hedging it around by every enactment, breaking down every barrier that surrounds it, and defeating the three hundred thousand bayonets behind which it is intrenched." Mr. Conness moved to refer the bill to the Committee on Slavery and

Freedmen. Mr. Wilson objected to the recommitment of the bill, and modified his amendment by withdrawing the second section. Mr. Conness said it was not in a condition that he could vote for it. He hoped the Senate would come to a vote on the motion to recommit. Mr. Carlile would refer it to the Judiciary Committee. He thought the difficulties that had been suggested as to ascertaining who are the wife and children of the party will not be found to be great in practical operation. "The great question," he said, "which stands in my way in support of this bill, is the question of power." Mr. Clark opposed recommitment. It would return from the Judiciary Committee with the same question embarrassing it. He would discuss the question in the Senate. He said, "Here you desire to put soldiers in your army, and those soldiers have their wives and their children. You are desirous of putting those soldiers in the service at the earliest moment; and the people who want to prevent those soldiers from going into the army take these very means to torment the soldier, so that he shall not go in. The master says to him, in effect, 'If you go into the armies of the United States, and fight the battles of the country, I will sell your wife; I will abuse your children.' That is very much worse than the rendition of a fugitive slave; and an amendment of the Constitution which would take place months hence does not cure or remedy the evil." Mr. Doolittle asked Mr. Clark if he had evidence that loyal masters "abused their women and children." — "We know," replied Mr. Clark, "that everywhere in these loyal States there are men who are in sympathy with the Rebellion. We know that men in the loyal States are opposed to the negroes going into the service. Many of those men — I will not say all — would be willing to punish the negro if he went in, if they are in sympathy with the Rebellion, by the abuse of his wife and children. They wish to deter him from going into the service if they can; and they say to him, 'Not only shall your wife and children have no care, no food, no protection, but they shall be sold into slavery; and, when you return from fighting the battles of the Union, you shall find your home desolate, your wife gone no one knows where in slavery, and your children all sent away.'" Mr. Howard hoped this bill would not be referred to the Judiciary Committee. He said, "There may be some difficulty in the apprehension of some gentlemen, perhaps, as to who can claim to be the wife or the child of a slave; inasmuch as the laws of the slaveholding States do not recognize the relation of husband and wife, and of parent and child, in that class. I know of no other mode of solving this difficulty than this: that that person shall be held to be the wife of the slave who recognizes the slave to be her husband, and whose husband recognizes the woman to be his wife; adopting the same principle of the common law that applies in other cases, — a simple recognition of the relation of husband and wife, and of parent and child." Mr. Fessenden said, "My doubt of course was, in the beginning, whether, in taking persons of this description, and insisting that they should render military service, we could go so far as to liberate other persons connected with them. That was a very serious difficulty; but, sir, I have been convinced that we can do any thing that is necessary to be done in order to accomplish the purpose that we have in view, and which is not only a legal, but a necessary purpose,—the salvation and perpetuation of the Republic."

The Senate, on the 21st, resumed the consideration of the bill. Mr. Wilson said, "I desire, after consulting with some senators, to modify the amendment that I offered to the bill, by adding, after the word 'wife,' the words, 'meaning thereby the woman regarded and treated by him as such.'"—"I move," said Mr. Davis, "to amend the amendment by adding to it, 'and the loyal owner or owners of the wife or children of all slaves taken into the military service of the United States shall be entitled to a just compensation for such wife and children of said slaves.'" He maintained that slaves were property; that, as such, they could only be taken for public use by paying a just compensation. "The party in power are grinding us to the dust by the weight and tyrannies of an organized military despotism. These usurpers and oppressors are seizing upon our able-bodied negro slaves, and organizing them into a standing army already numbering nearly one hundred thousand men, and to be augmented far beyond those figures, to hold us in hapless and hopeless political, social, and commercial servitude to themselves. Belshazzar and his host are now drunk and feasting; but Cyrus and the Persians will soon be upon them. The aroused American freemen will effect their own deliverance at the ides of next November."—"This bill," said Mr. Wilkinson, "is to give freedom to the wives and children of the soldiers who fight our battles for the Government and for freedom. It has been claimed, that, if this bill shall pass, it will work the emancipation of the whole negro race within the United States. While the noblest and the best sons of the loyal States were reddening every rivulet in Virginia with their blood, and almost every sod of the Old Dominion was pressing upon the grave of a blue-eyed soldier of the North, we turned our backs coldly upon the only friends we had in the rebellious States, and said to them, 'You are black, and are not worthy to suffer and die for freedom: we would rather lose our own liberties than to give freedom to a nation of slaves.' I do not know but that it was the design of Providence to blind the eyes of the people of the North to their true interests, until they had paid the full penalty for their participation in the great crime of human slavery in this Government. There is a retributive justice in this war, as the senator from Maryland said, and it is visited alike upon the North and the South; for the North as well as the South has been a guilty participator in the foulest crime that ever blackened the character of a nation."

On the 22d, the Senate resumed the consideration of the bill; and Mr. Willey (Union) of West Virginia addressed the Senate. He said he was disposed to believe the cases of vindictive cruelty to which allusions had been made were "more justly attributable to the impending universal emancipation of slavery in Missouri than to any exasperation of the master growing out of the enlistment of his slave." He thought the passage of the bill would "lead to very distressing difficulties in the States where these slaves live. There can be," he declared, "in Virginia, between slaves, no legal marriage; there can be no wife in the eye of the law; there can be no children of slaves in the eyes of the law." The bill was not brought to a vote in the Senate.

In the Senate, on the 18th of May, Mr. Wilson introduced a joint resolution to encourage enlistments, and to promote the efficiency of the military forces of the United States. This resolution provided that the wife and children of any person that has been or may be mustered into the military or naval service of the United States shall be for ever free, any law, usage, or custom whatsoever, to the contrary notwithstanding; that, in determining who is the wife and who are the children of the enlisted person, evidence that he and the woman claimed to be his wife have lived together, associated as husband and wife, and so continued to live or associate at the time of the enlistment, or that a form of marriage, whether the same was or was not authorized or recognized by law, has been celebrated between them, and that the parties thereto thereafter lived together or associated as husband and wife, and so continued to live or associate at the time of the enlistment, shall be deemed sufficient proof of a marriage; and the children of any such marriages born while the same continued, although it had ceased at the time of enlistment, shall be deemed and taken to be the children mentioned in this resolution. The provisions of this resolution were reported, moved as amendments to several bills, but failed to be brought to the test of the vote of the Senate. The joint resolution to make free the wives and children of colored soldiers is pending in the Senate, and will doubtless be pressed at the next session.

CHAPTER XVII.

A BUREAU OF FREEDMEN.

MEMORIAL OF THE MASSACHUSETTS EMANCIPATION LEAGUE. — MR. ELIOT'S BILL. — SELECT COMMITTEE ON EMANCIPATION. — FREEDMEN'S BILL REPORTED BY MR. ELIOT. — REMARKS OF MR. ELIOT. — MR. COX. — MR. COLE. — MR. BROOKS. — MR. KELLEY. — MR. DAWSON. — MR. PRICE. — MR. KNAPP. — MR. PENDLETON. — PASSAGE OF MR. ELIOT'S BILL. — MR. SUMNER'S BILL. — MR. ELIOT'S BILL REPORTED BY MR. SUMNER, WITH AN AMENDMENT. — MR. SUMNER'S SPEECH. — MR. SUMNER'S AMENDMENT AMENDED AND ADOPTED IN THE SENATE. — THE HOUSE POSTPONE THE BILL TO THE NEXT SESSION.

IN the Senate, on the 12th of January, 1863, Mr. Wilson (Rep.) presented the memorial of the Emancipation League of Massachusetts, setting forth the needs of the new-made freedmen and the duty of the Government, and praying for the immediate establishment of a Bureau of Emancipation; which was ordered to be printed, and referred to the Committee on Military Affairs. In the House, on the 19th, Mr. Eliot (Rep.) of Massachusetts introduced a bill to establish a Bureau of Emancipation; which was referred to the Select Committee on Emancipation, of which Mr. White (Rep.) of Indiana was Chairman.

On the 14th of December, 1863, Mr. Eliot introduced a bill to establish a Bureau of Emancipation; which was referred to a select committee of nine, consisting of Mr. Eliot (Rep.) of Massachusetts, Mr. Kelley (Rep.) of Pennsylvania, Mr. Knapp (Dem.) of Illinois, Mr. Orth (Rep.) of Indiana, Mr. Boyd (Rep.) of Missouri, Mr. Kalbfleisch (Dem.) of New York, Mr. Cobb (Rep.) of Wisconsin, Mr. Anderson (Union) of Kentucky, and Mr. Middleton (Dem.) of New Jersey. On the 23d, Mr. Eliot reported from the Select Committee a bill to establish a Bureau of Emancipation; which was ordered to be printed, and recommitted to the committee. On the 13th of January, 1864, Mr. Eliot reported back the bill with an amendment. Mr. Kalbfleisch made a minority report. On the 10th of February, the bill came up for consideration. Mr. Eliot offered a substitute for the original bill. Mr. Holman (Dem.) of Indiana moved to lay the bill on the table, and Mr. Cox (Dem.) of Ohio moved to refer it to the Committee of the Whole. The Speaker ruled that Mr. Eliot held the floor. Mr. Eliot addressed the House in favor of his bill in an earnest and able speech. He said the freedmen were "the children of the Government. Quick to learn; appreciating kindnesses, and returning them with veneration and affection; earnest to acquire property, because that, too, is proof of manhood, — they ask but opportunity and guidance and education for a season, and then they will repay you, some thirty, some sixty, and some an hundred fold. . . . So shall this, your act, give to the freedmen of the South, and to all the freemen whom you represent, 'beauty for ashes, the oil of joy for mourning, and the garment of praise for the spirit of heaviness.'"

On the 17th, the House proceeded to the consideration of Mr. Eliot's bill, and Mr. Cox spoke against its enactment. He declared that "not merely has the President's proclamation been made a *living lie,* but the thousands of corpses daily hurried out of the contraband hovels and tents along the Mississippi prove it to have been a *deadly lie*. Neither the judgment of man nor the favor of God can be invoked without mockery upon a fanatical project so fraught with misery to the weak, and wholesale slaughter to its deluded victims." Mr. Cole (Rep.) of California followed on the 18th in an earnest speech in favor of the bill and the policy of freedom. Mr. Kalbfleisch, on the 19th, spoke in opposition to the measure. Mr. Brooks (Dem.) of New York said, "The bill is vast in its territory, vast in its objects, vast in its purposes, vast in its intentions." He declared, " Whenever a gentleman from Massachusetts in these our latter days introduces any bill or propounds any proposition for the consideration of the House, I always listen to him with attentive ears, with apprehension, with something of awe; nay, with that deep interest that the Roman of old must have listened to the unrolling of the leaves of the Sibyl, or the Greek to the utterings of the oracle in Delphos. Massachusetts is now the leading power in this country. Whatever she decrees is in all probability to be law. She exercises the same control over this vast country, which stretches from the Passamaquoddy to the Rio Grande, and from the Rio Grande to the Pacific, that was exercised by imperial Rome, on the little Tiber, from the Pillars of Hercules to the Euphrates and Tigris. Boston, her capital, is well called the hub of our universe, with her spokes now inserted in New York, Pennsylvania, Ohio, the great West, and the great North-west, the rim of whose wheel now runs with frightful, crushing velocity from that Passamaquoddy to that Rio Grande.

... I know the spirit of Massachusetts. I know her inexorable, unappeasable, demoniac energy." He thought "this freedmen's bill not worthy of the practical mind of Massachusetts.... It must have come from some of the freedmen's commissioners, — perhaps from Robert Dale Owen; for the bill is Socialistic, Fouricristic, Owenistic, erotic." On the 23d, Mr. Kelley, a member of the Select Committee that reported the bill, spoke eloquently in favor of its passage. In reply to Mr. Brooks, he said, "I am no son of Massachusetts or New England, as the gentleman is, but I remember, that in my wayward youth, being free from the indenture that had bound me to a long apprenticeship, but not having attained manhood, I wandered from my native Pennsylvania, counter to the current tide of emigration, in pursuit of employment, and found a home in Massachusetts; and I may be pardoned if I pause for a moment to feebly testify my gratitude to her, in whom I found a gentle and generous foster-mother. I thank God for the Puritan spirit of Massachusetts. A boy, poor, friendless, and in pursuit of wages for manual toil, I found open to me, in the libraries of Boston, the science, history, and literature of the world. At a cost that even the laboring man did not feel, I found, night after night, and week after week, in her lyceums and lecture-rooms, the means of intercourse with her Bancrofts, her Brownsons, her Everetts, her Channings, her Prescotts, her Emersons, and scores of others as learned and as able sons as these, though perhaps less distinguished. I thus learned what it was to be an American citizen, and to what a height American civilization will be carried; and I found four years of life spent at well-

paid toil worth to me what the same number of years
in a college might have been. . . . You need not fear
that this black race will fade away. The glowing South,
the land of the tropics, genial to them, invites its own
development, and will insure that of this race."

The House resumed the consideration of the bill on
the 24th; and Mr. Dawson (Dem.) of Pennsylvania
made an elaborate and able speech in opposition to the
policy of the Administration. Mr. Davis of Maryland
followed on the 25th in a speech of eloquence and power. Mr. Knapp (Dem.) of Illinois addressed the House
on the 1st of March in opposition to the passage of the
bill. Mr. Price (Rep.) of Iowa spoke for the bill, and
sharply replied to Mr. Cox. Mr. Eliot moved the previous question, which was sustained by the House. Mr.
Eliot yielded a portion of his hour to close the debate
to Mr. Pendleton (Dem.) of Ohio, who spoke briefly
but forcibly against the right to enact the bill. He
thought the freedmen, numbering more than half a million, "long for the repose and quiet of their old homes,
and the care of their masters; that freedom has not been
to them the promised boon; that even thus soon it has
proven itself to be a life of torture, ending only in
certain and speedy death." Mr. Wadsworth, by the
courtesy of Mr. Eliot, spoke briefly against the passage
of the bill. Mr. Eliot, being anxious to take the vote,
declined to close the debate. Mr. Brooks's motion to
recommit the bill was lost, and the substitute moved
by Mr. Eliot was agreed to. Mr. Mallory (Dem.) of
Kentucky moved to lay the bill on the table, — yeas 62,
nays 68. Mr. Mallory demanded the yeas and nays on
the passage of the bill; and they were ordered. The

question was taken, — yeas 69, nays 67. So the bill passed the House.

In the Senate, on the 2d of March, Mr. Eliot's bill was referred to the Select Committee on Slavery, of which Mr. Sumner was chairman. On the 12th of April, Mr. Sumner reported from the Select Committee on Slavery a bill to establish a Bureau of Freedmen; which was read, and ordered to a second reading. On the 25th of May, Mr. Sumner reported back from the Select Committee on Slavery Mr. Eliot's bill, with an amendment to strike out the original bill, and insert his bill in lieu of it. On the 8th of June, the Senate proceeded to the consideration of the House bill, the pending question being on the substitute reported by Mr. Sumner as an amendment. Mr. Sumner explained the provisions of his substitute for the House bill, and earnestly and eloquently pressed the importance of prompt action. "The opportunity," he declared, "must not be lost, of helping so many persons who are now helpless, and of aiding the cause of reconciliation, without which peace cannot be assured." Mr. Richardson (Dem.) of Illinois opposed the bill, and bitterly assailed the Administration.

On the 14th, Mr. Sumner moved to proceed to the consideration of the House bill to establish a Bureau of Freedmen's Affairs. Mr. M·Dougall demanded the yeas and nays, — yeas 23, nays 11. Several important amendments were made; not, however, changing the general features of the measure. Mr. Carlile (Dem.) of Virginia moved to postpone the further consideration of the bill to the first Monday of December next, — yeas 13, nays 23. Mr. Willey (Union) of West Virginia, earnestly opposed and severely criticised the bill, and Mr. Sumner sharply replied to Mr. Willey's remarks. On the 27th, the Senate resumed the consideration of the bill; and several amendments were offered by the friends and opponents of the measure. Mr. Trumbull moved to amend the bill by adopting a new section, repealing the last clause of a joint resolution explanatory of the Confiscation Act. On the 28th, the vote was taken on Mr. Trumbull's amendment; and it was adopted, — yeas 23, nays 15. Mr. Doolittle moved that all assistant commissioners and superintendents and other officers be so far considered in the military service as to be liable to trial by court martial; and the amendment was agreed to. Mr. Willey moved to authorize the commissioners to open a correspondence with the governors and municipal authorities, to aid in securing homes for the freedmen; and it was adopted, — yeas 19, nays 15. Mr. Wilson moved to strike out of the substitute the word "treasury," and insert "war." — "I have moved this amendment, because, in my judgment, it is better, in every aspect in which the case can be viewed, that this bureau should be in the War Department, because the War Department controls the armies. The rebel States are divided into military departments; and all the law we administer there is military law, and all the government we exercise over them is military government. Why we should take these people, who now flock to the army, and have gathered around it for protection and support, from under the control of the War Department, and put them under the control of speculating treasury agents, is a thing I cannot comprehend." Mr. Sumner hoped the amendment would not be adopted. He declared, "If it should be adopted, I shall consider the bill worse than nothing." "I do not wish," replied Mr. Wilson, "to take the responsibility of giving a turn to this bill contrary to the wishes of my colleague, who has had the direction of it; and, having stated my opinion, I withdraw the amendment." Mr. Sumner's substitute for the House bill was then agreed to, and the bill reported to the Senate as amended. Mr. Johnson moved to strike out the word "treasury," and insert the word "war," — yeas 15, nays 20. Mr. Davis spoke in opposition to the bill, and in denunciation of the policy of the Administration; and Mr. Wilkinson sharply replied to Mr. Davis. Mr. Hendricks opposed the passage of the bill, and Mr. Chandler earnestly advocated the policy of using the negro to put down the Rebellion. "A secession traitor," he declared, "is beneath a loyal negro. I would let a loyal negro vote; I would let him testify; I would let him fight; I would let him do any other good thing; and I would exclude a secession traitor. I say this deliberately, that in Kentucky, in Tennessee, in Alabama, in Louisiana, in South Carolina, in every single rebel State, I consider a loyal negro better than a secession traitor, and I will treat him better. Make the most of it." — "The policy," said Mr. M·Dougall, "proposed by this bill, is an outrage upon Christianity and humanity; and as such, with a severe sense of duty, I denounce it." Mr. Buckalew called for the yeas and nays on the passage of the bill; and they were ordered, — yeas 21, nays 9. So the bill "to establish a Bureau of Freedmen" passed the Senate on the 28th of June.

In the House, on the 2d of July, Mr. Eliot, from the

Select Committee on Emancipation, reported back his bill and the amendment of the Senate, and moved that the amendment of the Senate be non-concurred in. Mr. Washburne (Rep.) of Illinois expressed the hope that Mr. Eliot would withdraw his report, and let the call of the committees go on. Mr. Eliot could not consent to that. Mr. Griswold (Dem.) of New York wished to know if it would be in order to move to lay the bill on the table. Mr. Washburne suggested that he could move the postponement to the next session. Mr. Griswold moved to postpone the further consideration of the bill to the 20th of December next. The motion was agreed to; and the bill will come up for consideration at the next session.

CHAPTER XVIII.

RECONSTRUCTION OF REBEL STATES.

MR. HARLAN'S BILL. — MR. SUMNER'S RESOLUTIONS. — MR. ASHLEY'S BILL. — MR. HARRIS'S BILL. — MR. WINTER DAVIS'S RESOLUTION. — SELECT COMMITTEE ON RECONSTRUCTION. — MR. DAVIS'S BILL. — REMARKS OF MR. DAVIS, MR. BEAMAN, MR. ALLEN, MR. SMITHERS, MR. NORTON, MR. BROOMALL, MR. SCOFIELD, MR. DAWSON, MR. WILLIAMS, MR. BALDWIN OF MASSACHUSETTS, MR. DONNELLY, MR. PERHAM, MR. GOOCH, MR. FERNANDO WOOD, MR. KELLEY, MR. BOUTWELL, MR. PENDLETON. — MR. DAVIS'S SUBSTITUTE. — PASSAGE OF MR. DAVIS'S BILL. — HOUSE BILL REPORTED BY MR. WADE. — MR. BROWN'S AMENDMENT. — MR. SUMNER'S AMENDMENT. — PASSAGE OF MR. BROWN'S SUBSTITUTE. — HOUSE NON-CONCUR. — SENATE RECEDE. — PASSAGE OF THE BILL. — THE PRESIDENT REFUSES TO APPROVE IT.

IN the Senate, on the 26th of December, 1861, Mr. Harlan (Rep.) of Iowa introduced a bill to establish a provisional government in each of the districts of country embraced within the limits of the Confederate States of Georgia, Alabama, Mississippi, Louisiana, Texas, Arkansas, and Tennessee; which was referred to the Committee on Territories. Mr. Sumner, on the 11th of February, 1862, introduced a series of resolutions declaratory of the relations between the United States and the territory once occupied by certain States, and now usurped by pretended governments without constitutional or legal right. These resolutions declare that slavery, being a local institution, ceased to exist when the States no longer exist; that it is the duty of Congress to see that everywhere, in this extensive territory, slavery shall cease to exist practically, as it has already ceased to exist constitutionally or legally; and that any recognition of slavery, or surrender of pretended slaves, besides being a recognition of the pretended governments, giving them aid and comfort, is a denial of the rights of persons, who, by the extinction of the States, have become free, so that, under the Constitution, they cannot again be enslaved. No action was taken on these resolutions.

In the House, Mr. Ashley (Rep.) of Ohio, on the 12th of March, reported, from the Committee on Territories, a bill for a provisional government over the territory in rebellion. Mr. Pendleton (Dem.) of Ohio declared that "this bill ought to be entitled a bill to dissolve the Union, and abolish the Constitution;" and moved that it be laid upon the table. Mr. Bingham (Rep.) of Ohio demanded the yeas and nays, — yeas 65, nays 56. So the bill was laid upon the table.

Mr. Harris (Rep.) of New York, on the 14th of February, introduced into the Senate a bill to establish provisional governments in certain cases; which was referred to the Committee on the Judiciary. Mr. Harris repeatedly pressed the consideration of the measure; but no action was taken upon it. On the 3d of March, 1863, the Senate, on motion of Mr. Harris, proceeded to the consideration of the bill; and Mr. Harris proposed to amend it by striking out six sections, and inserting three new sections. The third section of the amendment provided that no law, whereby any person has heretofore been held to service or labor in any such State, shall be recognized or enforced by any court or officer constituted or appointed under the provisions of this act; and all laws providing for the trial and punishment of white persons in any such State shall be deemed, and are hereby declared to be, applicable to the trial and punishment of all persons whomsoever within the jurisdiction of such court or officer. Mr. Carlile (Dem.) of Virginia moved to strike out those words. Mr. Davis (Dem.) of Kentucky moved to lay the bill on the table, — yeas 15; nays 21. The Senate, by a vote of 22 to 13, on motion of Mr. Wilkinson (Rep.) of Minnesota, postponed the consideration of the bill, to take up the bill for the organization of Idaho.

In the House of Representatives, on the 15th of December, 1863, Mr. Stevens (Rep.) of Pennsylvania proposed that so much of the President's message as relates to the condition and treatment of the rebellious States be referred to a Select Committee of nine. Mr. Davis (Rep.) of Maryland moved to amend the resolution, so as to appoint a committee of nine, to whom so much of the President's message as relates to the duty of the United States to guarantee a republican form of government to the States shall be referred, which shall report the bills necessary and proper to carry into execution that guaranty. After a brief debate, the amendment of Mr. Davis was carried, — yeas 91, nays 80; and the Speaker appointed as the select committee Mr. Davis (Rep.) of Maryland, Mr. Gooch (Rep.) of Massachusetts, Mr. J. C. Allen (Dem.) of Illinois, Mr. Ashley (Rep.) of Ohio, Mr. Fenton (Rep.) of New York, Mr. Holman (Dem.) of Indiana, Mr. Smithers (Rep.) of Delaware, Mr. Blow (Rep.) of Missouri, and Mr. English (Dem.) of Connecticut.

On the 15th of February, Mr. Davis reported a bill to guarantee to certain States whose governments have been usurped a republican form of government; which was read twice, ordered to be printed, and recommitted to the committee.

On the 22d of March, on motion of Mr. Davis, the House proceeded to the consideration of the bill guaranteeing to certain States a republican form of government. The bill, among other things, provided that the State constitutional conventions to be held shall incorporate into the constitutions of the States that involuntary servitude is for ever prohibited, and the freedom of all persons is guaranteed. The bill also provided that all persons held to involuntary servitude or labor in the rebel States are emancipated and discharged, and they and their posterity shall be for ever free; and, if they or their posterity shall be restrained of liberty under pretence of any claim to such service or labor, the courts of the United States shall, on *habeas corpus* discharge them. The bill also provided, that if any person declared free by this act, or any law of the United States, or any proclamation of the President, be restrained of liberty, with intent to be held in or reduced to involuntary servitude or labor, the person convicted before a court of competent jurisdiction of such act shall be punished by fine of not less than fifteen hundred dollars, and be imprisoned not less than five nor more than twenty years. Mr. Davis addressed the House eloquently in support of his bill. Mr. Beaman (Rep.) of Michigan earnestly advocated the measure. He closed his speech by the emphatic declaration, " By no consent of mine shall a single one of the wayward

States ever be permitted to participate in shaping the destinies of this nation, until she has by her organic law for ever prohibited involuntary servitude, except as a punishment for crime, within all her borders; nor, while I have life and strength, will I cease to urge by all constitutional means the freedom of every inhabitant of the United States, without regard to color or race."

On the 19th of April, the House resumed the discussion of the bill; and Mr. J. C. Allen, a member of the Select Committee, addressed the House in opposition to its passage. "Some one," he said, "had suggested, that, when slavery was buried, upon its tombstone should be written, 'Slavery, — died of the Rebellion.' I warn gentlemen to beware, lest beside the grave of Slavery be found another grave and another tombstone, whereon History will write, 'Civil Liberty, — died of Revolution.'" Mr. Smithers of Delaware made an earnest and able speech in advocacy of the measure. " I do not," he said, " trust wholly to presidential proclamations. I prefer to rest the security of the Republic upon the safer and more irrefragable basis of Congressional enactments. I would not forego any possible precaution against the recurrence of fraternal strife. Homogeneity of institutions is our only safeguard; universal freedom, the only possible solution." Mr. Norton (Rep.) of Illinois spoke in favor of the measure, and sharply criticised the speeches made in favor of the policy of peace. He was followed by Mr. Broomall (Rep.) of Pennsylvania in earnest advocacy of the bill. "Let us at last," he exclaimed, "do justice to our mother-tongue,—that in which the great English and the greater American charter were written; that which, from its infancy, proclaimed the rights of men, and denounced the crimes of tyrants. Let us learn, that, sublime as it is for the utterance of grand truths, *it is no language to lie in.*" Mr. Scofield (Rep.) of Pennsylvania spoke eloquently in favor of the policy of emancipation. He thought we had exhausted "all concessions within the range of possibility, which, if made, would conciliate the slave power. Even James Buchanan, so gifted in abasement, could find nothing more in the shape of theory to give them, and in its stead tendered the low villany of Lecompton." Mr. Dawson (Dem.) of Pennsylvania opposed the enactment of the bill. Mr. Williams (Rep.) of Pennsylvania followed in a speech of rare beauty and masterly power. He paid a glowing tribute to New England and to Massachusetts. "Leave out," he exclaimed, "Massachusetts in the cold! What matters it that no tropical sun has fevered her Northern blood into the delirium of treason? I know no trait of tenderness more touching and more human than that with which she received back to her arms the bodies of her lifeless children. 'Handle them tenderly' was the message of her loyal governor. Massachusetts desired to look once more upon the faces of her martyred sons, 'marred as they were by traitors.' She lifted gently the sable pall that covered them. She gave them a soldier's burial and a soldier's farewell; and then, like David of old, when he was informed that the child of his affections had ceased to live, she rose to her feet, dashed the teardrop from her eye, and in twenty days her iron-clad battalions were crowning the heights, and her guns frowning destruction over the streets, of the rebel city.

Shut out Massachusetts in the cold! Yes: you may blot her out from the map of the continent: you may bring back the glacial epoch, when the arctic ice-drift that has deposited so many monuments on her soil swept over her buried surface, — when the polar bear, perhaps, paced the driving floes, and the walrus frolicked among the tumbling icebergs : but you cannot sink her deep enough to drown the memory of Lexington and Concord, or bury the summit of the tall column that lifts its head over the first of our battle-fields. 'With her,' in the language of her great son, 'the *past* at least is secure.' The Muse of History has flung her story upon the world's canvas in tints that will not fade, and cannot die." Mr. Baldwin (Dem.) of Michigan opposed the bill and the emancipation measures of the Administration. "Fanatical radicalism," he declared," has gained the ascendency ; and the war for the last eighteen months has been prosecuted, not for the restoration of the Union, but for the destruction of the South." Mr. Thayer (Rep.) of Pennsylvania advocated the policy of taking security for the future peace of the nation. Mr. Yeaman (Union) of Kentucky did not see our power to legislate away the laws and institutions of States. "Viewing the bill from the stand-point of those who desire universal abolition, it would seem to be idle and premature legislation, because, without military success, the law is a dead letter ; and with military success, under the present programme, abolition is accomplished without the law." Mr. Longyear (Rep.) of Michigan spoke in favor of the passage of the bill.

On the 2d of May, Mr. Donnelly (Rep.) of Minnesota addressed the House in its favor. "I cannot," he said, "perceive the advantage, to any man, of the degradation of any other man; and I feel assured of the greatness and perpetuity of my country, only in so far as it identifies itself with the uninterrupted progress and the universal liberty of mankind." Mr. Dennison (Dem.) of Pennsylvania opposed the measure and the general policy of the Administration. Mr. Stevens spoke in advocacy of the bill, and of a radical antislavery policy. Mr. Strouse (Dem.) of Pennsylvania severely denounced the policy of the Administration; and Mr. Cravens (Dem.) of Indiana followed in a general assault upon the principles and measures of the Administration.

On the 3d, Mr. Perham (Rep.) of Maine spoke earnestly for the measure, and Mr. Keenan (Dem.) of New York strenuously opposed it. Mr. Gooch (Rep.) of Massachusetts supported, and Mr. Perry (Dem.) of New Jersey opposed, the passage of the bill. Mr. Fernando Wood, the leader of the unconditional peace Democrats, made an elaborate speech against it. "We of this generation," he said, "may not be able to estimate the full measure of the misery that will follow the realization of the fantastic theory, which, promising to remove the yoke from every shoulder, will curse the earth with sterility, and man with vice and poverty." Mr. Kelley (Rep.) of Pennsylvania would pass this bill "as a means of organizing conquest and peace." The debate was resumed by Mr. Cox of Ohio on the 4th. "I ask for this people justice," said Mr. Boutwell (Rep.) of Massachusetts, "in the presence of these great events, in this exigency, when the life of the nation is in peril, and when every reflecting person must see that the cause of that peril is in the injustice we have done to the negro race. I ask that we shall now do justice to that race. They are four millions. They will remain on this continent. They cannot be expatriated. They await the order of Providence. Their home is here. It is our duty to elevate them, to provide for their civilization, for their enlightenment, that they may enjoy the fruits of their labor and their capacity." Mr. Pendleton (Dem.) of Ohio spoke strongly against the passage of the bill. He declared, "It creates unity; it destroys liberty; it maintains integrity of territory, but destroys the rights of the citizen." Mr. Davis moved a substitute for the bill. Mr. Ancona (Dem.) of Pennsylvania moved that the bill and substitute be laid on the table. The motion was lost. The question was taken on Mr. Davis's substitute; and it was adopted. Mr. Cox demanded the yeas and nays on the passage of the bill; and they were ordered, — yeas 73, nays 59. So Mr. Davis's bill passed the House of Representatives.

In the Senate, the bill was referred to the Committee on Territories, of which Mr. Wade was chairman. On the 27th of May, Mr. Wade reported back the bill with amendments. On the 1st of July, Mr. Wade moved to take up the bill for consideration. Mr. Lane of Kansas opposed the motion, and Mr. Pomeroy advocated it. Mr. Powell demanded the yeas and nays; and they were ordered, — yeas 20, nays 11. Mr. Wade opposed all amendments. Mr. Lane of Kansas demanded the yeas and nays on the amendment to strike out the word "white" before the word "male;" and the question, being taken by yeas and nays, resulted — yeas 5, nays 24. Mr. Brown (Rep.) of Missouri moved to strike out all after the enacting clause, and insert, that when the inhabitants of any State have been declared in a state of insurrection by the proclamation of the President, by force and virtue of the act of the 13th of July, 1861, they shall be incapable of casting any vote for President, or of electing senators and representatives in Congress. Mr. Wade expressed the hope, that the amendment would not be adopted. Mr. Carlile opposed the original bill. The question being on Mr. Brown's amendment, Mr. Conness (Union) from California demanded the yeas and nays; and they were ordered, — yeas 17, nays 16: so Mr. Brown's amendment was agreed to. Mr. Sumner moved to amend the bill by adding, "That the proclamation of emancipation issued by the President of the United States on the first day of January, 1863, so far as the same declares that the slaves in certain designated States, and portions of States, thenceforward should be free, is hereby adopted, and enacted as a statute of the United States, and as a rule and article for the government of the military and naval forces thereof." Mr. Hale opposed the amendment to Mr. Brown's substitute, as he did not wish it embarrassed by any other question. Mr. Sumner thought it impossible for any person who recognizes the proclamation of emancipation to vote against the amendment. "I wish," he said, "to make the present sure, and to fix it for evermore and immortal in an act of Congress." Mr. Saulsbury (Dem.) of Delaware declared that "an Administration soon, thank God, will be in power, which will wipe out all this species of legislation, and will do it without blood-shedding too." Mr. Brown was in favor of Mr. Sumner's amendment as an independent proposition, but not on the pending bill. The question was taken on Mr. Sumner's amendment, — yeas 11, nays 21. Mr. Wilson demanded the yeas and nays on Mr. Brown's amendment; and they were ordered, — yeas 20, nays 13. The yeas and nays were then taken on the passage of the bill as amended, — yeas 26, nays 3. So the bill passed the Senate.

The House of Representatives, on motion of Mr. Davis, non-concurred in the Senate amendment, and asked a Committee of Conference; and Mr. Davis of Maryland, Mr. Ashley of Ohio, and Mr. Dawson of Pennsylvania, were appointed conferrees. The Senate, on motion of Mr. Wade, by a vote of 18 yeas to 14 nays, receded from Mr. Brown's amendment. Mr. Davis's bill passed the Senate on the 2d of July, but did not receive the approval of the President of the United States.

CHAPTER XIX.

CONFINEMENT OF COLORED PERSONS IN THE WASHINGTON JAIL.

MR. WILSON'S JOINT RESOLUTION. — REMARKS OF MR. WILSON, MR. CLARK, MR. HALE, MR. WILSON, MR. FESSENDEN, MR. SUMNER. — MR. CLARK'S RESOLUTION. — MR. GRIMES'S BILL. — REMARKS OF MR. GRIMES. — MR. POWELL'S AMENDMENT. — REMARKS OF MR. PEARCE, MR. POWELL, MR. CARLILE, MR. WILSON, MR. FESSENDEN, MR. LATHAM, MR. COWAN. — PASSAGE OF THE BILL. — MR. WILSON'S BILL. — REMARKS OF MR. WILSON. — MR. GRIMES'S AMENDMENT. — REMARKS OF MR. M'DOUGALL, MR. HALE, MR. WILSON, MR. PEARCE, MR. SUMNER. — MR. BINGHAM'S BILL.

IN the Senate, on the 4th of December, 1861, Mr. Wilson (Rep.) of Massachusetts introduced a joint resolution, that "all persons who may have been arrested as fugitives from service or labor, and confined in the county jail in the District of Columbia, shall be discharged therefrom." Mr. Wilson stated that he had "visited the jail, and such a scene of degradation and inhumanity he had never witnessed. There were persons almost entirely naked; some of them without a shirt. Some of those persons were free; most of them had run away from disloyal masters, or had been sent there by disloyal persons, for safe keeping until the war is over." He read the report of Mr. Allen, a government-officer, in regard to sixty of the persons confined there. Mr. Clark (Rep.) of New Hampshire heartily concurred in the desired object; but he thought the names should be put in the resolution.

"I am very glad," said Mr. Hale (Rep.) of New Hampshire, "that this report has been made and presented here, because it will help to answer a question that was put to me a great many times long and long ago,—what the North had to do with slavery. I think, when the Northern States find out that they are supporting here in jail the slaves of rebels who are fighting against us; that we are keeping at the public expense their slaves for them until the war is over,—it will have a tendency to enlighten some minds in regard to the proper answer to that question. If there be any duty which this Congress owes to humanity and to itself, it is to look into the administration of justice in this District, and to see to it that those who have been ground to the earth heretofore may not be ground still more under your auspices and your reign." Mr. M'Dougall (Dem.) of California moved to refer the joint resolution to the Judiciary Committee. Mr. Wilson was willing his resolution should go to the Judiciary Committee, or to the Committee on the District of Columbia. "I hope," he said, "that these persons will be discharged as speedily as possible, and then that a law will be passed punishing anybody for arresting such persons; and that all the laws in the District of Columbia, oppressive or degrading to any portion of the people, will be wiped from the statute-book, and that all the ordinances of the city of that character will be annulled; and then I trust that judicial tribunals will be established worthy of us, and that a system for selecting jurors will be adopted which will secure the ends of justice; and then I hope that slavery will be swept away for ever from the District, and the national capital freed from its pollution. The prison which stands in this city is a burning shame and a disgrace to our country; and I hope it will be levelled with the dust, and that a prison fit to keep human beings in will be erected. The other day, the French legation carried to that prison gentlemen who had traversed the world examining prisons, — gentlemen who were investigating the subject of prisons, and their construction and discipline. The jailer told me yesterday, that, after they had gone through this prison, they observed that they had never seen anywhere such a prison, with one exception; and that was in Austria. If senators will go to the prison; if they can bear to go there, and contemplate for a few moments what their eyes will look upon, — I think they will then be disposed, at any rate, to liberate those poor creatures, who are confined there for no offence whatever, and to construct a prison worthy of a Christian people." Mr. Fessenden (Rep.) of Maine saw but one remedy; and he had been hoping to see the day when Congress would " sweep all the courts of this District out of existence, and remodel the whole affair. . . . But with reference to runaways, men who have escaped from rebel masters, if the abuse which has been brought to our notice exists here, or exists anywhere, I wish now to say before the country, — for this matter has excited some interest, not only in our armies, but elsewhere, — that I am for rendering the most ample justice to them, whenever it can be done legally and constitutionally; and there are few instances, I trust, in which both these conditions will not be found to agree in reference to that matter." "There is," said Mr. Sumner, "a black code in this

District, derived from the old legislation of Maryland, which is a shame to the civilization of our age. If any one wishes to know why such abuses exist in our prisons and in our courts here as have been to-day so eloquently pointed out, I refer him to that black code. You will find in that black code an apology for every outrage that is now complained of. If, therefore, senators are really in earnest; if they are determined that the national capital shall be purified, that the administration of justice here shall be worthy of a civilized community, — they have got to expunge that black code from the statute-book: but to expunge that black code from the statute-book is to expunge slavery itself; and that brings us precisely to the point. Senators will mistake if they undertake to meet this question merely on the threshold, merely at the outside. They have got to meet it in its essence, in its substance. Why is that prison such an offensive place as I know it to be? — for it has been my fortune to visit it repeatedly. It is on account of slavery: it is the black code which prevails in this District. Why is justice so offensively administered in this District? It is on account of those brutal sentiments generated by slavery, sanctioned by the black code which the courts in this District enforce." Mr. M'Dougall, at the suggestion of Mr. Trumbull, modified his motion so as to refer the joint resolution to the Committee on the District of Columbia; and it was so referred.

On the 9th, the Senate, on motion of Mr. Clark, adopted a resolution, "That the Marshal of the District of Columbia be directed to inform the Senate by what authority he receives slaves into the jail of the District at the request of their masters, and holds them in confinement until discharged by their masters."

Mr. Grimes, on the 2d of January, 1862, introduced a bill in regard to the administration of criminal justice in the District of Columbia. It was referred to the District Committee, and reported back by Mr. Grimes, on the 6th, with amendments. The bill provided that all persons not held in final judgment, who were confined prior to the last term of the criminal court, were to be discharged; and the judge of the criminal court was to cause an order to be entered on the records of the court before the final adjournment of each term, requiring a general delivery of all persons confined in the jail before the grand jury for that term were impanelled, and against whom no indictment was found by them. "I am not," said Mr. Grimes, "very fresh in my reading of history; but, from my recollection of the descriptions of prisons I have read of, I think that there never was a place of confinement that would be compared with the Washington Jail as it was at the commencement of the present session, except the French Bastille and the dungeons of Venice. When I visited the jail the other day, I had hardly entered the threshold before a colored boy stepped up to me, and tapped me on the shoulder. He happened to know who I was. Said he, 'I have been here a year and four days.' I asked him for what offence. He said he was confined as a runaway. I asked him if any one claimed him. 'No.'—'Are you a free boy?'—'Yes.' Turning around to the jailer, I asked him if that was so. He said it was. I asked him, 'How do you know it to be so?' I found that the boy had been confined, not twelve months only, but thirteen months and four days, merely on the charge of being a runaway."

On the 14th, the Senate resumed the consideration of the bill; the pending question being on the motion of Mr. Powell (Dem.) of Kentucky to amend the bill, so as not to discharge fugitive slaves. Mr. Grimes commented upon the communication just received from Ward H. Lamon, the Marshal of the District, in regard to the rule he had adopted, excluding members of Congress from the jail without a written permission from him. Mr. Pearce (Dem.) of Maryland was opposed to the enactment of the bill. "You cannot," he said, "expect success in restoring the Union, if it be known that your policy is one of emancipation. Mr. Powell thought the sole object of the bill was the liberation of fugitive slaves. "The effect of the bill," he said, "clearly will be to release every fugitive slave from jail." Mr. Pomeroy (Rep.) of Kansas, and Mr. Morrill (Rep.) of Maine, advocated the passage of the measure. Mr. Carlile (Dem.) of Virginia would not vote for the bill: but he desired "to act upon it, and get rid of it; and thus one peg, at least, will be taken from gentlemen, upon which they hang their sympathetic speeches for the negro race." Mr. Morrill sharply replied to the remarks of Mr. Carlile. Mr. Wilson read a letter from Dr. Samuel G. Howe of Massachusetts, stating that the same atrocities were practised in the jail at Alexandria. He pronounced the jail in Washington "a dishonor and a disgrace to the nation, and it should be levelled with the dust." — "I have three sons in the army, out of four," said Mr. Fessenden; "and I never would have consented that one of them should be there if his life was to be perilled, exposed to sickness or other dangers, under the authority of men who ordered him to arrest fugitive slaves, and return them to their masters." He denounced the return of fugitive slaves by officers of the army as "an outrage to which he would not submit, unless he was compelled to submit to it." Mr. Latham (Dem.) of California would vote for the bill without amendment. Mr. Collamer earnestly opposed Mr. Powell's amendment not to discharge persons claimed as fugitive slaves. He protested utterly against confining a negro until an owner was found for him. The yeas and nays were taken on Mr. Powell's amendment, and it was lost,— yeas 5, nays 35. Mr. Cowan (Rep.) of Pennsylvania inquired if there was "any law in the District which allows slaves to be impounded in the common jail as estrays are impounded in other countries." Mr. Sumner replied, that "it was certainly the practice." — "If it be the law," said Mr. Cowan, "I do not see in what way this bill is going to operate to prevent it." Mr. Clark moved to amend the bill, so that no person could be committed without a warrant; and the amendment was agreed to. Mr. Powell demanded the yeas and nays on the passage of the bill, — yeas 31, nays 4. So the bill passed the Senate.

On the 12th of February, Mr. Wilson introduced a bill for the appointment of a warden of the jail in the District of Columbia, and it was referred to the Committee on the District of Columbia. He said the jail was "under the control of Mr. Phillips, the Deputy-Marshal; and under the superintendency of a negro thief by the name of Wise." This Wise had stolen a negro from a Rhode-Island regiment within a few days, and had tied a negro, held as a fugitive slave, for attempting to escape from the jail, over a barrel, and "cobbed" him. "Now, sir, I want it understood in the Senate and in the country, and by the men who, on their bended knees and over their Bibles, prayed, in the year 1860, for an end to these crimes against humanity, that this man Wise, this negro thief, who is the superintendent of the jail, is there to-day by our votes and our influence, and we are responsible for it before the nation and before Almighty God; and, for one, I wash my hands of the crime, and I denounce it."

On the 13th, Mr. Grimes reported back the bill with an amendment; and, on the 14th, the Senate proceeded to its consideration. The committee proposed as an amendment to strike out all of the original bill, and insert a substitute. Mr. M'Dougall opposed the passage of the bill, and Mr. Morrill and Mr. Hale advocated it. Mr. Wilson said, "The night after I introduced the bill, our man Wise, our negro thief, whom we keep there, went out into the city, and stole a woman who declares herself free, and her mother says she is free." Mr. Pearce opposed the bill. "I am glad," said Mr. Sumner, "this subject has been brought before the Senate. I feel personally obliged to my colleague for the way in which he did it, and also to the committee on the District of Columbia for their prompt report of the bill; but I hope the chairman of that committee will pardon me if I say that I do not think his committee went far enough. He ought to have reported a bill to abolish the office of marshal. There is an old saying, that 'he gives twice who quickly gives;' and surely there is no occasion for the application of that saying more pertinent than a case of injustice like this: surely we ought to be prompt, and every moment of delay is a shame upon us." The bill was then passed without a division.

In the House of Representatives, on the 9th of December, 1861, Mr. Bingham (Rep.) introduced a joint resolution "in regard to the commitment of negroes to the jail of the District of Columbia." The resolution declared that all acts, and parts of acts, in force in the District of Columbia, which authorize the commitment, to the jails of said District, of persons as runaways, or suspected or charged with being runaways, and all acts, and parts of acts, which authorize the sale of persons so committed for charges of commitment or jail fees, be, and the same are, repealed; and so to commit or imprison or sell any person for the causes aforesaid within said District is hereby declared a misdemeanor. This joint resolution was referred to the Judiciary Committee, but no action was taken upon it; nor were the bills relating to the jail passed by the House of Representatives. But the exposure, in Congress, of the shameful abuses in that prison, brought redress to the victims of "black codes" and dishonest officials. On the 25th of January, 1862, the Hon. William H. Seward, Secretary of State, addressed to Marshal Lamon the following order: —

"The President of the United States being satisfied that the following instructions contravene no law in force in this District, and that they can be executed without waiting for legislation by Congress, I am directed to convey them to you. As Marshal of the District of Columbia, you will not receive into custody any persons claimed to be held to service or labor within the District or elsewhere, and not charged with any crime or misdemeanor, unless upon arrest or commitment pursuant to law as fugitives from such service or labor; and you will not retain any such fugitives in custody beyond a period of thirty days from their arrest and commitment, unless by special order of competent civil authority. You will forthwith cause publication to be made of this order; and, at the expiration of ten days therefrom, you will apply the same to all persons so claimed to be held to service or labor, and now in your custody. This order has no relation to any arrests made by military authority."

CHAPTER XX.

NEGRO TESTIMONY.

THE BILL TO ABOLISH SLAVERY IN THE DISTRICT OF COLUMBIA. — MR. SUMNER'S AMENDMENT. — SUPPLEMENTARY BILL TO ABOLISH SLAVERY IN THE DISTRICT OF COLUMBIA. — MR. SUMNER'S AMENDMENT. — MR. SUMNER'S BILL. — MR. SUMNER'S AMENDMENT TO THE CIVIL APPROPRIATION BILL. — REMARKS OF MR. SUMNER, MR. SHERMAN. — MR. BUCKALEW'S AMENDMENT. — REMARKS OF MR. SAULSBURY, MR. HOWARD. — MR. SUMNER'S AMENDMENT ADOPTED.

THE original bill for the abolition of slavery in the District of Columbia, introduced by Mr. Wilson (Rep.) of Massachusetts on the 16th of December, 1861, provided that the claimant may be summoned before the commissioners, and examined on oath; and that the party for whose service compensation is claimed may also be examined before the commissioners, and may testify. This provision simply secured to the person claimed to owe service or labor the right to testify before the commissioners.

Mr. Sumner (Rep.) of Massachusetts, on the 3d of April, moved to amend the bill by empowering the commissioners to take testimony, " without the exclusion of witnesses on account of color." Mr. Saulsbury (Dem.) of Delaware demanded the yeas and nays; and they were ordered, — yeas 26, nays 10. This amendment empowered the commissioners appointed to assess the sum to be paid for each slave claimed to own service or labor; to examine and take the testimony in the pending cases of colored witnesses, free or slave.

On the 7th of July, the Senate having under consideration Mr. Wilson's supplementary bill for the release of certain persons held to service or labor in the District of Columbia, Mr. Sumner moved to add as a new section, "That, in all the judicial proceedings in the District of Columbia, there shall be no exclusion of any witness on account of color." Mr. Powell (Dem.) of Kentucky demanded the yeas and nays; and they were ordered, — yeas 25, nays 11.

In the Senate, on the 25th of June, 1864, Mr. Sumner moved to amend the third section of the Civil Appropriation Bill by adding, "that, in the courts of the United States, there shall be no exclusion of any witness on account of color." In support of his amendment, Mr. Sumner read a note from a member of the Virginia Constitutional Convention, stating that, unless the freedmen were allowed to give testimony, "their persons and property will be at the mercy of every vagabond who may happen to have a black heart instead of a black skin. It is hard," he said, "to be obliged to argue this question. I do not argue it. I will not argue it. I simply ask for your votes. Surely Congress will not adjourn without redressing this grievance. The king, in Magna Charta, promised that he would deny justice to no one. Congress has succeeded to this promise and obligation." Mr. Sherman said he had always voted, and always should vote, to make no distinction in the color, condition, form, or nation, of a man as a witness; "but I beseech the senator from Massachusetts not to load down this, the last of the appropriation bills, with amendments that are likely to create controversy between the two Houses." Mr. Carlile would " appeal to the senator from Massachusetts to withdraw this amendment." He demanded the yeas and nays upon it; and they were ordered. Mr. Buckalew (Dem.) of Pennsylvania moved to add to Mr. Sumner's amendment, " or because he is a party to or interested in the issue tried." Mr. Sumner was in favor of the proposition taken by itself, but did not wish it put upon his amendment. Mr. Brown reminded Mr. Sumner, that that is just what other people said about his amendment. Mr. Sumner understood that, but wished " to secure this justice." Mr. Buckalew wished " to secure the additional justice provided for by his amendment." Mr. Saulsbury did not wish " to say any thing about the ' nigger ' aspect of the case. It is here every day; and I suppose it will be here every day for years to come, till the Democratic party comes into power, and wipes out all legislation on the statute-book of this character, which I trust in God they will soon do."— " Is it to be presumed at the outset," said Mr. Howard (Rep.) of Michigan, " that, because a man has a black skin, he either cannot or will not tell the truth in court? It seems to me that those persons, who object to the examination of black persons as witnesses on the ground that they are black, put it upon this most unphilosophical, and, I may add, most inhuman and cruel presumption, that a negro either cannot or will not tell the truth in any case. I shall be guilty of presuming no such thing." Mr. Wilkinson (Rep.) of Minnesota suggested to Mr. Buckalew the modification of his amendment, so as to apply only to civil actions; and he so modified it. Mr. Sumner hoped the amendment would not be adopted. The vote was taken, and Mr. Buckalew's amendment to Mr. Sumner's amendment was agreed to, — ayes 21, noes not counted. The question being then taken on the amendment as amended, it was adopted, — yeas 22, nays 16. The Civil Appropriation Bill was approved by the President on the 2d of July, 1864: so that no witness is now excluded in the courts of the United States on account of color.

CHAPTER XXI.

THE COASTWISE SLAVE-TRADE.

MR. SUMNER'S BILL. — MR. SUMNER'S AMENDMENT TO THE CIVIL APPROPRIATION BILL. — REMARKS OF MR. SHERMAN, MR. SUMNER, MR. JOHNSON, MR. HENDRICKS, MR. COLLAMER, MR. JOHNSON, MR. SAULSBURY, MR. DOOLITTLE. — ADOPTION OF MR. SUMNER'S AMENDMENT.

IN the Senate, on the 23d of March, 1864, Mr. Sumner (Rep.) of Massachusetts, from the Select Committee on Slavery and Freedmen, reported a bill to prohibit commerce in slaves among the several States, and the holding or transportation of human beings as property in any vessel within the jurisdiction of the National Government. The bill provided that there shall be no commerce in slaves among the several States, by land or by water; and any person attempting or aiding to transport slaves as an article of commerce from one State to another State, or any person who shall take part in such commerce, either as seller, buyer, or agent, shall be deemed guilty of a misdemeanor, and, being convicted thereof, shall suffer imprisonment for not more than five years, and be fined not exceeding five thousand dollars; and every slave so treated as an article of commerce shall be free; and no human being shall be held or transported as property in any vessel on the high seas, or sailing coastwise, or on any navigable water, within the jurisdiction of the United States; and every vessel violating the provisions of this act shall be forfeited to the United States. But this bill was not taken up for consideration.

The Senate, on the 24th of June, proceeded, as in Committee of the Whole, to the consideration of the Civil Appropriation Bill. Mr. Sumner (Rep.) of Massachusetts moved as an amendment, that sections eight and nine of the act entitled "An act to prohibit the importation of slaves into any port or place within the jurisdiction of the United States from and after the first day of January, in the year of our Lord 1808," which said sections undertake to regulate the coastwise slave-trade, are hereby repealed. Mr. Sherman (Rep.) of Ohio would not oppose the amendment on an ordinary bill. He had read the two sections referred to in the amendment, and felt disposed to repeal them; but he trusted the Senate would keep the bill free from disputed political questions. Mr. Sumner regretted the opposition of Mr. Sherman, though it was one of form only. "In moving it now," he said, " on an appropriation bill, I follow approved precedents : it is in conformity with order and with usage. . . . I propose," he said, "to remove from the statute-book odious provisions in support of slavery. Whoever is in favor of those provisions, whoever is disposed to keep alive the coastwise slave-trade, or whoever wishes to recognize it in our statutes, will naturally vote against my motion. And yet let me say that I am at a loss to understand how at this moment, at this stage of our history, any senator can hesitate to unite with me in this work of expurgation and purification." Mr. Johnson of Maryland contended that the repeal of these sections of the act of 1807 would leave the slave-trade open to unrestrained abuses. Mr. Sumner differed "radically from the senator from Maryland. He is always willing to interpret the Constitution for slavery: I interpret it for freedom. He proceeds as if those old days still continued, when slavery was installed supreme over the Supreme Court, giving immunity to slavery everywhere. The times have changed, and the Supreme Court will yet testify to the change. To me it seems clear, that, under the Constitution of the United States, no person can be held as a slave on shipboard within the national jurisdiction, and that the national flag cannot cover a slave. The senator thinks differently, and relies upon the Supreme Court; but I cannot doubt that this regenerated tribunal will yet speak for freedom, as in times past it has spoken for slavery. And I trust, should my life be spared, to see the senator from Maryland, who bows always to the decisions of that tribunal, recognize gladly the law of freedom thus authoritatively pronounced."

Mr. Hendrick (Dem.) of Indiana expressed surprise that any senator should oppose the proposition, as it would eventually be adopted. He regretted to see all the laws made by the fathers to carry out the Constitution fall, one after another. Mr. Sumner proposed to amend his amendment by adding at the end, "and the coastwise slave-trade is prohibited for ever." Mr. Collamer (Rep.) of Vermont asserted, that, "if it be true that Congress can prohibit the carrying of slaves as articles of commerce from one State to another, they can allow it from one State to another; and the State cannot prevent it. I say, if they can prohibit it or regulate it, they can allow it and license it; and no

State can prevent it. . . . In my judgment, all laws, I do not care when they are attempted to be made nor when they were made, that undertake to deal with slaves, who are persons under the Constitution and our laws, as articles of merchandise in any form, under any regulations of trade whatever, are unconstitutional; and I believe to make a law now to prohibit the carrying of slaves from one State to another for sale is totally unauthorized. . . . Therefore, inasmuch as the sections of the law to which our attention is now called, and which it is proposed to repeal, are of that character, and attempt to deal with the subject as of that character, I say, repeal them." Mr. Johnson did not concur in the views expressed by Mr. Collamer; and that senator, on the 25th, replied to his criticisms. Mr. Sumner said, that, "in view of the minute and ample legislation of Congress on the subject of passengers and of the coasting-trade, I submit there can be no question that Congress can go farther, and, by a final regulation, declare, that, in that coasting-trade, there shall be no such thing as the slave-trade." The question, being taken by yeas and nays, resulted — yeas 13, nays 20. So the amendment was lost in Committee of the Whole.

After the Civil Appropriation Bill was reported to the Senate, Mr. Sumner again moved as an additional section to the bill, that sections eight and nine of the act entitled "An Act to prohibit the importation of slaves into any port or place within the jurisdiction of the United States from and after the first day of January, in the year of our Lord 1808," which sections undertake to regulate the coastwise slave-trade, are hereby repealed, and the coastwise slave-trade prohibited for ever. "It seems to me," he said, "this Congress will do wrong to itself, wrong to the country, wrong to history, wrong to our national cause, if it separates without clearing the statute-book of every support of slavery. Now, this is the last support that there is in the statute-book; and I entreat the Senate to remove it." Mr. Saulsbury (Dem.) of Delaware moved the indefinite postponement of the bill; and the motion was rejected. Mr. Doolittle (Rep.) of Wisconsin voted against the proposition; but as other amendments had been put on the bill, and he was in favor of the abolition of the coastwise slave-trade, he should vote for it. The vote was then taken, and resulted — yeas 23, nays 14. So the amendment was agreed to, and the bill approved by the President on the 2d of July, 1864.

CHAPTER XXII.

COLOR NO DISQUALIFICATION FOR CARRYING THE MAILS.

MR. SUMNER'S BILL. — PASSAGE IN THE SENATE. — REPORTED BY MR. COLFAX IN THE HOUSE. — REMARKS OF MR. COLFAX. — MR. DAWES. — MR. WICKLIFFE. — BILL LAID ON THE TABLE. — MR. SUMNER'S BILL. — MR. COLLAMER'S AMENDMENT. — REMARKS OF MR. COLLAMER. — MR. LANE OF INDIANA. — MR. LANE OF KANSAS. — MR. SAULSBURY. — MR. SUMNER. — MR. POWELL. — MR. HENDRICKS. — MR. POWELL'S AMENDMENT. — REMARKS OF MR. CONNESS. — MR. JOHNSON.

IN the Senate, on the 18th of March, 1862, Mr. Sumner (Rep.) of Massachusetts introduced a bill to abolish all disqualification of color in carrying the mails; which was referred to the Committee on Post-offices and Post-roads; and, on the 27th, Mr. Collamer reported it back without amendment. The Senate, on the 11th of April, proceeded to consider the bill to remove all disqualification of color in carrying the mails. It provided, that, from and after its passage, no person, by reason of color, should be disqualified from employment in carrying the mails; and all acts, and parts of acts, establishing such disqualification, including especially the seventh section of the act of March 3, 1825, are repealed. Mr. Powell (Dem.) of Kentucky demanded the yeas and nays on the passage of the bill; and they were taken, — yeas 24, nays 11. So the bill passed the Senate.

Mr. Colfax (Rep.) of Indiana, on the 20th of May,

reported it from the House Post-office Committee, with the recommendation that it do not pass. He explained the reasons for the action of the committee. "It does not," he said, "affect exclusively the blacks of the country. It will throw open the business of mail contracting, and of thus becoming officers of the Post-office Department, not only to blacks, but also to the Indian tribes, civilized and uncivilized; and to the Chinese, who have come in such large numbers to the Pacific coast. . . . It would allow all over the South the employment by the slaveholder of his slaves to carry the mail, and to receive compensation for the labor of such slaves out of the Federal treasury. By the present law, not a dollar is ever paid out of the post-office treasury to any slaveholder for the labor of his slave." It was necessary to have testimony to convict mail depredators; "and colored men were not allowed to testify in the courts of many of the States." Mr. Dawes (Rep.) of Massachusetts inquired of Mr. Colfax "whether he supposes depredators upon the mails are tried in the State courts, or whether they are tried in the United-States courts; and, if the latter, whether he and I do not make the laws of the United States and the courts of the United States, prescribing who shall testify, and who shall not." Mr. Wickliffe (Dem.) of Kentucky stated that "the law which this bill proposes to repeal was originally enacted to exclude some men in the South who were in the habit of obtaining mail contracts, and employing their negroes to drive their stages and carry the mails." Mr. Colfax moved to lay the bill on the table. Mr. Fessenden (Rep.) of Maine demanded the yeas and nays; and they were ordered. On the 21st, the vote to lay the bill on the table was taken, and resulted — yeas 82, nays 45.

On the 18th of January, 1864, Mr. Sumner introduced a bill to remove all disqualification of color in carrying the mails; which was referred to the Post-office Committee. Mr. Collamer, on the 11th of February, reported it back with an amendment. The Senate, on the 26th, proceeded to its consideration; the question being on the amendment reported by the committee, to add, "that, in the courts of the United States, there shall be no exclusion of any witness on account of color." Mr. Collamer said, "The bill is sufficiently explicit in itself; but the committee were of the opinion, that if persons of color were to be employed, and rendered eligible to be employed, as carriers of the mail, by those who have contracted to carry it, and who wish to employ them, it would be unsafe to commit to their hands the mail, when they could not themselves be witnesses against those who should violate that mail, steal it, rob it, and commit depredations upon it." Mr. Lane (Rep.) of Indiana had voted, and would vote, against the measure. "I am proud," said Mr. Lane (Rep.) of Kansas, "that I represent a State, the people of which have intelligence sufficient to sift all testimony presented, and justice enough to receive the truth from the lips of individuals, without reference to color." Mr. Saulsbury (Dem.) of Delaware declared, "We are legislating against reason, against our own race, by such enactments as this." Mr. Sumner read a letter from Postmaster-General Gideon Granger to Senator Jackson of Georgia, to show that the "origin of the offensive legislation sought to be removed grew out of a proposition to sustain slavery." Mr. Powell denounced the bill as "fanatical and radical legislation:" he demanded the yeas and nays, and they were ordered. Mr. Hendricks (Dem.) of Indiana was not "content to see a law passed by the Congress of the United States, placing the negro upon the platform of equality with the white race in the courts of the country, the sanctuary of our rights. Standing alone, the white race has progressed for a thousand years, without a step backward. Standing alone, the negro race has gone downward and downward for a thousand years." Mr. Harlan (Rep.) of Iowa inquired of Mr. Hendricks, "if, in his opinion, riding in a public conveyance with another either creates or becomes evidence of social equality between the parties." — "I did not refer," replied Mr. Hendricks, "to any particular action of this body; but I referred to the general tendency of our proceedings, giving nearly all the time of the Senate to the consideration of the interests of the negro, but very little of it to the white man." Mr. Powell proposed to amend the amendment, so that it would only apply to "cases for robbing or violating the mails." This limitation was opposed by Mr. Conness (Union) of California, whose purpose was "to receive testimony and proof from any source that is human." Mr. Johnson of Maryland regretted the introduction of the measure; but, if adopted, he trusted it would be confined to free persons of color. The bill was not further considered, and is pending in the Senate.

CHAPTER XXIII.

NO EXCLUSION FROM THE CARS ON ACCOUNT OF COLOR.

MR. SUMNER'S AMENDMENT. — REMARKS OF MR. SAULSBURY, MR. JOHNSON, MR. SUMNER, MR. MORRILL. — MR. SUMNER'S AMENDMENT. — REMARKS OF MR. SHERMAN, MR. HENDRICKS, MR. WILLEY, MR. SUMNER, MR. WILSON, MR. TRUMBULL, MR. SUMNER, MR. WILSON, MR. GRIMES, MR. POWELL. — AMENDMENT AGREED TO.

IN the Senate, on the 27th of February, 1863, Mr. Sumner moved to amend the House bill to extend the charter of the Washington and Alexandria Railroad Company, by adding to the first section, "that no person shall be excluded from the cars on account of color." The yeas and nays were ordered; and, being taken, resulted — yeas 19, nays 18. So the amendment was agreed to, was concurred in by the House, and approved by the President on the 3d of March, 1863.

In the Senate, on the 16th of March, Mr. Sumner proposed to amend the bill to incorporate the Metropolitan Railroad Company by adding, "that there shall be no regulation excluding persons from any car on account of color." Mr. Saulsbury expressed his surprise that there should be such a strong disposition manifested on the part of white men and the representatives of white men to ride in the cars with negroes. "Has any gentleman, any man who was born a gentleman, or any man who has the instincts of a gentleman, felt himself degraded by the fact that he was not honored by a seat by the side of some free negro? Has any lady in the United States felt herself aggrieved from the fact that she was not honored with the company of Miss Dinah or Miss Chloe on board these cars?" Mr. Johnson, on the 17th, maintained, in reply to Mr. Saulsbury, that colored persons had a legal right to ride in the cars; and, if excluded, they had the same rights as white men to appeal for redress to the courts: but whether a white man is to ride in a car with black passengers, or whether a black man is to ride in a car appropriated to white passengers, is a matter that he did not think touched any of the great issues now before the country. Mr. Sumner agreed with Mr. Johnson, that "colored people have the legal right to enter the cars, and the proprietors are trespassers when they undertake to exclude them." Mr. Carlile thought it better to leave the subject to the courts, that are open alike to the white and the black man. Mr. Doolittle thought the amendment entirely unnecessary. Mr. Morrill replied in a speech of eloquence and power to Mr. Saulsbury. In reply to the remark of Mr. Saulsbury, that this question between the races had better be left to the gentlemanly instincts of the superior race and to the principles of Christianity, Mr. Morrill said, "Christianity is an inspiration of love and good-will to man,— purifying, elevating, emancipating; not a law of force, — binding, inthralling:" but, "under the influence of the gentlemanly instincts of the superior race, slavery has come to be cherished, — cherished as a benefaction to the race; cherished as a great social good;

cherished as the corner-stone upon which you are to rear American institutions, — the corner-stone of civil and religious liberty." The question being taken on Mr. Sumner's amendment, it was agreed to, — yeas 19, nays 17. The House concurred, and the President approved the bill.

On the 21st of June, Mr. Sumner moved to amend " the bill to amend the charter of the Washington and Georgetown Railroad Company " by adding, " that there shall be no exclusion of any person from any car on account of color." Mr. Sherman thought " the amendment ought not to be adopted." Mr. Hendrick opposed the amendment, because it tended to depreciate the value of investments made on the faith of former legislation. Mr. Willey would vote against the amendment. The Committee on the District of Columbia, and the Senate, had deliberately decided that negroes " had the same right under the original charter to go into any car, as white persons." — " I presume," said Mr. Sumner, " the senator will vote against this proposition; for he would not act naturally if he did not." — " He can ride with negroes if he sees proper," replied Mr. Willey; " so may I : but, if I see proper not to do so, I shall follow my natural instincts, while he follows his." — " I shall vote for this amendment," said Mr. Wilson; " and my own observation convinces me that justice, not to say decency, requires that I should do so. Some weeks ago, I rode to the capital in one of these cars. On the front part of the car, standing with the driver, were, I think, five colored clergymen of the Methodist-Episcopal Church, dressed like gentlemen, and behaving like gentlemen. These clergymen were riding with the driver on the front platform; and inside the car were two drunken loafers, conducting and behaving themselves so badly, that the conductor threatened to turn them out." Mr. Trumbull denied that any right would be secured to the colored man by the amendment. "This provision," he said, "can give no additional right to the negro." Mr. Sumner said, "I always regarded the Wilmot Proviso, if the Constitution were properly interpreted, surplusage: yet I never hesitated, in season and out of season, to vindicate it; and I believe the senator never hesitated, in season and out of season, to do the same. . . . And, on the same principle, I insist that this proviso also should be adopted." — "The senator from Illinois tells us," said Mr. Wilson, "that the colored people have a legal right to ride in these cars now. We know it; nobody doubts it: but this company into which we breathed the breath of life outrages the rights of twenty-five thousand colored people in this District, in our presence, in defiance of our opinions. They may act according to their prejudices; and I would not offend their prejudices, unless it were necessary to protect the rights of others. I tell the senator from Illinois, that I care far more for the rights of the humblest black child that treads the soil of the District of Columbia than I do for the prejudices of this corporation, and its friends and patrons. The rights of the humblest colored man in the capital of this Christian nation are dearer to me than the commendations or the thanks of all persons in the city of Washington who sanction this violation of the rights of a race. I give this vote, not to offend this corporation, not to offend anybody in the District of Columbia, but to protect the rights of the poor and the lowly, trodden under the heel of power. I trust we shall protect rights, if we do it over prejudices and over interests, until every man in this country is fully protected in all the rights that belong to beings made in the image of God. Let the free man of this race be permitted to run the career of life; to make of himself all that God intended he should make, when he breathed into him the breath of life." Mr. Grimes desired to know if these colored men would not be compelled to enforce their rights in the courts if the amendment should pass, and "the company goes on, and does exactly what it has been doing." — "The company," replied Mr. Sumner, "will not dare to continue this outrage in the face and eyes of a positive provision of statute." — "Poor, helpless, and despised inferior race of white men," exclaimed Mr. Saulsbury, "you have very little interest in this Government; you are not worth consideration in the legislation of the country: but let your superior, Sambo's interests come in question, and you will find the most tender solicitude in his behalf! What a pity it is there is not somebody to lampblack white men, so that their rights could be secured." Mr. Powell thought the senator from Massachusetts should, "the next time one of his Ethiopian friends comes to complain to him on this subject that he has been wronged and outraged, volunteer to bring an action in the courts, and teach this heartless corporation that they must treat these persons properly, and not deny them any of their legal rights. The senator has indicated to his fanatical brethren — those people who meet in free-love societies, the old ladies, the sensation preachers, and those who live on fanaticism — that he has offered it; and I see no reason why we should take up the time of the Senate eternally with squabbling over the senator's amendments introducing the negro into every wood-pile that comes along." Mr. Sumner called for the yeas and nays; and they were ordered, and, being taken, resulted — yeas 14, nays 16. The bill was then reported to the Senate. Mr. Sumner renewed his amendment; and it was agreed to, — yeas 17, nays 16. The House concurred in the amendment; and the Washington and Georgetown Railroad Company was forbidden to exclude persons from their cars on account of color.

CHAPTER XXIV.

CONCLUSION.

THE annals of the nation bear the amplest evidence that the patriots and statesmen who carried the country through the Revolution from colonial dependence to national independence, framed the Constitution, and inaugurated the Federal Government, hoped and believed that slavery would pass away at no distant period under the influences of the institutions they had founded. But those illustrious men tasted death without witnessing the realization of their hopes and anticipations. The rapid development of the resources of the country under the protection of a stable government, the opening-up of new and rich lands, the expansion of territory, and perhaps, more than all, the wonderful growth and importance of the cotton culture, enhanced the value of labor, and increased many fold the price of slaves. Under the stimulating influences of an ever-increasing pecuniary interest, a political power was speedily developed, which early manifested itself in the National Government. For nearly two generations, the slaveholding class, into whose power the Government early passed, dictated the policy of the nation. But the Presidential Election of 1860 resulted in the defeat of the slaveholding class, and in the success of men who religiously believe slavery to be a grievous wrong to the slave, a blight upon the prosperity, and a stain upon the name, of the country. Defeated in its aims, broken in its power, humiliated in its pride, the slaveholding class raised at once the banners of treason. Retiring from the chambers of Congress, abandoning the seats of power to men who had persistently opposed their aggressive policy, they brought to an abrupt close the record of half a century of SLAVERY MEASURES IN CONGRESS. Then, when slavery legislation ended, antislavery legislation began. A condensed summary of the ANTISLAVERY MEASURES IN CONGRESS, briefly traced in the preceding pages, may perhaps convey to the reader more distinctly their scope and magnitude.

When the Rebellion culminated in active hostilities, it was seen that thousands of slaves were used for military purposes by the rebel forces. To weaken the forces of the Rebellion, the 37th Congress decreed that such slaves should be for ever free.

As the Union armies advanced into the rebel States, slaves, inspired by the hope of personal freedom, flocked to their encampments, claiming protection against rebel masters, and offering to work and fight for the flag whose stars for the first time gleamed upon their vision with the radiance of liberty. Rebel masters and rebel sympathizing masters sought the encampments of the loyal forces, demanding the surrender of the escaped fugitives; and they were often delivered up by officers of the armies. To weaken the power of the insurgents, to strengthen the loyal forces, and assert the claims of humanity, the 37th Congress enacted an article of war, dismissing from the service officers guilty of surrendering these fugitives.

Three thousand persons were held as slaves in the

District of Columbia, over which the nation exercised exclusive jurisdiction: the 37th Congress made these three thousand bondmen freemen, and made slaveholding in the capital of the nation for evermore impossible.

Laws and ordinances existed in the national capital, that pressed with merciless rigor upon the colored people: the 37th Congress enacted that colored persons should be tried for the same offences, in the same manner, and be subject to the same punishments, as white persons; thus abrogating the "black code."

Colored persons in the capital of this Christian nation were denied the right to testify in the judicial tribunals; thus placing their property, their liberties, and their lives, in the power of unjust and wicked men: the 37th Congress enacted that persons should not be excluded as witnesses in the courts of the District on account of color.

In the capital of the nation, colored persons were taxed to support schools, from which their own children were excluded; and no public schools were provided for the instruction of more than four thousand youth: the 38th Congress provided by law that public schools should be established for colored children, and that the same rate of appropriations for colored schools should be made as are made for schools for the education of white children.

The railways chartered by Congress excluded from their cars colored persons, without the authority of law: Congress enacted that there should be no exclusion from any car on account of color.

Into the territories of the United States, — one-third of the surface of the country, — the slaveholding class claimed the right to take and hold their slaves under the protection of law: the 37th Congress prohibited slavery for ever in all the existing territory, and in all territory which may hereafter be acquired; thus stamping freedom for all, for ever, upon the public domain.

As the war progressed, it became more clearly apparent that the rebels hoped to win the Border slave States; that rebel sympathizers in those States hoped to join the rebel States; and that emancipation in loyal States would bring repose to them, and weaken the power of the Rebellion: the 37th Congress, on the recommendation of the President, by the passage of a joint resolution, pledged the faith of the nation to aid loyal States to emancipate the slaves therein.

The hoe and spade of the rebel slave were hardly less potent for the Rebellion than the rifle and bayonet of the rebel soldier. Slaves sowed and reaped for the rebels, enabling the rebel leaders to fill the wasting ranks of their armies, and feed them. To weaken the military forces and the power of the Rebellion, the 37th Congress decreed that all slaves of persons giving aid and comfort to the Rebellion, escaping from such persons, and taking refuge within the lines of the army; all slaves captured from such persons, or deserted by them; all slaves of such persons, being within any place occupied by rebel forces, and afterwards occupied by the forces of the United States, — shall be captives of war, and shall be for ever free of their servitude, and not again held as slaves.

The provisions of the Fugitive-slave Act permitted disloyal masters to claim, and they did claim, the return of their fugitive bondmen: the 37th Congress enacted that no fugitive should be surrendered until the claimant made oath that he had not given aid and comfort to the Rebellion.

The progress of the Rebellion demonstrated its power, and the needs of the imperilled nation. To strengthen the physical forces of the United States, the 37th Congress authorized the President to receive into the military service persons of African descent; and every such person mustered into the service, his mother, his wife and children, owing service or labor to any person who should give aid and comfort to the Rebellion, was made for ever free.

The African slave-trade had been carried on by slave pirates under the protection of the flag of the United States. To extirpate from the seas that inhuman traffic, and to vindicate the sullied honor of the nation, the Administration early entered into treaty stipulations with the British Government for the mutual right of search within certain limits; and the 37th Congress hastened to enact the appropriate legislation to carry the treaty into effect.

The slaveholding class, in the pride of power, persistently refused to recognize the independence of Hayti and Liberia; thus dealing unjustly towards those nations, to the detriment of the commercial interests of the country: the 37th Congress recognized the independence of those republics by authorizing the President to establish diplomatic relations with them.

By the provisions of law, white male citizens alone were enrolled in the militia. In the amendment to the acts for calling out the militia, the 37th Congress provided for the enrolment and drafting of citizens, without regard to color; and, by the Enrolment Act, colored persons, free or slave, are enrolled and drafted the same as white men. The 38th Congress enacted that colored soldiers shall have the same pay, clothing, and rations, and be placed in all respects upon the same footing, as white soldiers. To encourage enlistments, and to aid emancipation, the 38th Congress decreed that every slave mustered into the military service shall be free for ever; thus enabling every slave fit for military service to secure personal freedom.

By the provisions of the fugitive-slave acts, slave-masters could hunt their absconding bondmen, require the people to aid in their recapture, and have them returned at the expense of the nation. The 38th Congress erased all fugitive-slave acts from the statutes of the Republic.

The law of 1807 legalized the coastwise slave-trade: the 38th Congress repealed that act, and made the trade illegal.

The courts of the United States receive such testimony as is permitted in the States where the courts are holden. Several of the States exclude the testimony of colored persons. The 38th Congress made it legal for colored persons to testify in all the courts of the United States.

Different views are entertained by public men relative to the reconstruction of the governments of the seceded States, and the validity of the President's proclamation of emancipation. The 38th Congress passed a bill providing for the reconstruction of the governments of the rebel States, and for the emancipation of the slaves in those States; but it did not receive the approval of the President.

By the provisions of law, colored men are not permitted to carry the mails; there is pending in the Senate a bill introduced by Mr. Sumner, and reported by Mr. Collamer, to repeal the law, and make it legal to allow colored men to carry the mails of the United States.

The wives and children of colored soldiers may be held as slaves, and sold, while they are absent fighting the battles of the country; there is pending in the Senate a joint resolution, introduced by Mr. Wilson, and reported by him from the Committee on Military Affairs, to make free the wives and children of colored soldiers.

There is pending, in the House of Representatives, Mr. Eliot's bill to establish a Freedmen's Bureau; which passed the House, and was amended in the Senate by the adoption of Mr. Sumner's substitute.

There is also pending, in the House, Mr. Ashley's motion to reconsider the vote rejecting the Senate joint resolution, submitting to the people an amendment to the Constitution, prohibiting slavery in the United States.

Such are the "ANTISLAVERY MEASURES" considered by the Thirty-seventh and Thirty-eighth Congresses during the past three crowded years. But, while Congress has been engaged in this antislavery legislation, other agencies have been working to the consummation of the same end. The new State of West Virginia has adopted a system of gradual emancipation. Missouri has followed in the adoption of a gradual system, which will doubtless be speedily changed to a plan of immediate emancipation. A Constitutional Convention in Maryland has just framed a free Constitution, which will doubtless be accepted by her people. Delaware is preparing to adopt emancipation; and an emancipation party is rapidly rising in Kentucky. The rebel States of Arkansas and Louisiana have, by the action of their loyal men, framed and adopted free State constitutions. The loyal men of Tennessee are taking steps to call a Constitutional Convention, with a view of placing that State in the list of free commonwealths. Attorney-General Bates officially pronounces the negro a citizen of the United States. The colored man now travels the world over, bearing the passport of Secretary Seward that he is a citizen of the United States. The President of the United States has, by proclamation, declared henceforward and for ever free more than three millions of slaves in the rebel States. Christian men and women are following the loyal armies with the agencies of mental and moral instruction, to fit and prepare the enfranchised freedmen for the duties of the higher condition of life opening before them.

THE END.

Boston: Printed by John Wilson and Son.

Recent Standard Publications.

THE DANGER OF SLAVERY, AND THE SAFETY OF EMANCIPATION.

THE learned and justly celebrated French author, M. AUGUSTIN COCHIN, has written two remarkable volumes, forming together the most *complete and exhaustive* HISTORY OF SLAVERY, both as an institution and a principle, ever offered to the world; showing conclusively from *past experience*, and giving the "facts and figures" to prove, that in *Freedom* only is safety for any nation. The volumes are entitled —

THE RESULTS OF SLAVERY.
12mo. $1.75.

THE RESULTS OF EMANCIPATION.
12mo. $1.75.

These works are not only invaluable, but *indispensable*, to every man desirous of fully understanding the momentous questions at issue in this nation at this time. The volumes are the *unprejudiced* work of a foreigner, and are not partisan, but cool, logical, and *practical*.

SPEECHES, LECTURES, AND LETTERS.
BY WENDELL PHILLIPS.

No recent contribution to distinctively American literature is so timely, so suggestive, so pregnant, as this eloquent volume.

One vol. 8vo, elegantly printed, bound in vellum, gilt top, or bevelled boards, red edges; *with the finest Portrait of Mr. Phillips ever made.* Price $2.50.

"No ancient orator was ever more brilliant with keen sarcasm, splendid invective, or destructive satire, scattered like diamond handfuls in every direction. . . . They are classic, as products of rare genius, aristocratic culture, stern moral purpose, historic permanence." — *Methodist Quarterly Review.*

THE REJECTED STONE;
Or, Insurrection vs. Resurrection in America.
By a Native of Virginia (Rev. M. D. CONWAY).
16mo. 75 cents.

WALKER, WISE, & CO., Publishers,
245, Washington Street, Boston.

The Three New War-Books.

The Color Guard; being a Corporal's Notes of Military Service in the Nineteenth Army Corps. By Rev. J. K. HOSMER, who volunteered as Private in the Fifty-second Massachusetts, and went through the campaign. 12mo. $1.50.

It is undoubtedly the most piquant and readable sketch ever made of the *interior life of a great army in active service*, and made *from the inside*, by a hand entirely competent.

"His story," says the *Daily Advertiser*, "is written in a delightfully graphic epistolary style, and is really one of the most sterling books that the war has called into existence. It will be read with great interest by soldiers everywhere, and by civilians with equal interest. It forms the counterpart of DANA's 'Two Years before the Mast,' and ought to become as popular."

Everybody should send a copy to *some* soldier in camp or hospital. No gift can be more acceptable.

The Whip, Hoe, and Sword; or, The Gulf Department in '63. By Rev. GEO. H. HEPWORTH. 12mo. $1.50.

Mr. HEPWORTH went out to New Orleans as Chaplain of the 47th Massachusetts, but was subsequently commissioned by General BANKS as First Lieutenant in the Fourth Louisiana Native Guards (colored). He was detailed to superintend the plantations; and this volume is the result of his experience more particularly in that department of duty. It throws a flood of light upon the vexed question of paid labor upon the plantations, and abounds with interesting facts, anecdotes, and sketches of Southern life and character.

Chaplain Fuller; being a Life-Sketch of a New-England Clergyman and an Army Chaplain. 12mo. Portrait. Price $1.50.

This volume has a wide interest from the graphic picture of CAMP AND FIELD LIFE which it presents, and the vast amount of important information on the subject of the conduct and progress of the war not elsewhere obtainable.

The narrative of the *remarkable duel* between the MERRIMACK and the MONITOR is the only full account in print from the pen of an actual *eye-witness* of the whole affair.

The *New-York Tribune* devotes three and a half columns to a favorable review of the book.

The *Methodist* pronounces Mr. Fuller "a model army chaplain," and adds, "He was one whose qualities it is good to commemorate; who in his home and public life afforded constant examples of genial virtue and of earnest piety well worthy of the imitation of young Americans. The biography of a such a man is always a desirable gift to the reading public."

☞ All these Books SENT FREE BY MAIL on receipt of the price.

WALKER, WISE, & CO.,
245, Washington Street, Boston

www.ingramcontent.com/pod-product-compliance
Lightning Source LLC
Chambersburg PA
CBHW020105010526
44115CB00008B/703